The UN Charter

"Written by two towering figures in the field, this extraordinary book is a must read for anyone interested in the future of international law and diplomacy in these turbulent times. On the 80th anniversary of the UN Charter, Ellis and Scheffer provide a masterful analysis of the origins, interpretation, impact, and continuing relevance of history's most important secular document."

—Michael P. Scharf, *President of the American Branch of the International Law Association and Dean of Case Western Reserve University School of Law from 2013–2024*

"This is an extraordinary book. An excellent combination of history and future. It should definitely be used widely in educating present and coming generations about the importance of the UN and international law. It should also be read by representatives of UN member states, in particular of the P5 of the UN Security Council. It is unacceptable that all of them do not consequently perform as required by the UN Charter."

—Hans Corell, *Former Under-Secretary-General for Legal Affairs and the Legal Counsel of the United Nations*

"Our world is now fraught with peril from natural and human-made disasters. In this context, Scheffer and Ellis make a timely and compelling call for universal respect for, and commitment to, the cornerstone of international law—the Charter of the United Nations. The authors demonstrate that in this 80th anniversary year of the Charter coming into force, its core provisions remain as relevant and vital as they did in 1945."

—Richard Goldstone, *Former Prosecutor of the International Criminal Tribunals of the former Yugoslavia and Rwanda*

"This book is a brilliant and timely reminder of why law matters. Bravo!"

—Baroness Helena Kennedy LT KC

"For eight decades, the United Nations has stood as a beacon of hope, diplomacy, and collective action on the global stage. In "The UN Charter: Five Pillars for Humankind" Scheffer and Ellis provide a compelling retrospective that highlights the organization's landmark achievements, challenges overcome, and its unwavering commitment to fostering peace, security, and human rights worldwide.

This superb and important volume brings to life the pivotal moments and remarkable figures that have shaped the UN's history—from its founding in the aftermath of World War II to its evolving role in today's complex geopolitical landscape.

Whether you are a history enthusiast, a student of international relations, or simply someone inspired by the ideals of global cooperation, "The UN Charter: Five Pillars for Humankind" provides an enriching and celebratory tribute to the enduring spirit of the United Nations."

—Leila Nadya Sadat, James Carr, *Professor of International Law, Washington University School of Law*

"This is an authoritative, comprehensive and timely work on the occasion of the 80th anniversary of the UN Charter, by two leading experts in international human rights, humanitarian and criminal law. A must read."

—The Honourable Irwin Cotler, *P.C., O.C., O.Q., Ad.E.; former Minister of Justice and Attorney General of Canada; Founder & International Chair, Raoul Wallenberg Centre for Human Rights*

David J. Scheffer · Mark S. Ellis

The UN Charter

Five Pillars for Humankind

Springer

David J. Scheffer
School of Politics and Global Studies
Arizona State University
Washington, DC, USA

Mark S. Ellis
International Bar Association
London, UK

ISBN 978-3-031-94865-7 ISBN 978-3-031-94866-4 (eBook)
https://doi.org/10.1007/978-3-031-94866-4

This Springer imprint is published by the registered company Springer Nature Switzerland AG
The registered company address is: Gewerbestrasse 11, 6330 Cham, Switzerland

Foreword

Throughout decades of public service at the national and international levels, I have regarded the United Nations Charter as the foundational constitutional document to guide governments, international organizations, and the global populace. The U.N. Charter establishes, for the ages, both aspirational goals and the institutional means (particularly through the United Nations and its specialized agencies) to achieve them. The fact that the U.N. Charter is sometimes overshadowed in the chaos of daily policymaking across the world or challenged by skeptics questioning its relevance does not diminish its significance. Just as wise leaders derive authority from national constitutions and legal frameworks, they ultimately turn to the Charter to reinforce the credibility and legitimacy of their actions. In a sense, the Charter is the great leveler among nations, reminding each one that there are common principles and procedures to honor in the pursuit of national interests amidst the constellation of factors shaping a multilateral world.

With the 80th anniversary of the U.N. Charter unfolding in the year 2025, David J. Scheffer and Mark S. Ellis have written this book honoring the continuous and critical relevance of the Charter in the management of world affairs. They make the case that the Charter indeed remains "the world's most important secular document." I know from my own lifetime of experiences the truth of that maxim. In the defense of human rights, creation of international law, maintenance of international peace and security, building of sustainable economies and societies, and striving for peaceful resolution of disputes, there has been one battered but indispensable body of words to draw upon for the last eight decades.

In *The UN Charter: Five Pillars for Humankind*, Scheffer and Ellis, whom I have known for decades, write with refreshing and highly readable prose about the origins of the Charter in the 1940's, many of its most important tenets, and how they should be interpreted in the modern world. The future, of course, belongs to younger generations who would be remiss to overlook this evergreen document explained so artfully in a contemporary book written primarily for them.

Where else in a dangerously fractured and vastly digitized world can one draw inspiration but in the "determined" rendering of the Charter's opening words: "to save succeeding generations from the scourge of war…and to reaffirm faith in foundational human rights, in the dignity and worth of the human person, in the equal rights of men and women and of nations large and small, and to establish conditions under which justice and respect for the obligations arising from treaties and other sources of international law can be maintained, and to promote social progress and better standards of life in larger freedom…" One can build an entire life grounded in these precepts of human civilization. Scheffer and Ellis invite all of us to try.

Mary Robinson

Mary Robinson formerly served as President of Ireland, U.N. High Commissioner for Human Rights, Chancellor of the University of Dublin, U.N. Special Envoy on Climate Change, and Chair of The Elders. She received the Presidential Medal of Freedom in 2009 and is author of Climate Justice (Bloomsbury Publishing, 2018).

Acknowledgements

The authors would like to acknowledge the International Bar Association (IBA) for its indispensable support in making this book possible. The IBA is the world's largest organization of international legal practitioners, bar associations and law societies. The IBA's present membership is comprised of more than 80,000 individual international lawyers from most of the world's leading law firms and some 190 bar associations and law societies spanning more than 170 countries. The IBA was established in 1947. Based on the founding principles of the United Nations, its aim is to protect and advance the rule of law globally. The IBA was born out of the conviction that an organization of legal practitioners could contribute to global stability and peace through the administration of justice. Thus, it is not surprising that the IBA viewed this book as an important expression of its mission. However, it was the IBA's Special Project Fund that ultimately decided to allocate funding to this project so that the authors could secure research assistance and other support. Without this funding, completing this important book would not have been possible. We are indebted to the IBA and its Special Project Fund.

The authors would also like to thank Hans Corell, Under-Secretary-General for Legal Affairs and the Legal Counsel of the United Nations (1994–2004), for his reading of the manuscript and Nicholas Lower and Julia Katsovich for their research assistance and Talia Dove for her valuable administrative support.

Contents

About the Authors

David J. Scheffer is Professor of Practice in the School of Politics and Global Studies at Arizona State University. He was the Mayer Brown/Robert A. Helman Professor of Law at Northwestern University Pritzker School of Law (2006–2020) and is Director Emeritus of the Center for International Human Rights. He was the International Francqui Professor at KU Leuven in 2022. Scheffer was the first U.S. Ambassador at Large for War Crimes Issues (1997–2001) and negotiated the creation of five war crimes tribunals. He was the U.N. Secretary-General's Special Expert for U.N. Assistance to the Khmer Rouge Trials (2012–2018) and was Senior Adviser and Counsel to Dr. Madeleine Albright during her tenure as the U.S. Permanent Representative to the United Nations, when he also represented the U.S. Mission to the United Nations on the National Security Council's Deputies Committee (1993–1997). Scheffer was Vice President of the American Society of International Law (2020–2022). He authored *All the Missing Souls: A Personal History of the War Crimes Tribunals* (Princeton, 2012) and *The Sit Room: In the Theater of War and Peace* (Oxford, 2019). Among his honors, he received the American Bar Association's 2024 Eleanor Roosevelt Prize for Global Human Rights Advancement and the Berlin Prize in 2013. Scheffer is a graduate of Harvard, Oxford, and Georgetown Universities and is a member of the New York, District of Columbia and Supreme Court Bars.

Mark S. Ellis is the Executive Director of the International Bar Association (IBA). Previously, he directed the ABA's Central European and Eurasian Law Initiative (CEELI). He served as Legal Advisor to the Independent International Commission on Kosovo and was appointed by the OSCE to advise on creating Serbia's War Crimes Tribunal. Ellis was actively involved with the ICTY *Tadic* case and the Iraqi High Tribunal and acted as legal consultant to the defense team of *Nuon Chea* at the Cambodian War Crimes Tribunal (ECCC). He previously served as Chair of the ICTY Advisory Panel and the UN-created Advisory Panel on Matters Relating to Defence Counsel of the Mechanism for International Criminal Tribunals. Ellis is presently an adjunct Professor at Florida State University College of Law. Twice a Fulbright Scholar at the Economic Institute in Zagreb, Croatia, he earned his J.D.

and B.S. (Economics) degrees from Florida State University and his Ph.D. in Law from King's College, London. He has published extensively on international humanitarian law, war crimes tribunals, and the development of the rule of law. Among his honors, Ellis is the recipient of the ABA's *World Order Under Law Award,* Florida State University's *Distinguished Graduate Award* and *Torch Award*, the University's College of Social Sciences & Public Policy *Distinguished Alumni Award*, the College of Law's *Distinguished Alumni Award* and the *International Impact Award* from King's College London. In 2024, Ellis was made a *Fellow* of Kings College.

List of Figures

Chapter 1
Introduction

The United Nations Charter is the world's most important secular document. It affirms the universal principles of human character and conduct that every nation has confirmed by signing the U.N. Charter, albeit often honored in the breach. Most of the existential challenges now dominating the global agenda—climate change, wars of aggression, pandemics, massive migration, authoritarianism, nuclear annihilation, misinformation, and artificial intelligence—may initially appear disconnected from the Charter's words drafted during the final year of World War II. But one would be mistaken to relegate the Charter to the archives of the twentieth century. Indeed, the Charter means more to the fate of the world today than at any other time during its 80-year history. Just as Americans explore the text of the U.S. Constitution, particularly its Bill of Rights, to unravel complex issues confronting modern public and private life, they and other citizens of the world are governed by one secular document—the Charter—that is grounded in history's lessons and expressive of the "forever law" that at least in theory guides global society.

We have written this book about the U.N. Charter for two primary reasons. First and foremost, we aim to reintroduce the Charter to current generations of global citizens and to explain the Charter's lasting significance in managing life on Planet Earth. Gaps in embracing the Charter in contemporary literature and popular imagination need to be filled. Second, the 80th anniversary of the U.N. Charter occurs in 2025. The final text of the Charter was first signed by diplomats in San Francisco on June 26, 1945. The Charter entered into force as a binding treaty for 29 nations, including the United States, on October 24, 1945. The 80th year in the Charter's evolution invites a fresh look at its words and relevance for the modern world.

The full text of the U.N. Charter, recited in Appendix I and illuminated throughout this book, entered the global stage during the final battles of World War II and just prior to the dawn of the nuclear age at Hiroshima and Nagasaki. Throughout the conflict and carnage of that war and as early as 1941, core principles to guide world affairs emerged from the fora convened by the Allied powers fighting the Axis powers of Germany, Italy, and Japan. These meetings focused primarily on confirming the

D. J. Scheffer and M. S. Ellis, *The UN Charter*,
https://doi.org/10.1007/978-3-031-94866-4_1

will of the United States, United Kingdom, Soviet Union (at that time), and other nations to fight and defeat, unconditionally, the Axis powers. But each one of these gatherings turned the leaders' attention towards the kind of international system that should emerge in the aftermath of the war. That this happened is testament to the courage and foresight of primarily U.S. President Franklin D. Roosevelt, joined by British Prime Minister Winston Churchill, each of whom were willing to think boldly about the future and their responsibility to build a saner world.

Roosevelt had the more natural instinct for the endeavor. He appreciated the Wilsonian vision of self-determination of peoples and nations, which was a cornerstone of the Treaty of Versailles after World War I.[1] That vision guided Roosevelt in grappling with the looming post-World War II reality of previously occupied countries of the Axis powers. But the remaining colossus of colonialism would remain during the war as a futures project and one drafted into the U.N. Charter. Churchill, who led the British Empire, could not imagine de-colonizing the many British possessions, including India, around the world.[2] But the logic of fighting a world war against the atrocity warfare and tyranny of the Axis powers made the aspiration of liberated nations and democratic governance a powerful ideal, at least in these pre-Charter declarations and statements. Churchill needed Roosevelt's, and America's, support to defeat Hitler so desperately that he refrained from voicing outright opposition to de-colonization, a governance revolution that, when unleashed in later years, indeed would decimate the British Empire. As for Joseph Stalin, he had his own expansionist agenda for the Soviet Union, particularly in Eastern Europe, in the aftermath of the war regardless of whatever was pledged at the pre-Charter meetings. He wanted the end game to be preserving the veto power of the major victor nations, preserving the sacrosanct principle of sovereignty, and ensuring non-interference in the internal affairs of any nation.[3] He would not be disappointed in the outcome.

The most notorious pre-Charter document that failed to prevent World War II was the Covenant of the League of Nations.[4] Forged in the post-World War I Paris negotiations of 1919 that resulted in the Treaty of Versailles, the Covenant created a new diplomatic world of multilateralism. While 63 nations ultimately ratified the Covenant and became member states of the League of Nations, the United States failed to join despite President Woodrow Wilson's tireless but futile campaign for Senate ratification which finally led to his disabling stroke in October 1919.[5]

The Covenant of the League of Nations offered a ponderous and meandering methodology for deterring and ending warfare, one that proved hopelessly ineffective between the world wars. The language of the Covenant created a convoluted artifice of dispute settlement procedures at the prospect or outbreak of war and mandated arbitration or, if arbitration were not chosen, a report prepared by the "Council," which consisted of the Allied victors of World War I and a rotating group of other members

---

[1] Treaty of Versailles (28 Jun 1919); Danspeckgruber and Gardner (2024).

[2] Kennedy (2006), p. 42; Schlesinger (2003), pp. 61, 99, 235.

[3] Schlesinger (2003), pp. 50, 58.

[4] Treaty of Versailles, Part I, Covenant of the League of Nations (28 Jun 1919).

[5] The United Nations Office at Geneva (2024a); U.S. Office of the Historian (2016b).

of the League, as the presumptive gateway to resolve disputes. The Covenant required members to "carry out in full good faith any [arbitration] award that may be rendered" and not resort to war against any member that complies with such award.[6] But in the event of non-compliance, the Covenant acquiesced to war commencing as soon as three months after an arbitration ruling or issuance of a Council report but still obligated the Council to propose the steps to be taken to achieve such compliance.[7]

Adding to the imponderables, Article 15 of the Covenant required unanimous approval by all member states (excluding the nations in dispute) of the Council's report on the facts and recommendations regarding a dispute before they were all obligated *not* to go to war with a nation that complied with the recommendations of such report. Article 15 further stipulated that if the Council failed to produce a unanimous report (again, excluding the contesting nations) in a dispute, then the League's member states (presumably alone or collectively) could exercise "the right to take such action as they shall consider necessary for the maintenance of right and justice."[8]

Finally, Article 16 of the Covenant explained that a member state failing to invoke a bevy of dispute settlement procedures in the Covenant and then pursuing war would be "deemed to have committed an act of war against all other Members of the League…"[9] This is similar to Article 5 under the NATO treaty which obligates collective response to any armed attack against a NATO member state.[10] But the Covenant did not authorize unleashing military force in response to any such de facto declaration of war by the violating nation. Rather, all member states of the League of Nations would be obligated to ostracize the violating member state with economic and financial sanctions and to terminate interactions with all nationals of that country. The League's Council did not have to convene, discuss, or decide upon these punitive non-military actions as the Covenant mandated that they be implemented automatically while remaining silent on use of armed force. As an enforcement remedy, the Covenant proved largely ineffective when Japan invaded China and Italy invaded Ethiopia during the 1930s.[11] Japan and Germany, which had reoccupied the Rhineland, withdrew from the League of Nations in 1933 and Italy did so in late 1937.[12]

Although the League of Nations was not formally dissolved until April 1946, its viability was overtaken by World War II, which blasted through the Covenant's fragile guardrails for peace and security.[13] The catastrophic global war compelled leaders, particularly at first U.S. President Franklin D. Roosevelt, who was then followed somewhat reluctantly by British Prime Minister Winston Churchill, to

[6] Treaty of Versailles, Part I, Covenant of the League of Nations, Art. 13 (28 Jun 1919).

[7] *Id.*, Art. 12; *Id.*, Art. 15.

[8] Treaty of Versailles, Part I, Covenant of the League of Nations, Art. 15 (28 Jun 1919).

[9] *Id.*, Art. 16.

[10] North Atlantic Treaty, Art. 5 (4 Apr 1945).

[11] Harry S. Truman Library (2024); Foreign Affairs (2022).

[12] U.S. Office of the Historian (2016a); The New York Times (1937).

[13] The United Nations Office at Geneva (2024b).

imagine creating a far more potent international organization, guided by an inspiring and resilient charter that would be enforced by powerful victor nations once the war had ended.

The Atlantic Charter, agreed to by Roosevelt and Churchill on the *U.S.S. Augusta* in Placentia Bay, Newfoundland, on August 14, 1941—at a time when it remained highly doubtful that the United States would even enter the war—expressed "common principles" for a future world at peace, enjoying self-government and living in economic prosperity.[14] The idealistic vision embodied in the eight common principles, one of which expressed their belief in the "abandonment of the use of force" by all nations, would resonate years later in the U.N. Charter, albeit with variance of wording and emphasis.[15] The Atlantic Charter thus emerged as one of the signature statements issued during World War II, setting forth an idealistic vision for the post-war world.

The term "United Nations" arose to describe the allied coalition of nations fighting the Tripartite Pact (Germany, Italy, and Japan), which were the principal Axis Powers. Roosevelt is credited with introducing the term, which framed the 182-word Declaration of United Nations backing the "purposes and principles embodied in" the Atlantic Charter and committing "full resources, military or economic," to the defeat of the Tripartite Pact.[16] The Declaration was signed by the United States, United Kingdom, Soviet Union, and China on January 1, 1942, followed the next day by

---

[14] Joint Declaration by the President and the Prime Minister (The Atlantic Charter) (1941).

[15] *Id.* The eight principles of the Atlantic Charter are as follows: "First, their countries, seek no aggrandizement, territorial or other; Second, they desire to see no territorial changes that do not accord with the freely expressed wishes of the peoples concerned; Third, they respect the right of all peoples to choose the form of government under which they will live; and they wish to see sovereign rights and self government restored to those who have been forcibly deprived of them; Fourth, they will endeavor, with due respect for their existing obligations, to further the enjoyment by all States, great or small, victor or vanquished, of access, on equal terms, to the trade and to the raw materials of the world which are needed for their economic prosperity; Fifth, they desire to bring about the fullest collaboration between all nations in the economic field with the object of securing, for all, improved labor standards, economic advancement and social security; Sixth, after the final destruction of the Nazi tyranny, they hope to see established a peace which will afford to all nations the means of dwelling in safety within their own boundaries, and which will afford assurance that all the men in all lands may live out their lives in freedom from fear and want;

Seventh, such a peace should enable all men to traverse the high seas and oceans without hindrance;

Eighth, they believe that all of the nations of the world, for realistic as well as spiritual reasons must come to the abandonment of the use of force. Since no future peace can be maintained if land, sea or air armaments continue to be employed by nations which threaten, or may threaten, aggression outside of their frontiers, they believe, pending the establishment of a wider and permanent system of general security, that the disarmament of such nations is essential. They will likewise aid and encourage all other practicable measure which will lighten for peace-loving peoples the crushing burden of armaments.".

[16] Declaration by the United Nations, A Joint Declaration by the United States, the United Kingdom, the Union of Soviet Socialist Republics, China, Australia, Belgium, Canada, Costa Rica, Cuba, Czechoslovakia, Dominican Republic, El Salvador, Greece, Guatemala, Haiti, Honduras, India, Luxembourg, Netherlands, New Zealand, Nicaragua, Norway, Panama, Poland, South Africa, Yugoslavia (1 Jan 1942); Schlesinger (2003), p. 39.

22 other nations. (The "China" referenced for the period spanning World II and the negotiations of the U.N. Charter is the Republic of China, which governed during those years. The membership of China in the United Nations transitioned from the Republic of China to The People's Republic of China on October 25, 1971.) By 1945, 47 nations from across the globe had signed the Declaration and they became the collective body that drafted the U.N. Charter.[17] Only countries that signed the Declaration qualified to engage in the San Francisco negotiations and then sign the U.N. Charter on June 26, 1945.

Subsequent declarations further emphasized both defeat of the Tripartite Pact and creation of a new world order in the aftermath of the war. The four Moscow Declarations of October 30, 1943, saw only the major Allied powers–the United States, United Kingdom, Soviet Union, and China—signing the documents.[18] The first declaration recognized "the necessity of establishing at the earliest practicable date a general international organization, based on the principle of the sovereign equality of all peace-loving states, and open to membership by all such states, large and small, for the maintenance of international peace and security."[19] So it was in Moscow, bastion of Leninist communism and brutal nationalism, where the first prominent vision of the United Nations as an international organization appeared on the horizon.

The fourth declaration signed in Moscow that day focused on the atrocities of the Nazi regime and called for domestic prosecutions of Germans responsible for such atrocities by the governments of liberated countries where the crimes occurred. The "Declaration on Atrocities" did not explicitly call for what later would become the International Military Tribunal at Nuremberg in 1945, but it pronounced that "German criminals whose offenses have no particular geographical localization…will be punished by joint decision of the governments of the Allies."[20]

The Moscow Declarations were followed a month later by the Tehran Declaration, signed in Iran on December 1, 1943, by Roosevelt for the United States, Churchill for the United Kingdom, and Stalin for the Soviet Union.[21] These leaders affirmed their determination to achieve victory in the war and recognized the responsibility of the war-fighting coalition of the "United Nations to make a peace which will command the good will of the overwhelming mass of the peoples of the world and banish the scourge and terror of war for many generations."[22] That aim for the "United Nations" would soon stir the task of creating an international organization guided by a charter. The Tehran Declaration continued, "We shall seek the cooperation and active participation of all nations, large and small, whose peoples in heart and mind are dedicated, as are our own peoples, to the elimination of tyranny and slavery,

---

[17] Only countries that signed the Declaration qualified to engage in the San Francisco negotiations and then sign the U.N. Charter on June 26, 1945.

[18] The Moscow Declarations (Oct 1943).

[19] *Id.*, Joint Four-Nation Declaration.

[20] *Id.*, Statement on Atrocities.

[21] The Tehran Declaration (1 Dec 1943).

[22] *Id.*

oppression and intolerance. We will welcome them, as they may choose to come, into a world family of democratic nations."[23] Though "democratic nations" would not come to define the full membership in the United Nations, the principles articulated in the Tehran Declaration briefly signified what would later be stressed in the Charter.

The hard work of Charter drafting began at Dumbarton Oaks in Washington, D.C., during the months of August, September, and October 1944 as the war raged intensively on both the Atlantic and Pacific fronts.[24] Spurred by the Moscow and Tehran Declarations, the three major Allied powers—the United States, the United Kingdom, and the Soviet Union—set out to transform idealistic notions into operational text for a charter of the United Nations. This planning for what would be erected in the wake of the world war demonstrated foresight often lacking in modern day conflicts, where planning for the post-war revival and governance of one or more nations sometimes becomes an afterthought or is deemed so complicated, risky, and costly that paralysis takes hold among politicians and diplomats. Not so in the minds of the Charter's founders, particularly Roosevelt who was determined throughout the war to bury the ghost of Versailles by ensuring that the Charter was completed before the war's end.[25] He quickly approved the designation of Dumbarton Oaks, which remains today an elegant institute and museum of Byzantine studies resting on a large acreage of flower beds, cherry blossom trees, and other foliage on the northern edge of colonial Georgetown in the American capital city.[26]

A century before World War II, Vice President and then Senator John C. Calhoun of South Carolina—a staunch champion of slavery—lived in the main building at Dumbarton Oaks. Adjacent to the estate is Oak Hill Cemetery, where American Civil War generals of both Union and Confederate stripe are buried, as is Abraham Lincoln's son Willie and Confederate President Jefferson Davis. Harvard University owned Dumbarton Oaks in 1944 and continues that stewardship to the present day. The estate was deemed the perfect site, despite Calhoun's legacy and Washington's muggy summer heat, for a drafting exercise among diplomats accustomed to such elegant and historic settings.

Throughout this book we return to Dumbarton Oaks and the enormous challenge undertaken there as we parse the origins of the Charter provisions while projecting into the future about what the Charter should mean for the modern world. But in general, the document that emerged on October 7, 1944, followed two months of negotiations and drafting at Dumbarton Oaks to establish the textual template for the Charter. Since the Dumbarton Oaks draft was well known by governments long before the final drafting conference convened in San Francisco in late April 1945, the relatively detailed draft facilitated the warp speed completion of the Charter two months later. Inspired by Roosevelt, a massive public relations campaign was

---

[23] *Id.*

[24] The history of the Dumbarton Oaks talks is told in Hilderbrand (2001); Schlesinger (2003), pp. 46–51.

[25] Schlesinger (2003), p. 31.

[26] Dumbarton Oaks (2024).

launched in late 1944 throughout the United States to circulate the text of the "Dumbarton Oaks Proposals for a General International Organization" and hold town hall meetings and other community gatherings in order to prepare the American public to support what would follow—the U.N. Charter—and thus lay the groundwork for rapid U.S. Senate ratification of the treaty when it was completed.[27] That alone was a masterstroke of consensus-building behind what would become the U.N. Charter and accelerate ratification by the Senate.

And yet, before San Francisco one more conference intervened and was held at Yalta in early February 1945.[28] At that time Yalta, which has long been a resort city in Crimea on the Black Sea, was a Ukrainian city but also part of the Soviet Union. Since Ukraine's independence in 1991, Yalta has been part of the territory of the sovereign nation of Ukraine. At the time of this writing, Russia continues to occupy Yalta as part of the annexed territory of Ukraine's region of Crimea (a move rejected repeatedly by the U.N. General Assembly following an aggressive intervention in 2014 that was amplified by Russia's massive war of aggression against Ukraine launched in February 2022).[29]

Roosevelt, Churchill, and Stalin met at Yalta only two months before Roosevelt's death and three months before the end of World War II in the European theater. Bowing to Stalin's insistence on meeting in remote Yalta, Roosevelt courageously made the arduous trip there despite the rapidly deteriorating health of not only himself but also of Harry Hopkins, his top aide.[30] But Roosevelt was determined to remove impediments to finalizing the U.N. Charter and Stalin was priority number one on that list.

Publicly, the Yalta Conference's primary aims were to defeat Japan and persuade Stalin to commit the massive Soviet army to join in that conquest. But off script discussions at Yalta resulted in the United States, United Kingdom, and Soviet Union agreeing to the American proposal—backed by the Dumbarton Oaks draft—for a U.N. Security Council with five permanent members: the United States, United Kingdom, France, Soviet Union, and China (the "P-5"). Perhaps more significantly, the three leaders agreed to vest each such permanent member with the power to veto any Security Council resolution, an outcome that soon would be reflected in Article

[27] Schlesinger (2003), pp. 53–55.

[28] U.S. Office of the Historian (2016c).

[29] Countries that have voted against UN resolutions condemning the Russian annexation of Crimea include, but are not limited to, Armenia, Belarus, Bolivia, Cuba, Nicaragua, North Korea, Russia, Sudan, Syria, Venezuela, and Zimbabwe. UNGA, Resolution 68/262 Territorial integrity of Ukraine, UN Doc A/RES/68/262 (27 Mar 2014); UNGA, Resolution 74/17 Problem of the militarization of the Autonomous Republic of Crimea and the city of Sevastopol, Ukraine, as well as parts of the Black Sea and the Sea of Azov, UN Doc A/RES/74/17 (9 Dec 2019); UNGA, Resolution 74/168 Situation of human rights in the Autonomous Republic of Crimea and the city of Sevastopol, Ukraine, UN Doc A/RES/74/168 (18 Dec 2019); UNGA, Resolution 75/29 Problem of the militarization of the Autonomous Republic of Crimea and the city of Sevastopol, Ukraine, as well as parts of the Black Sea and the Sea of Azov, UN Doc A/RES/75/29 (7 Dec 2020); Pifer (2020); Walker (2024).

[30] Schlesinger (2003), pp. 53–72.

27(3) the U.N. Charter, would often cripple the United Nations from acting effectively during the Cold War, and steadily fracture the P-5 along ideological grounds far into the 21st Century and to the present day.[31] Indeed, the veto power had already appeared months earlier, in 1944, in Chapter VI, Section C(3) of the Dumbarton Oaks draft, which required all non-procedural matters to receive the concurring votes of the five permanent members of the Security Council. However, at Yalta Roosevelt labored, successfully, to gain Stalin's approval that simply initiating a discussion about a question would be considered a procedural matter requiring only a majority of Security Council member votes, no option for a veto, and no nation engaged in the actual dispute at issue entitled to cast a vote.[32] Yalta sealed that deal although weeks later the Soviet delegation in San Francisco had to be accommodated on it once again during painful negotiations.[33]

Thousands of delegates and their staffs ultimately representing 50 nations descended on San Francisco, California, for the "United Nations Conference on International Organization," which commenced on April 25, 1945.[34] Adolf Hitler would die by suicide five days later in a Berlin bunker and the war in the European theater would end on May 9.[35] The war in the Pacific theater would outlast the conference and the initial signing of the final text of the Charter on June 26. But the defeat of Japan in August 1945 facilitated the Charter's founding governments to reach the required majority, including the "Big Five" nations (China, France, Soviet Union, United Kingdom, and United States) comprising the Permanent Five of the Security Council, to ratify the Charter by October 24, 1945, thus bringing it into force as a binding treaty and the launch of the United Nations as the premier international organization.[36] Every year thereafter that date has been celebrated as United Nations Day.

Administrative committees for the San Francisco Conference and committees responsible for drafting individual portions of the Charter were quickly established at the beginning of the conference. Delegates convened in buildings that still stand as iconic cultural centers: the War Memorial Opera House and the Herbst Theater auditorium in the Veterans War Memorial Building next door, and scores of offices throughout them.[37] In 1995 co-author David Scheffer attended the 50th anniversary of the U.N. Charter, held in the opulent Opera House with a full audience addressed by U.S. President Bill Clinton and the U.S. Permanent Representative to the United Nations, Dr. Madeleine Albright, for whom Scheffer was senior adviser and counsel at the time.[38] In their speeches Clinton focused on reforming the United Nations so

---

[31] *Id.*, pp. 58–59; U.S. Office of the Historian (2016c).

[32] Schlesinger (2003), pp. 203–206.

[33] *Id.*, pp. 215–223.

[34] United Nations (2024).

[35] U.S. Holocaust Memorial Museum (2021).

[36] National Archives (2022).

[37] San Francisco Opera (2024); San Francisco War Memorial & Performing Arts Center (2024).

[38] San Francisco Opera (2024).

as to adapt it to the realities of the modern world while Albright stressed the legacy that the Charter bestows on the children of the world.[39]

One particular room in San Francisco served as a critical venue for some of the toughest drafting endeavors. Located in the iconic Fairmont Hotel on Nob Hill, the Garden Room was the setting for small gatherings of delegates to iron out the Charter wording (see Figs. 1.1 and 1.2).[40] Today the Garden Room is usually vacant (except for occasional events such as wedding receptions) and seemingly without historic purpose save for a plaque outside the door noting the role it played in 1945. Yet it was in the Garden Room where some of the most critical negotiations were held in shaping the final version of the U.N. Charter. The notoriously young (aged 45) and prematurely grey-haired U.S. Secretary of State Edward R. Stettinius Jr. conveniently resided in the hotel's penthouse apartment and held daily meetings there with his delegation, the senior delegates and aides of the Big Five, as well as some other nations playing key roles in the talks—all with the aim of ironing out thorny issues.[41]

Signifying the hotel's centrality to the entire exercise, U.S. President Harry S. Truman arrived at the Fairmont Hotel on June 25, 1945, to meet negotiators and, the next day, attend the signing ceremony and deliver his historic public address before the delegates.[42] Only two months earlier, on April 16, Truman had stood as president for the first time before Congress following Roosevelt's death and closed his brief remarks with reference to "a United Nations deeply devoted to the highest ideals. With great humility, I call upon all Americans to help me keep our nation united in defense of those ideals which have been so eloquently proclaimed by Franklin Roosevelt."[43]

Working from the proposals negotiated at Dumbarton Oaks, 850 delegates and advisors in San Francisco spent nine weeks crafting the U.N. Charter. They debated and ultimately resolved contentious issues, but not until after some very tough negotiations, particularly with the Soviet delegation, compelling President Truman to request an emergency mission to Moscow in June 1945 by Harry Hopkins, who had been Roosevelt's most trusted but seriously ill aide, to secure Stalin's explicit approval on the Security Council voting formula, although negotiators in San Francisco still had to labor over how to finalize the relevant Charter language.[44]

The Latin American bloc of nations, which proved to be a powerful voting group in San Francisco, held Stettinius's feet to the fire over their insistence that Argentina

---

[39] Clinton W J, Remarks on the 50th Anniversary of the United Nations Charter in San Francisco, California (26 Jun 1995) The American Presidency Project; Albright, Madeleine, Remarks on the 50th Anniversary of the United Nations Charter in San Francisco, California (26 Jun 1995), C-SPAN at https://www.c-span.org/program/white-house-event/united-nations-50th-anniversary/156379.

[40] Fairmont San Francisco (2024).

[41] Schlesinger (2003), p. 160.

[42] Truman H S, Address in San Francisco at the Closing Session of the United Nations Conference (26 Jun 1945) The American Presidency Project.

[43] Truman H S, Address Before a Joint Session of the Congress (16 Apr 1945) The American Presidency Project.

[44] Schlesinger (2003), pp. 209–225.

Fig. 1.1 Co-author David Scheffer standing in the Fairmont Hotel's Garden Room where the U.N. Charter was negotiated in 1945 (*Source* David Scheffer)

be allowed to sign the U.N. Charter along with the other nations represented in San Francisco, including many from Latin America, as a precondition to casting their essential votes to admit Soviet-dominated Ukraine and Belarus as voting member states of the United Nations in addition to the Soviet Union. In reality, Stalin insisted on this mathematical lift to counter the West's larger vote count in the emerging United Nations and he strongly objected to admitting Argentina. That government had expressed pro-Nazi sympathies throughout World War II and only turned against Berlin several weeks before the German surrender in April 1945. (Roosevelt had countered, perhaps half-seriously, during an earlier phase of the dispute that the United States should add a few votes of its own from among its 48 federal states of the union.) Stalin's man in San Francisco, Foreign Minister Vyacheslav Molotov, failed to defeat the final vote that invited Argentina to join the United Nations.[45]

In the end, however, the Soviet Union ultimately prevailed in its bid to rig the system so that Poland would be admitted to the United Nations with a largely pro-Soviet government that ensured its subservience to Moscow despite what Roosevelt and Churchill had negotiated at Yalta. So, for the price of Argentina's admission to the United Nations, Stalin gained Poland, Ukraine, and Belarus in his U.N. column of faithful votes for Soviet interests thanks to the San Francisco bartering. Moscow would dominate these three nations, and many others, throughout the Cold War.

[45] *Id.*, pp. 127–142.

Fig. 1.2 The plaque at the entrance to the Fairmont Hotel's Garden Room in San Francisco (*Source* David Scheffer)

There were many diplomatic battles waged in San Francisco during those fateful weeks when Roosevelt's vision of a world body dedicated to international peace and security, economic and social progress, and the protection of human rights was on the knife-edge of success, overshadowed by critical moments of despair among the founders of the Charter. Some of those stories will emerge in the chapters that follow as the legacy of Roosevelt, Churchill, and Truman is remembered.

President Truman, who had long advocated creation of a world organization and led in the Senate on the issue since March 1943, made critical decisions frequently during the San Francisco conference as policy judgments were presented to him by Secretary of State Stettinius for final determination of the American position.[46] His stake in the outcome was profoundly important and was guided in part by what would satisfy the U.S. Senate to ratify the Charter within a few weeks of its signing in San Francisco. (Truman's thinking likely also was steered by, "What would FDR do?") Those few weeks are unparalleled speed for any treaty, particularly one of such significance and political complexity as the Charter.

Truman wanted the United States to lead the world in supporting the document and so he delivered three key addresses in connection with the Charter between June and October 1945. He opened the San Francisco conference by radio address and then,

[46] *Id*., pp. 77–78.

at the closing session of that conference on June 26, Truman signaled the prospect of further change.

> This Charter, like our own Constitution, will be expanded and improved as time goes on. No one claims that it is now a final or a perfect instrument. It has not been poured into any fixed mold. Changing world conditions will require readjustments—but they will be the readjustments of peace and not of war."[47] He continued, "We all have to recognize—no matter how great our strength—that we must deny ourselves the license to do always as we please. No one nation, no regional group, can or should expect, any special privilege which harms any other nation. If any nation would keep security for itself, it must be ready and willing to share security with all. That is the price which each nation will have to pay for world peace. Unless we are all to pay that price, no organization for world peace can accomplish its purpose.[48]

In presenting the signed U.N. Charter to the Senate for ratification six days later, on July 2, 1945, Truman astutely acknowledged resolutions adopted in the Senate and the House of Representatives more than a year and a half earlier, under his leadership when he was a senator, favoring the creation of such an international organization with American participation. The congressional hand, he said, shaped "the Dumbarton Oaks Proposals, upon which the Charter has been based." Then he pointed out, with the clarity that a seasoned lawmaker like himself knew well how to deliver, the basic objectives and challenge of the Charter:

> It seeks to prevent future wars.
>
> It seeks to settle international disputes by peaceful means, in conformity with the principles of justice.
>
> It seeks to promote worldwide progress and better standards of living.
>
> It seeks to achieve universal respect for, and observance of, human rights and fundamental freedoms for all men and women—without distinction as to race, language, or religion.
>
> It seeks to remove the economic and social causes of international conflict and unrest.
>
> It is the product of many hands and many influences. It comes from the reality of experience in a world where one generation has failed twice to keep the peace. The lessons of that experience have been written into this document.
>
> The choice before the Senate is now clear. The choice is not between this Charter and something else. It is between this Charter and no Charter at all.
>
> Improvements will come in the future as the United Nations gain experience with the machinery and methods which they have set up. For this is not a static treaty. It can be improved—and, as the years go by, it will be—just as our own Constitution has been improved.[49]

The Senate ratified the U.N. Charter on July 28, 1945, with a stunning bipartisan vote of 89 to 2 compared to what one would normally expect given contemporary standards of raw partisanship on Capitol Hill.[50]

---

[47] *Id.*, p. 290.

[48] *Id.*, p. 292; Truman (1945).

[49] Truman H S, Address Before the Senate Urging Ratification of the Charter of the United Nations (2 Jul 1945) The American Presidency Project.

[50] VoteView (2024).

Finally, on October 23, 1945, Truman addressed the opening session of the U.N. General Assembly in New York City, an event made possible because the Charter had just entered into force with the ratifications of China, France, the United Kingdom, the Soviet Union, and the United States as well as a majority of the other signatory nations in San Francisco. Truman opened his address with pride that the United Nations had chosen the United States for its headquarters. "This meeting," he said, "symbolizes the abandonment by the United States of a policy of isolation." He then grounded his address on the "four essential freedoms" that Roosevelt committed himself and the United States to early in the war and which are often turned to when illuminating the Charter: freedom of speech, freedom of religion, freedom from want, and freedom from fear.[51]

Truman declared that these "are fundamental freedoms to which all the United Nations are pledged under the Charter." He continued,

> [E]very member of the United Nations is legally and morally bound by the Charter to keep the peace. More specifically, every member is bound to refrain in its international relations from the threat, or use, of force against the territorial integrity or political independence of any state….
>
> We shall attain freedom from fear when every act of every nation, in its dealings with every other nation, brings closer to realization the other freedoms—freedom of speech, freedom of religion, and freedom from want. Along this path we can find justice for all, without distinction between the strong and the weak among nations, and without discrimination among individuals.[52]

Abundant historical evidence entertains critics and cynics of the Charter because so much of its aspirational language has been challenged by the darker forces of human nature and power since World War II.[53] Battle-scarred and yet preserving words that at times seem to survive on life support, the Charter remains a universally vibrant document of hope and vision that no nation or people should abandon. In contrast to the Charter's World War II origins, today a new constellation of powers competes for influence while existential challenges dominate the global agenda. We need to rediscover the Charter and explore pragmatic modern interpretations of its words to help nations and peoples navigate the highly uncertain terrain of the future.

The following chapters of this book examine the text of the Charter in five fields of human endeavor: human rights and fundamental freedoms, international law, international peace and security, social and economic progress, and peacemaking. The final chapter summarizes how the Charter should be understood and applied in the modern world. The various chapters of this book touch on interconnected issues addressed in other chapters, based on their shared focus on the Charter as a foundational document shaping global governance, human rights, and international law.

What follows is a modest effort to bring to life words that form the bedrock of global governance.

---

[51] These four freedoms are examined further in Chapter 2.

[52] Truman H S, Address in New York City at the Opening Session of the United Nations General Assembly (23 Oct 1945) The American Presidency Project.

[53] Gold (2005); Moloney (2020); Schaefer (2022).

References

Danspeckgruber W, Gardner A (2024) Self-setermination. In: Encyclopedia princetoniensis. Princeton University. https://pesd.princeton.edu/node/656 Self-Determination. Accessed 3 Dec 2024

Dumbarton Oaks (2024) Dumbarton oaks. https://www.doaks.org/. Accessed 2 Dec 2024

Fairmont San Francisco (2024) Event venues. https://www.fairmont-san-francisco.com/gather/venues/. Accessed 3 Dec 2024

Foreign Affairs (2022) Fascist Italy invades Ethiopia. https://www.foreignaffairs.com/lists/fascist-italy-invades-ethiopia. Accessed 2 Dec 2024

Gold D (2005) Tower of babble: how the United Nations Has Fueled Global Chaos. Crown Forum

Harry S. Truman Library (2024) Invasion of Manchuria. https://www.trumanlibrary.gov/education/presidential-inquiries/invasion-manchuria. Accessed 2 Dec 2024

Hilderbrand RC (2001) Dumbarton Oaks: the origins of the United Nations and the search for postwar security, 1st edn. University of North Carolina Press

Kennedy P (2006) The parliament of man. Vintage Books

Moloney W (2020) The long, sad decline of the United Nations. https://thehill.com/opinion/international/495071-the-long-sad-decline-of-the-united-nations/. Accessed 9 Dec 2024

New York Times (1937) Italy leaves the league. https://timesmachine.nytimes.com/timesmachine/1937/12/13/118995646.html?pageNumber=26. Accessed 2 Dec 2024

https://history.state.gov/milestones/1937-1945/yalta-conf.

Pifer S (2020) Crimea: six years after illegal annexation. In: Foreign policy, Center on the United States and Europe. Brookings Institution. https://www.brookings.edu/articles/crimea-six-years-after-illegal-annexation/Crimea: Six years after illegal annexation. Accessed 3 Dec 2024

San Francisco Opera (2024) War memorial opera house. https://www.sfopera.com/about/venue/war-memorial-opera-house/. Accessed 3 Dec 2024

San Francisco War Memorial & Performing Arts Cener (2024) Herbst theatre. https://sfwarmemorial.org/herbst-theatre/. Accessed 3 Dec 2024

Schaefer B D (2022) Is the United Nations a failure? https://www.heritage.org/global-politics/commentary/the-united-nations-failure. Accessed 9 Dec 2024

Schlesinger S (2003) Act of Creation: The Founding of the United Nations. Westview Press

The United Nations Office at Geneva (2024) The League of Nations. https://www.ungeneva.org/en/about/league-of-nations/overview. Accessed 2 Dec 2024 ("The United Nations Office at Geneva (2024a)")

The United Nations Office at Geneva (2024) Transition to the United Nations. https://www.ungeneva.org/en/about/league-of-nations/transition. Accessed 2 Dec 2024 ("The United Nations Office at Geneva (2024b)")

United Nations (2024) The San Francisco conference. https://www.un.org/en/about-us/history-of-the-un/san-francisco-conference. Accessed 3 Dec 2024

University of Virginia Miller Center (1943) December 1, 1943: The Tehran declaration. https://millercenter.org/the-presidency/presidential-speeches/december-1-1943-tehran-declaration. Accessed 2 Dec 2024

U.S. Holocaust Memorial Museum (2021) World War II dates and timeline. https://encyclopedia.ushmm.org/content/en/article/world-war-ii-key-dates. Accessed 3 Dec 2024

U.S. National Archives (2022) United Nations Charter (1945). https://www.archives.gov/milestone-documents/united-nations-charter. Accessed 3 Dec 2024

U.S. Office of the Historian (2016) The covenant of the league of nations (Art. 1 to 26). https://history.state.gov/historicaldocuments/frus1919Parisv13/ch10subch1. Accessed 6 Dec 2024 ("U.S. Office of the Historian (2016a)")

U.S. Office of the Historian (2016) The league of nations, 1920. https://history.state.gov/milestones/1914-1920/league. Accessed 2 Dec 2024 ("U.S. Office of the Historian (2016b)")

U.S. Office of the Historian (2016) The Yalta conference, 1945. https://history.state.gov/milestones/1937-1945/yalta-conf. Accessed 17 Dec 2024 ("U.S. Office of the Historian (2016c)")

VoteView (2024) 79th Congress > Senate > Vote 65: Executive F. (79th Cong., 1st Sess.) Charter of the U.N. Ratification. https://voteview.com/rollcall/RS0790065. Accessed 10 Dec 2024

Walker N (2024) Conflict in Ukraine: A timeline (current conflict, 2022 – present). In: Research briefings. House of Commons Library. https://researchbriefings.files.parliament.uk/documents/CBP-9847/CBP-9847.pdf Conflict in Ukraine: A timeline (current conflict, 2022 – present). Accessed 3 Dec 2024

Chapter 2
Protect Human Rights and Fundamental Freedoms

Introduction

On any objective measurement, the international community is facing extraordinary challenges. The post-World War II legal, or "rules-based," international order—the bedrock of today's global statecraft—is under threat. Principles such as the equal application of the law, unfettered elections, judicial independence, pluralism and tolerance, and media freedom are unraveling rapidly. In their place is emerging a legal order embedded in authoritarianism fueled by a dramatic rise of populism and nationalism. The number of democracies is declining; individual human rights and fundamental freedoms are eroding.[1] This is the new normal. When contrasted with the establishment of human rights that emerged from the ashes of World War II, the present situation shows that the pendulum has dramatically shifted. The question is: can these negative trends be reversed? History, with its lessons and examples, gives us both guidance and hope in this endeavor.

In the immediate aftermath of World War II, a transformative shift emerged, with political leaders focusing on creating a legal structure that would establish and, ideally, uphold human rights for all people. This idea would partially upend the Westphalian legal order (which emerged after the end of the Thirty Years' War in 1648) that was premised on absolute state sovereignty, including the non-interference in the internal affairs of another state, even for flagrant violations of citizens' rights. State sovereignty would no longer be seen as manifestly superior to the rights of individuals.[2] The new legal priority marked by the U.N. Charter was a significant departure from the previous attempt to "internationalize" law through the League of Nations in 1920. The League, despite the grand aspirations of U.S. President Woodrow Wilson, failed in large part due to the U.S. Senate's refusal to ratify the Versailles Treaty, leaving the League of Nations crippled and too often a mere shell

[1] Repucci and Slipowitz (2021) and V-Dem Institute (2024).
[2] Reus-Smit (2013, pp. 68–105).

D. J. Scheffer and M. S. Ellis, *The UN Charter*,
https://doi.org/10.1007/978-3-031-94866-4_2

of an organization.[3] The 1928 Kellogg-Briand Pact, aimed at outlawing war, failed to achieve its aim with the outbreak of World War II.[4] As the march towards that world war grew stronger during the 1930s, the League of Nations eventually withered away. The United Nations would represent the second attempt at internationalizing peace, with a renewed focus on social and economic rights and, significantly, human rights and fundamental freedoms for the individual.

This chapter reviews the journey of human rights and fundamental freedoms to their emplacement as core principles of the U.N. Charter. It is a journey that includes the early formation of the Charter and the Herculean efforts by state and non-state actors to create an international structure inspired by these rights and freedoms. Both accentuated the individual and were intentionally drafted into the U.N. Charter as a way to prevent future wars. While the function of states in the international system was a prominent feature of the Charter from its inception, the unique emphasis on individual rights is what makes the Charter so uniquely important.

Human rights and fundamental freedoms remain two of the foundational tenets of the U.N. Charter. In the inspiring language of the preamble, the drafters employed imagery reflected on history's dark passage of world wars to motivate states to embrace a new international organization where protecting the rights and freedoms of individuals would become permanent:

> WE THE PEOPLES OF THE UNITED NATIONS DETERMINED
>
> to save succeeding generations from the scourge of war, which twice in our lifetime has brought untold sorrow to mankind, and to reaffirm faith in fundamental human rights, in the dignity and worth of the human person, in the equal rights of men and women and of nations large and small, and to establish conditions under which justice and respect for the obligations arising from treaties and other sources of international law can be maintained, and to promote social progress and better standards of life in larger freedom…[5]

The language above did not appear miraculously. As the Introduction relates, it resulted from over five years of conferences, debates, drafts, and, most importantly, political will. The U.N. Charter was a remarkable manifestation of states' willingness to give up a significant degree of their sovereign power to an international organization and to cede power to their citizens by granting them fundamental rights.

Throughout the early stages of this journey, the drafters of the Charter did not hold any preconceived notions of the exact meaning of human rights and fundamental freedoms; that would come later. However, the Charter's drafters intuitively knew that advancing these rights was critical to maintaining peace and security in the post-war era. If the world's governments could not uphold these principles, the lessons of the wars would be lost, leaving the world doomed to future catastrophes. The drafters also knew that the Charter had to be seen as created by the will of all people; thus, the words "[W]e the Peoples of the United Nations." And though the word "Peoples" is closely aligned to the countries in which they live, it was drawn directly from the U.S. Constitution ("We the People of the United States") to demonstrate a collective

---

[3] Henig (2010).

[4] Hathaway and Shapiro (2017).

[5] Charter of the United Nations 1 UNTS XVI (26 June 1945), Preamble.

commitment by states to ensure fundamental rights to all "peoples" regardless of within which sovereign territory they reside.

The Charter's emphasis on human rights and fundamental freedoms is grounded on four historical events occurring under the pressure of global warfare. The first arose in the United States when President Franklin D. Roosevelt delivered his annual State of the Union address on January 6, 1941, known as the "Four Freedoms" speech. Roosevelt articulated almost one year before America entered into World War II an all-encompassing concept of human rights that belonged to all humankind: (1) freedom of speech and expression, (2) freedom of religion, (3) freedom from want, and (4) freedom from fear.[6] The famous American painter Norman Rockwell depicted these principles in his painting entitled, "Four Freedoms." Roosevelt's address set into motion the journey that ultimately would lead to the creation of the United Nations. His "Four Freedoms" theme was the common thread throughout all significant discussions of the Charter's human rights agenda, weaving together differing ideologies, cultures, and perspectives through masterful statesmanship that ultimately created a cohesive tapestry of the post-war international legal order.

The speech's influence was not confined to the United States. Within the country, Roosevelt faced a dramatic isolationist movement that he needed to counter. During his speech, which he redrafted many times, Roosevelt stated, "[I]n the future days, which we seek to make secure, we look forward to a world founded upon four essential human freedoms." His commitment to freedom of expression and religion was not alien to Americans, but he wanted them to see these freedoms as relevant to the world community. One of Roosevelt's boldest wishes was "freedom from want—which, translated into world terms, means economic understandings which will secure to every nation a healthy peacetime life for its inhabitants—everywhere in the world." It showed Roosevelt's understanding that individual economic prosperity facilitates a world of security and that there would need to be a new international organization built upon the rubble of the League of Nations.

In addition to Roosevelt's indispensable role in conceptualizing the fundamental freedoms, there were three other events critical to these components of the U.N. Charter—the Atlantic Charter, the Dumbarton Oaks Conference, and the San Fransisco Conference—that ultimately secured consensus for the codification of human rights and fundamental freedoms in the Charter. They offer us a glimpse into the remarkable commitment of so many governments and non-governmental actors to establishing a legal instrument to uphold these principles for all humankind. That collective commitment still resonates today despite the many struggles at all levels of global society challenging these principles.

---

[6] Roosevelt F D, Annual Message to Congress (January 6, 1941) Records of the United States Senate (SEN 77A-H1).

The Atlantic Charter

British Prime Minister Winston Churchill's primary goal for the Atlantic Charter, which he signed with Roosevelt in August 1941, was "to get the Americans into the war." He had hoped that the United States would increase its military aid to Great Britain and, in doing so, deter Japan from taking any aggressive actions in the Pacific.[7] Roosevelt was of the same view and hoped to overcome the American people's reluctance to back American intervention in the war, as they eventually would do on December 8, 1941 on the day after the Japanese attack on Pearl Harbor. Churchill believed that a joint declaration of a robust alliance would raise the morale of the British public and align the interests of the United States with Great Britain.[8]

However, the most compelling issue discussed by the two leaders was their desire to outline an international system that would emerge after the war despite enormous uncertainty about its outcome.[9] Churchill and Roosevelt each approached this issue differently. Churchill wanted the joint declaration to mention an "effective international organization." Roosevelt was cautious because of the American public's isolationist fervor and the U.S. Senate's negative view of the failed League of Nations, so he rejected any mention (yet) of such an entity.[10] This initial reluctance does not diminish Roosevelt's role in creating the architecture of the U.N. Charter. More than any other country, the United States under Roosevelt's leadership worked during World War II for a future of global peace and security through the U.N. Charter and its institutional embodiment in the United Nations.

The Atlantic Charter was the first of the sequenced international documents that alluded to the creation of international human rights. A key provision reads:

> Sixth, after the final destruction of the Nazi tyranny, they hope to see established a peace which will afford to all nations the means of dwelling in safety within their own boundaries, and which will afford assurance that all the men in all the lands may live out their lives in freedom from fear and want.

The fifth provision of the Atlantic Charter also refers to advancing social and economic rights to secure global peace and security:

> Fifth, they desire to bring about the fullest collaboration between all nations in the economic field with the object of securing, for all, improved labor standards, economic advancement, and social security...

Years later, at the 1945 San Francisco Conference (Fig. 2.1), delegates would reference the importance of economic and social security for all in the U.N. Charter.

Although not a binding treaty and lacking explicit reference to "human rights," the Atlantic Charter emphasized the notion of what became articulated as human rights and fundamental freedoms in the U.N. Charter. Roosevelt's influence was prominent.

---

[7] United States Office of the Historian (2016).

[8] The cabinet supported Churchill's recommendation and approved the charter. Id.

[9] Id.

[10] Meisler (1995).

Fig. 2.1 U.S. Secretary of State Edward R. Stettinius addressing the San Francisco Conference with President Harry S. Truman on June 26, 1945 (*Source* UN Photo)

Two of his "Four Freedoms" were explicitly invoked in the Atlantic Charter: freedom from want and freedom from fear. After the defeat of Nazi Germany, Roosevelt and Churchill hoped to see established a peace which will afford to all nations the means of dwelling in safety within their own boundaries, and which will afford assurance that "all the men in all lands may live out their lives in freedom from fear and want".[11]

The Dumbarton Oaks Conference

The Dumbarton Oaks Conference was the next major step toward the formation of the United Nations; it laid the groundwork for the San Francisco Conference, where human rights protections eventually would be embodied in the U.N. Charter. As described in the Introduction, the Dumbarton Oaks meeting of the four major powers—the United States, Great Britain, China and the Soviet Union—took place at a private estate in Washington, D.C., from August to October 1944. The small group of diplomats addressed a multitude of substantive and administrative issues. However, there was virtually no promotion of human rights at Dumbarton Oaks; the issue was mentioned only once, at the request of the United States.[12] Indeed, the Dumbarton Oaks proposals failed to use the words "human rights and fundamental freedoms" in Chapter I, which defined the purposes of the international organization to be created. Neither Britain nor the Soviet Union were keen on maintaining an aggressive human

[11] Joint Declaration by the President and the Prime Minister (The Atlantic Charter) (1941), provisions 2, 3, 5–6.

[12] Glendon (2002).

rights agenda that would define and structure the future United Nations. They wanted the Charter to mirror a peace treaty and focus on security, including collective defense against aggression. Although the intricate balance between state sovereignty and the rights of individuals, discussed earlier in the chapter, was hotly debated at Dumbarton Oaks, diverse coalitions contested the notion of eroding state sovereignty to facilitate fundamental human rights and freedoms. A number of delegates hoped that an "international bill of rights" would be attached to the preamble of the Charter, but that idea was rejected as the major powers were not enthusiastic about the concept. Instead, Chapter IX of the Dumbarton Oaks Proposals envisaged the creation of the Economic and Social Council that, among other responsibilities, would promote fundamental rights and freedoms. No definitions of these terms emerged at Dumbarton Oaks, but the table was set for their inclusion of major principles in the U.N. Charter seven months later in San Francisco.[13]

The San Francisco Conference

> Daily bread turns to stone unless eaten in freedom and with human dignity. (Trygve Halvdan Lie)[14]

Something extraordinary happened between the Dumbarton Oaks meetings in 1944 and the San Francisco Conference held from April to June 1945. The focus on human rights and fundamental freedoms was dramatically sharpened as 46 nations from across the world convened in San Francisco.[15]

Although discussions at the San Francisco Conference were often centered on the proposed veto power reserved for the permanent members of the Security Council, there was a growing awareness among the delegates of the need to support human rights. The speeches in San Francisco emphasized the importance of individual human rights as a core purpose of the Charter because the world war had exposed the weakness of state territorial sovereignty, particularly in protecting the rights of people. One of the main catalysts to this emphasis was the appearance of images emerging from liberated concentration camps in Europe.

The fog of war lifted in April 1945 as the liberation of, for example, the Buchenwald, Dachau, and Mauthausen camps by American soldiers exposed the atrocities committed by Nazi Germany.[16] The appalling sight of death and survival at the same

[13] United Nations (2024b).

[14] United Nations Conference on International Organization (1945a, p. 555) (per Lie T H).

[15] United Nations (2024a).

[16] Buchenwald Concentration Camp, Germany (April 17, 1945), National Archives, Record Group 111: Records of the Office of the Chief Signal Officer to Military Activities, 111-ADC-4199; Atrocities at Dachau, Germany (May 3, 1945), National Archives, Record Group 111: Records of the Office of the Chief Signal Officer to Military Activities, 111-ADC-4469; Concentration and Death Camp Mauthausen, Austria (May 11, 1945), National Archives, Record Group 111: Records of the Office of the Chief Signal Officer to Military Activities, 111-ADC-4319.

time that the world's nations were deliberating on the post-war world order would have a powerful impact. The delegates in San Francisco could not ignore these horrors, which shocked the conscience of humankind. They recognized the need for an international organization that would endeavor to prevent future atrocities. The representative from Czechoslovakia, whose citizens witnessed the Holocaust first-hand, attested:

> Last but not least, the suffering inhabitants of the terrible concentration camps and ghettos. My country, Fellow Delegates, has been one concentration camp since 1939. To make the world worthy of all their sacrifices and sufferings, to keep faith with our dead, this Conference has been convened. We who have survived in comparative safety have an almost crushing responsibility.[17]

The emerging view was that human rights were independent of territorial borders and transcended the interests of states. Mexico, for example, was among those espousing the view that the human individual enjoyed a universal standard of human rights no matter the location and "without any restriction" so as "to guarantee him a minimum standard of civilized justice."[18]

As stated earlier in the chapter, this view was exceptional, considering that historically, international law maintained strict principles of state sovereignty and non-interference in domestic affairs, including the view that the state decided what was best for its citizens. The concept of the universality of human rights was antithetical to this view but seen by a growing number of states as paramount and not to be diluted by national interests. In many ways, this concept was familiar. It can be found in early religious teachings and legal texts like the Magna Carta, the American Declaration of Independence, the French Declaration of the Rights of Man and of the Citizen, and the Declaration of the International Rights of Man.[19] This view also reflects the philosophy espoused by enlightened thinkers such as John Locke and Immanuel Kant, who emphasized that human rights were at the forefront of state responsibilities. Of course, the legal concept of sovereignty, as seen through the protective lens of head-of-state immunity and state immunity, would persist, such as in foreign state jurisdictions. Still, the delegates in San Francisco demonstrated an intention to chip away at rigid allegiance to state sovereignty so as to protect all citizens' human rights.

The United States' support of the position was critical. Roosevelt was determined to see that his "Four Freedoms" would not languish in obscurity but would be perfected. Again, it is impossible to exaggerate Roosevelt's instrumental role in consummating the Charter and guiding its core purposes to include human rights and fundamental freedoms. He never saw the Charter as a zero-sum proposition as he believed it would elevate the entire world community.

It is worth pausing and reflecting on how Roosevelt's death just two weeks before the San Francisco Conference affected the arriving delegations. His name was

[17] United Nations Conference on International Organization (1945a, p. 232).

[18] United Nations Conference on International Organization (1945b, p. 69).

[19] Finch (1941, pp. 663–664). The Declaration was adapted by the Institute of International Law, which recognized that all individuals have the right to life, liberty and property.

invoked at least 150 times during their opening speeches. The outpouring of grief was palpable. The participating states knew the extraordinary contributions Roosevelt had made. The representative of the Philippines summed up these feelings:

> May I pause here to pay tribute to the memory of Franklin Delano Roosevelt, the staunch defender of the human rights of those millions—a man who died an American, but whose grave is the world—the peerless leader who gave new meaning to our lives in the Far East because he was the champion not only of the forgotten man of his own nation, but of the forgotten man everywhere in the world. We turn our reverential thoughts to him today with a very deep sense of loss, because to us of the United Nations he is the symbol of all the ideals for which we are fighting in this war; and his passing away at this time deprives us of his guidance and inspiration. We find consolation and strength in the assurance that . . . his spirit marches on.[20]

The delegate from Chile also spoke eloquently about Roosevelt:

> The life of a great man is like the seed of an unknown tree. During his days on this earth we see its branches and flowers that may be splendid and modestly fragrant. The waters of death sometimes enhance this splendor into glory and season its fruits with intense flavor and beauty. Roosevelt has been a powerful tree of magnanimous and firm fruits and flowers, strong within the heart of this great people, and his foliage extends over the entire world. His death has been only a streak of lightning that has destroyed the mere form, the mortal form. Although sorrow weighs upon us for his apparent disappearance, we affirm that Roosevelt goes on in all parts of the earth. His death is as a strong light that sheds its light always with greater clarity—the light of a great statesman and a great leader of peoples.
>
> His spiritual work begins to grow and to spread throughout the earth. It is we, the United Nations, who have the solemn duty to be faithful to this noble heritage.[21]

The focus on human rights at the conference also significantly resonated with less developed countries. In hindsight, this may be one of the most extraordinary aspects of the journey to emphasize human rights and fundamental freedoms within the U.N. Charter. The less developed countries played an indispensable role. Together, they made up a global coalition that doggedly sought to include human rights in the Charter as a fundamental purpose of the United Nations.

When reading the speeches delivered at the San Francisco Conference by representatives from the "Global South," one is struck by the conviction and passion with which they articulated the need to enshrine human rights and fundamental freedoms within the new Charter.

For example, South Africa's representative, despite his country's racist and discriminatory society at the time, delivered a remarkable statement about the human spirit that the oppressed in South Africa must have been astonished to hear, assuming they were given the opportunity:

> The new Charter should not be a mere legalistic document for the prevention of war. [It] should contain at its very outset and in its Preamble, a declaration of human rights and of the common faith which has sustained the Allied peoples in their bitter and prolonged struggle for the vindication of those rights and that faith. . .

20 United Nations Conference on International Organization (1945a, p. 293).

21 Id., p. 121.

> We bravely fought for justice and decency and for the fundamental freedoms and rights which are basic to all human advancement and progress and peace. Let us, in this new Charter to humanity, give expression to this faith in us … [and] of the ideal of the faith in justice and the resolve to vindicate the fundamental rights of man. . .[22]

Time and time again, developing countries in 1945 aggressively and movingly gave voice to the human rights agenda that would transcend a more rigid interpretation of the post-war treaties. Granted, security in the post-war era was paramount since many smaller developing countries had suffered under the authority of the Axis powers. However, these countries also knew that security would collapse without an equal emphasis on human rights. India, poised to seek independence from the British Empire, certainly saw it that way:

> Those [human] rights are incapable of segregation or of isolation. There is neither border nor breed nor color nor creed on which those rights can be separated as between beings and beings. . . . [I]f we are laying the foundations for peace we can only lay them honestly and justly, to last for some time—for a couple of generations at least. Those fundamental human rights of all beings worldwide should be recognized, and men and women should be treated as equals in every sphere so far as opportunities are concerned.[23]

Another striking voice from the developing world was Cuba. During the San Francisco Conference, Cuba proposed the idea of a human rights document titled "Declaration on the Rights and Duties of the Individual."[24] Like many countries in the Americas, Cuba took an active part in the dialogue on what this new international organization would look like. Long before Cuba turned to a Communist form of government under Fidel Castro in 1965, Cuba's proposal in San Francisco explicitly invoked the U.S. Constitution:

WHEREAS:

> The fourteenth amendment to the Constitution of the United States provides that no state shall deprive any person of life, liberty, or property without due recourse of law, and shall not deny any person, whoever he may be, equal protection of the laws within its jurisdiction;
>
> This Supreme Court of the United States has decided unanimously that in accordance with the terms of the said amendment, it is applicable within the jurisdiction of the United States "to all persons, regardless of any difference of race or color or of nationality; and that the equal protection of the laws is a pledge of the protection of equal laws."[25]

The human rights language in the Charter also inferred that it would act as a shield of justice to combat future acts of aggression. Human rights and fundamental freedoms would undermine the premise for aggression by giving every person in the potentially aggressive nation social and economic security and peace through security. This aligned with two of Roosevelt's "Four Freedoms:" freedom from fear and freedom from want. Roosevelt pressed for disarmament in order to protect the individuals of every country. Without disarmament, there would be no trust in engaging

---

[22] Id., pp. 437–438.

[23] Id., p. 245.

[24] United Nations Conference on International Organization (1945b, p. 499).

[25] Id.

in economic and social programs that transcended borders. And without economic and social progress, social unrest would proliferate into acts of aggression. These two freedoms nourished each other, and Roosevelt, realizing this, had tied them together.[26]

Developing countries' unique and influential role in advocating for human rights in the Charter cannot be overstated. However, in contrast to its occasional forays into inconsistent positions on international human rights today, the United States maintained remarkably unfailing support for human rights during the negotiations to create the Charter in 1945. Mirroring Roosevelt's well-documented position, the United States repeatedly voiced its desire to strengthen human rights.[27] For example, the American delegation to the conference made it clear that "fundamental freedoms" included freedom of speech, which they argued was necessary for international relationships.[28] One extraordinary case in point was the United States championing an international bill of rights, as expressed by the new American president, Harry S. Truman:

> Under this document we have good reason to expect an international bill of rights, acceptable to all the nations involved. That bill of rights will be as much a part of international life as our own Bill of Rights is a part of our Constitution. The Charter is dedicated to the achievement and observance of human rights and fundamental freedoms. Unless we can attain those objectives for all men and women everywhere—without regard to race, language, or religion—we cannot have permanent peace and security in the world. ...[29]

The Charter's preamble asserts human rights and fundamental freedoms "to save succeeding generations from the scourge of war … and to reaffirm faith in fundamental rights."[30] Some scholars have argued that the term "Charter" was equivalent to a written constitution.[31] However, to ensure that these principles were legally binding upon treaty members, the drafters of the Charter added language to Article 1 to emphasize that human rights and fundamental freedoms are equal to the desire to maintain peace and security.[32] That original intent serves as interpretative guidance for subsequent provisions of the Charter.[33] For instance, Part 3 of Article 1 includes this phrase:

> To achieve international cooperation in solving international problems of an economic, social, cultural, or humanitarian character, and in promoting and encouraging respect for human rights and for fundamental freedoms for all without distinction as to race, sex, language, or religion...[34]

---

[26] Engel (2015).

[27] Waltz (2002, pp. 440–441).

[28] United Nations Conference on International Organization (1945a, pp. 684–685).

[29] Id., p. 683.

[30] Charter of the United Nations 1 UNTS XVI (26 June 1945), Preamble; Wolfrum (2012a, pp. 101–106).

[31] Wolfrum (2012b, pp. 108, 113–117).

[32] Id.

[33] Id.

[34] Id., pp. 107–120.

Later, in Article 55(c), the drafters called for

> universal respect for, and observance of, human rights and fundamental freedoms for all without distinction of race, sex, language, or religion.[35]

If another war was to be prevented, it was imperative to guarantee all human rights and fundamental freedoms to all peoples. This reflected Roosevelt's original vision.

As noted above, the Economic and Social Council was tasked with creating an official international bill of rights after the Charter was promulgated. The drafters wanted to rely on governments, previous tribunals, scholars, and renowned non-governmental organizations to determine which human rights and fundamental freedoms should be protected within an international bill of rights. They relied upon Roosevelt's "Four Freedoms," the prospective jurisprudence of the Nuremberg and Tokyo tribunals, and the Atlantic Charter when alluding to human rights and fundamental freedoms. This idea would be further actualized three years later with the Universal Declaration of Human Rights and subsequently with the Declaration's two follow-on and essential treaties, the International Covenants on Civil and Political Rights and on Economic, Social and Cultural Rights.

The Critical Role Played by Non-Government Organizations (NGOs)

Non-government organizations (NGOs) played a central role in achieving the inclusion of human rights standards in the U.N. Charter in 1945, and later, they were instrumental in building support for the Universal Declaration of Human Rights.

The term NGO originated in the United Nations. Before 1945, such organizations engaged with the League of Nations but under the term, "the Union of International Associations." After significant lobbying by civil society, the term NGO was first used by the United Nations in Article 71 of the charter with the creation of the U.N. Economic and Social Council (ESOSOC):

> The Economic and Social Council may make suitable arrangements for consultation with non-governmental organizations which are concerned with matters within its competence.[36]

A notable aspect of the San Francisco Conference was NGOs' decisive role in advocating that the U.N. Charter include human rights and fundamental freedoms. As we

[35] Riedel and Arend (2012, pp. 1565–1602).

[36] Future ECOSOC resolutions established the basis for NGOs to engage with the United Nations. In 1950, the ECOSOC Resolution 288 (X) defined an "international NGO" as an "international organization that is not founded by an international treaty." UN ECOSOC, Admission of Representatives of Non-Governmental Organizations Enjoying Consultative Status, Doc. E/2397 (April 10, 1953); In 1948, only 41 NGOs were recognizable by the ECOSOC. By 2024, over 6,494 NGOs were recognized by the U.N. United Nations Department of Economic and Social Affairs NGO Branch (2024) and Hobe (2012, pp. 1788–1815).

know today, both civil society and NGOs play an important role in protecting international human rights law. In a surprisingly similar way, two NGOs, in particular, played a pivotal role in conceptualizing Roosevelt's "Four Freedoms" and drove policy for creating an Economic and Social Council and an International Bill of Rights. States welcomed these NGOs' suggestions:

The Commission to Study the Organization of Peace

The Commission to Study the Organization of Peace (CSOP) was the first of these two vanguard NGOs. The Commission was founded in 1939 to help Americans consider the fundamentals of creating lasting peace. The Commission was adamant that human rights and economic interdependence were the most prudent ways to combat Fascism in the post-war world.

The CSOP included influential members in public international law, such as Philip Jessup, Eleanor Roosevelt, university professors, and officials in the U.S. State Department.[37] It is unclear how connected the Commission's members were with the U.S. federal government beyond Eleanor Roosevelt, but they regularly met with President Roosevelt. However, Eleanor indeed had a significant influence.[38] States in San Francisco regularly cited the CSOP's reports in their discussions on human rights.[39]

The CSOP's reports reflected the threads of Roosevelt's "Four Freedoms" speech, woven through the Atlantic Charter, the Dumbarton Oaks Proposals, and the San Francisco Conference.[40] For example, the CSOP released its third report on human rights in 1942 after the Declaration by the United Nations was signed in Washington, D.C.[41] In that report and others, the CSOP lauded those who argued that international law and policy should shift its focus to individuals and enlarge their freedoms with protection from the world community.

The Atlantic Charter was a significant norm-building document because it focused on the individual, a novel concept at the time. The CSOP was also aware that political willingness to ensure human rights might one day erode, so it focused on the idea of an international bill of rights as a necessary way to protect the "Four Freedoms."

The broad spectrum of human rights articulated by the "Four Freedoms" could not stand independently without a foundation. The CSOP believed that the foundation should be, and governments needed to provide, better economic, social and cultural benefits and opportunities. The CSOP highlighted the views of John Winant, the U.S. ambassador to the United Kingdom, delivered in his speech of June 6, 1942:

---

[37] Hillman (1998, pp. 485–486).

[38] Id.

[39] Id.

[40] Eichelberger (1943).

[41] Commission to Study the Organization of Peace (1943).

> What we want is not complicated. We have enough technical knowledge and organizing ability to respond to this awakening of social conscience. We have enough courage. We must put it to use. When war is done, the drive for tanks must become a drive for houses. The drive for food to prevent the enemy from starving us must become a drive for food to satisfy the needs of all people in all countries. The drive for physical fitness in the forces must become a drive for bringing death and sickness rates in the whole population down to the lowest possible level. The drive for manpower in war must become a drive for employment to make freedom from want a living reality. The drive for an all-out war effort by the United Nations must become a drive for an all-out peace effort based on the same cooperation and willingness to sacrifice.[42]

Winant's speech could have been made before the United Nations today. It directly addressed Roosevelt's freedom from want in the impending post-World War II era to ensure that the atrocities would not be repeated.

Another CSOP report that was issued before the Dumbarton Oaks Conference fleshed out what the post-war era international organization would look like:

> This [report] is concerned with Welfare. It is an attempt to outline the international mechanisms that will be needed to achieve what the great Chinese leader Sun Yat-sen once described as "the principle of livelihood"—what we now call "freedom from want." Its main purpose is to discuss the first steps that must be taken toward constructing means of international collaboration by which the work of the world may be organized to yield better living conditions and more secure livelihoods for the world's peoples.[43]

The CSOP envisaged an approach resembling an international government, focusing on security, justice, and welfare.

Although evidence of its impact is still evolving, the CSOP's work likely influenced the major powers in determining how the U.N. Security Council, General Assembly, and International Court of Justice would interact with one another. The CSOP's attention to the "political branch" and its responsibility for assuring justice and human rights likely influenced the creation of the Economic and Social Council, too.

The CSOP was cognizant that enforcing individual human rights would be seen as inherently undermining state sovereignty. It sought to remedy this by imposing responsibility and obligations on states to enforce human rights:

> Provision should be made for the creation of a Permanent United Nations Commission on Human Rights, which should include jurists of high standing, to deal with the protection of human rights wherever their violation is a matter of international concern but not adequately covered by existing treaties or agencies. Such protection of individual and group rights should be in accordance with minimum standards which may be agreed upon and in ways which utilize national machinery of law enforcement. This Commission should have as well the task of recommending the reformulation from time to time of the rights of individuals under international law and the relevant function of United Nations agencies in protecting them.[44]

The proposed U.N. Commission on Human Rights became a reality as discussed below.

---

[42] Id.

[43] Commission to Study the Organization of Peace (1944, pp. 68–69).

[44] Id., p. 19.

American Law Institute

The American Law Institute (ALI), the most prominent NGO promoting an international bill of rights, comprised a starter group of lawyers and academics dedicated to advocating the law. The ALI's primary purpose was to prevent future aggression through the codification of human rights, and ultimately it wanted the U.N. Charter to "secure peace, freedom, food, and education for all men. …"[45] The ALI project started only three months after Roosevelt's "Four Freedoms" speech in 1941 and was completed in 1944, a few months before the San Francisco Conference.[46]

The ALI created the "Statement of Essential Human Rights" to accomplish this aspirational goal. In doing so, it sought to gather past international documents and constitutions from around the world to draft a comprehensive human rights document representative of universal fundamental human rights.[47] This project formulated the most elaborate code of human rights the world had ever seen. The importance of the ALI's work is realized by the fact that its "Statement of Essential Human Rights" would be a central component when creating the Universal Declaration of Human Rights (UDHR). The U.N. Commission on Human Rights, created in 1946 to draft the UDHR, relied heavily on the ALI's work.

In fact, the ALI statement had been the basis for the proposed universal document on human rights, which had been proposed as early as the San Francisco Conference. There, the Panamanian delegation had suggested duplicating the ALI statement in the U.N. Charter.[48] Although, as noted above, the conference delegates rejected including a proposed bill of rights in the Charter's preamble, the focus on human rights became the starting point for subsequent negotiations that drafted the UDHR, which was adopted by the U.N. General Assembly in 1948. As discussed below, none of the post-1945 human rights instruments have had more impact than the UDHR.

---

45 Drafted by a committee representing principal cultures of the world, appointed by the American Law Institute; Ellingston (ed) (1945).

46 American Law Institute (2018); Drafted by a committee representing principal cultures of the world, appointed by the American Law Institute; Ellingston (ed) (1945); The ALI attached legislative intent through the form of comments for each article. The comments included how many state constitutions referenced that specific human right and explained what the right actually meant, including limitations and a state's obligation to preserve or promote that right. These comments were included to make the document as unambiguous and useful as possible for what would become the United Nations. This project by the ALI to create a draft international bill of rights included more than 30 appointed members and peoples from around the globe, including the cultures or countries of the Arabic, British, Canadian, Chinese, French, pre-Nazi German, Italian, Indian, Latin American, Polish, Soviet Russian and Spanish. Countries that helped create this document, like Panama, are the parties that championed its implementation into the U.N. Charter at the San Francisco Conference.

47 Id.

48 Id.

The Universal Declaration of Human Rights

As envisaged by its chairperson and driving champion, Eleanor Roosevelt, and inspired by President Roosevelt's "Four Freedoms" and the Charter, the UDHR became the most prominent doctrine of human rights in history. Eleanor Roosevelt reflected on the fact that throughout the world many people do not enjoy the fundamental rights which have come to be accepted in many other parts of the world as inherent rights of all individuals, without which no one can live in dignity and freedom.[49]

In 1946, the newly formed Economic and Social Council (ECOSOC) established the U.N. Commission on Human Rights,[50] which was led by individuals like Eleanor Roosevelt and Lord Dukeston who, though not jurists, were firm advocates of advancing human rights. The Commission quickly focused on drafting an international bill of rights that would become the UDHR. Its first session ran from January 27 to February 1, 1947, at Lake Success, N.Y. Eleanor Roosevelt maintained that individual human rights should eclipse national state sovereignty and "in the writing of the bill of rights, that we safeguard the fundamental freedoms of the individual."[51]

The delegates debated the articles of the UDHR between 1946 and 1948, which is not surprising considering the diversity of the nations represented. An essential point of contention was whether the UDHR would be an aspirational manifesto or a legally binding document. The Commission on Human Rights drafted both a "declaration" and a "convention." For all of her stalwart leadership and unabashed enthusiasm for universal human rights, Eleanor Roosevelt was also a realist. In her eyes, a legally binding treaty had significant risks — primarily the possibility that critical states such as the United States would refuse to ratify it. The failure of the League of Nations still haunted her, as it had her husband. The Soviet bloc was unenthusiastic about a binding document, either. However, other states, concerned that the proposed international bill of rights would be meaningless if not legally binding, were more vigorous in their support of a treaty rather than a declaration.

Ultimately, delegates settled to bifurcate the process: the UDHR became aspirational as a declaration adopted by the U.N. General Assembly, while two treaties on human rights would essentially implement the UDHR with binding obligations on states parties to those treaties.

On December 10, 1948 (one day after the U.N. General Assembly agreed upon the Genocide Convention), the same body adopted the UDHR: 48 states voted in favor, eight abstained, and none opposed. The declaration consists of only 30 concise articles presenting some of the most powerful words in the lexicon of international law. The aspirations of both Franklin and Eleanor Roosevelt had finally been realized.

In 1966, at the height of the Cold War, the U.N. General Assembly approved and opened to state ratification the International Covenant on Civil and Political Rights

---

[49] Roosevelt (1948).

[50] UN ECOSOC, Resolution 5(I) Commission on Human Rights with a Sub-Commission on the Status of Women, UN Doc E/RES/5(I) (16 February 1946).

[51] Glendon (2002, p. 40).

and the International Covenant on Economic, Social and Cultural Rights. Together with the UDHR, these instruments make up the "International Bill of Human Rights," the *magnum opus* of human rights in modern times.

The Legacy of San Francisco

When fifty countries signed the Charter on June 26, 1945, they launched the most significant international legal movement in history. Three years later, the UDHR was completed and approved by the General Assembly, laying the foundation of the modern-day human rights framework. The UDHR would not have been possible without the U.N. Charter and its powerful mandate on human rights. The legacies of both documents continue to this day.

Civil society and non-governmental organizations remain just as important in promoting and protecting human rights now as they were during the drafting of these two historic documents. The International Bar Association, established in 1947; Amnesty International, founded in 1961; and Human Rights Watch, created initially as Helsinki Watch in 1978, are just a few of the premier organizations. The IBA was created with the same intention as the United Nations: to contribute to global stability and peace by protecting and advancing the rule of law. These organizations provide essential information on the state of international human rights by conducting research and investigations, writing reports and articles, and actively working to educate citizens about their rights. The drafters of the UDHR put forward the crucial goal of educating people about their rights, and these organizations strive to fulfil that mission.

The UDHR inspired a number of subsequent treaties. There are now nine core treaties that constitute today's human rights structure: the International Convention on the Elimination of All Forms of Racial Discrimination,[52] the previously noted International Covenant on Civil and Political Rights[53] and International Covenant on Economic, Social and Cultural Rights,[54] the Convention on the Elimination of All Forms of Discrimination against Women,[55] the Convention against Torture and Other Cruel, Inhuman or Degrading Treatment or Punishment,[56] the Convention on the Rights of the Child,[57] the International Convention on the Protection of the

---

[52] International Convention on the Elimination of All Forms of Racial Discrimination 660 UNTS 195 (21 December 1965).

[53] International Covenant on Civil and Political Rights 999 UNTS 171 (16 December 1966).

[54] International Covenant on Economic, Social and Cultural Rights 993 UNTS 3 (16 December 1966).

[55] Convention on the Elimination of All Forms of Discrimination against Women 1249 UNTS 13 (18 December 1979).

[56] Convention against Torture and Other Cruel, Inhuman, or Degrading Treatment or Punishment 1465 UNTS 85 (10 December 1984).

[57] Convention on the Rights of the Child 1577 UNTS 3 (20 November 1989).

Rights of All Migrant Workers and Members of Their Families,[58] the International Convention for the Protection of All Persons from Enforced Disappearance,[59] and the Convention on the Rights of Persons with Disabilities.[60] Each of these treaties is overseen by its own treaty body, which is tasked with monitoring state-party compliance and providing interpretation of treaty provisions. The UDHR inspired these human rights treaties and they expand upon the principles articulated therein. The constitutional character of the Charter and the UDHR, which many of the drafters of these documents envisaged, came to pass as new treaties and enforcement mechanisms were created.

Regional human rights instruments have also been created since the adoption of the Charter; they all advance the aims of the UDHR and, in many ways, are more potent than the treaties originating at the United Nations. The Council of Europe (COE) is the preeminent regional human rights entity.[61] The COE's negotiation and creation of the European Convention on Human Rights (ECHR), established in 1950, is the benchmark for regional human rights systems.[62] Forty-six states on the European continent are currently parties to the ECHR.[63] The European Court of Human Rights (ECtHR) enforces the ECHR.[64] The ECtHR was the first legal mechanism to give binding force to the principles underlying the UDHR because they are largely replicated in the ECHR. The court is uniquely situated to uphold the rights guaranteed in the ECHR to ensure that national laws do not restrict the human rights of a country's citizens. The convention also provides citizens with direct standing before the ECtHR. This fulfills one of the U.N. Charter's core aims of protecting individual rights when threatened by the state, as individuals and NGOs may bring claims directly to the ECtHR. The court has made landmark decisions in human rights law that have defined and expanded the "Four Freedoms."[65]

Another vital legacy institution of the United Nations is the Organization of American States (OAS), whose charter was adopted in 1948.[66] Among other aims, the OAS promotes human rights in the Americas through its own Inter-American Commission on Human Rights, which was created in 1959.[67] Subsequently, the American Convention on Human Rights (ACHR) entered into force in 1978.[68] However, neither

---

[58] International Convention on the Protection of the Rights of All Migrant Workers and Members of their Families 2220 UNTS 3 (18 December 1990).

[59] International Convention for the Protection of All Persons from Enforced Disappearance 2716 UNTS 3 (20 December 2006).

[60] Convention on the Rights of Persons with Disabilities 2515 UNTS 3 (13 December 2006).

[61] Fella and Walker (2023, para 2.2).

[62] Directorate-General for External Policies of the European Union (2010, pp. 11–12).

[63] Council of Europe Treaty Office (2024).

[64] Convention for the Protection of Human Rights and Fundamental Freedoms 1955 UNTS 222 (4 November 1950), Articles 19–51.

[65] European Court of Human Rights (2011, p. 36).

[66] Charter of the Organization of American States 1952 UNTS 48 (30 April 1948).

[67] OAS, Statute of the Inter-American Commission on Human Rights, OAS Rec OEA/Ser.P/IX.0.2/80 447 (IX-0/79) (25 May 1960).

[68] American Convention on Human Rights 1144 UNTS 123 (22 November 1969).

the United States nor Canada has ratified the ACHR. The convention set in motion the creation of the Inter-American Court of Human Rights in 1979, a regional court that granted individuals standing to sue and produced a dynamic record of visionary human rights judgments over the decades.[69]

The African Charter on Human and Peoples' Rights entered into force in 1986.[70] It has been ratified by 54 states, all but one of which are members of the African Union. In 2004, the African Court of Human and Peoples' Rights became operational.[71] Under selected circumstances, NGOs and individuals can gain jurisdictional standing before the court.

The Arab Charter on Human Rights was adopted on May 22, 2004, by the Council of the League of Arab States.[72] The Arab Charter was a significant step for a region lacking a human rights court. Its Article 1 mirrors that of the UN Charter as its purpose is to "place human rights at the center of the key national concerns of Arab States, making them lofty and fundamental ideals that shape the will of the individual in Arab States and enable him to improve his life in accordance with noble human values." Article 4 of the Arab Charter reaffirms its reliance on the UDHR that all human rights are universal, indivisible, interdependent and interrelated.[73] Both the African and Arab Charters are aspirational human rights instruments drawing upon the legacy of the U.N. Charter.

At the United Nations, mechanisms inspired by the U.N. Charter work daily on advancing human rights. The Office of the High Commissioner on Human Rights (OHCHR) is the lead entity tasked with promoting and protecting human rights. Although the OHCHR did not exist until 1994, its remit can be discerned in the deliberations leading to the U.N. Charter.[74] The OHCHR serves as the secretariat of the U.N. Human Rights Council, which adopts resolutions on behalf of the global community regarding human rights violations.[75] The high commissioner is selected by the U.N. Secretary-General and has always been a highly respected human rights advocate.[76] The OHCHR also supports the work of special rapporteurs and experts tasked with monitoring and investigating human rights violations where they occur.[77]

---

69 OAS, Statute of the Inter-American Court on Human Rights, OAS Rec OEA/Ser.P/IX.0.2/80 (1 October 1979).

70 African Charter on Human and Peoples' Rights 1988 UNTS 245 (27 June 1981).

71 OAU, Protocol to the African Charter on Human and People's Rights on the Establishment of an African Court on Human and People's Rights, OAU Doc OAU/LEG/EXP/AFCHPR/PROT (III) (9 June 1998).

72 Arab Charter on Human Rights, [ST/HR/]CHR/NONE/2004/40/Rev.1 (22 May 2004).

73 Id.

74 Glendon (2002, p. 47).

75 UNGA, Resolution 48/141 High Commissioner for the promotion and protection of all human rights' UN Doc A/Res/48/141 (20 December 1993).

76 The former president of Ireland, Mary Robinson, the Jordanian diplomat Prince Zeid bin Ra'ad bin Zeid al-Hussein, and the former Canadian Supreme Court justice Louise Arbour. However, similar to the Human Rights Council, the high commissioner requires the political support of States to implement its policies and decisions. Too often, that is missing.

77 United Nations Sustainable Development Group (2024).

The U.N. special rapporteurs and experts cover a large number of human rights issues ranging from free expression to torture.[78] Their attention can vary from individual cases to broad concerns implicating multiple parties. One critical task is increasing public awareness of human rights, which has been a longstanding goal of the UDHR.

As with many international organizations, the effectiveness of all of these U.N. entities ebbs and flows. This was certainly the case with the U.N. Commission on Human Rights. By the turn of the twenty-first century, it had become so politicized that its credibility had been severely undermined. For example, Libya, notorious for human rights abuses, had been selected as the Commission's chairman in 2003. But in 2006 the Commission was replaced by the new U.N. Human Rights Council, which has not solved all of the credibility problems that beset the Commission but has established a firmer foothold for human rights concerns within the entire U.N. system.[79]

The Human Rights Council continues pursuing goals outlined in the U.N. Charter, in theory and often in practice focusing on protecting human rights and fundamental freedoms for both individuals and peoples at risk. It acts as the international mechanism for advancing human rights through primarily political pressure, in contrast to the treaty bodies discussed above, which advance human rights through the law.

---

[78] Forty-six thematic mandates: (1) Racial discrimination against people of African descent; (2) enjoyment of human rights by persons with albinism; (3) arbitrary detention; (4) human rights and transnational corporations and other business enterprises; (5) human rights in the context of climate change; (6) cultural rights; (7) the right to development; (8) rights of persons with disabilities; (9) enforced or involuntary disappearances; (10) the right to education; (11) the right to a clean, healthy and sustainable environment; (12) extrajudicial, summary or arbitrary executions; (13) the right to food; (14) effects of foreign debt and other related international financial obligations of States on the enjoyment of human rights; (15) right to freedom of opinion and expression; (16) rights to freedom of peaceful assembly and of association; (17) right to enjoyment of the highest attainable standard of physical and mental health; (18) adequate housing; (19) human rights defenders; (20) independence of judges and lawyers; (21) rights of Indigenous Peoples; (22) rights of internally displaced persons; (23) promotion of a democratic and equitable international order; (24) international solidarity; (25) elimination of discrimination against persons affected by leprosy; (26) use of mercenaries as a means of violating human rights and impeding the exercise of the right of peoples to self-determination; (27) human rights of migrants; (28) minority issues; (29) enjoyment of all human rights by older persons; (30) rights of peasants and other people working in rural areas; (31) extreme poverty and human rights; (32) right to privacy; (33) contemporary forms of racism, racial discrimination, xenophobia and related intolerance; (34) freedom of religion or belief; (35) sale, sexual exploitation and sexual abuse of children; (36) protection against violence and discrimination based on sexual orientation and gender identity; (37) contemporary forms of slavery; (38) promotion and protection of human rights and fundamental freedoms while countering terrorism; (39) torture and other cruel, inhuman or degrading treatment or punishment; (40) implications for human rights of the environmentally sound management and disposal of hazardous substances and wastes; (41) human trafficking; (42) promotion of truth, justice, reparation and guarantees of non-recurrence; (43) negative impact of unilateral coercive measures on the enjoyment of human rights; (44) violence against women and girls; (45) human rights to safe drinking water and sanitation; (46) discrimination against women and girls.

[79] UNGA, Resolution 60/251 Human Rights Council, UN Doc A/RES/60/251 (3 April 2006).

The Future

The United Nations remains the only international organization that is comprised of almost every country in the world. The U.N. Charter is embedded within the law of nations and its purpose and principles symbolize a degree of universality that had been missing before 1945. The drafters of the Charter strove to create an international entity that would uphold human rights and fundamental freedoms for everyone. Although they did not see human rights as a panacea for human suffering, this incredibly diverse group of states and individuals rejected a relativistic approach, arguing human rights exceptions. They believed these principles should bind all nations regardless of religious, cultural, or ethnic differences. Nor could states abandon these principles because of legal traditions, whether drawn from common law, civil law, or religious law.

The core human rights principles decreed in the Charter and subsequent U.N. instruments were designed to be absolute. They were not meant to be subverted by the actions of any state. The principles and norms would be meaningless if they were applied selectively or viewed in relative terms. The UDHR reinforced this belief with its explicit stake in a "universal" declaration of human rights principles.

While the UDHR is not a binding treaty among states parties, many of its articles are now considered part of "customary international law" because of the number of countries that have accepted them over time and have done so because they believe in the binding character of the legal principle. Some articles of the UDHR, like Article 4 on the prohibition of slavery and Article 5 on the prohibition of torture, are even examples of *jus cogens* norms, meaning immutable and "compelling law" that no treaty or law or custom can contradict. Customary international law and *jus cogens* principles bind all states, even the few that have not have gained membership in the United Nations. The U.N. Charter is an international treaty and clearly binds all of its states parties, each of which is a member nation of the United Nations. The International Covenants on Civil and Political Rights and on Economic, Social and Cultural Rights are similar as they embody some principles of customary international law binding on all nations regardless of whether they have ratified or acceded to the Covenants.[80]

However, the agreed-upon understanding of human rights and fundamental freedoms that emerged after World War II is deteriorating. Since that time, the estimated number of victims of human rights abuses has been staggering.[81] Yet justice for the victims has been minuscule. This is not necessarily due to a lack of accountability mechanisms but rather because of a lack of enforcement of the rule of law.

In this chapter we have described the journey that created internationally recognized human rights principles in the U.N. Charter and beyond, with monumental growth of human rights instruments since the formation of the United Nations. However, the same political will that catalyzed the modern-day human rights movement in 1945 has dramatically receded. There are many reasons for this decline:

[80] Human Rights Committee (2004, para 2).

[81] Bassiouni (ed) (2010).

the rise of nationalism, the blind adherence to populism, the escalation of authoritarianism, and the deplorable state of education—all movements that undervalue, ignore, and denigrate human rights.

To protect and advance the legacy of the Charter in promoting human rights and fundamental freedoms, we need a paradigm shift that emphasises the importance of human rights for all, regardless of borders, and foster a deep understanding and unwavering commitment to these principles among younger generations. It will require, in part, a reinterpretation of the Charter to strengthen its meaning. Fortunately, there remains a solid foundation. International human rights law has developed into an integrated system based on a global structure of treaties, conventions, state practice, and legal mechanisms. However, steps still need to be taken to reinforce the Charter's importance and focus on human rights.

Underlying the future evolution of the Charter in the realm of human rights is education. The UDHR's preamble already guides us: "Every individual and every organ of society … shall strive by teaching and education to promote respect for these rights and freedoms." The drafters of the Charter and the UDHR knew education was necessary to counter ideologies denigrating human rights. They knew that education remained the lifeblood of human rights as foreseen by Franklin Roosevelt.[82] Yet, today, there is a troubling decline in citizens' knowledge and appreciation of the sanctity of human rights. Alarmingly, a clear, inverse correlation exists between educational attainment and awareness and support for human rights.[83] This trend is concerning because it undermines the principles that form our global society's foundation. We must dedicate ourselves to a robust and comprehensive educational program for youth. Human rights must be integrated into academic curricula. This is no short-term prospect, but will take a long-term commitment.

Second, a similar and corresponding area of focus is civil society. This includes the critical voice of national bar associations and law societies. In the same way, non-government organizations played a crucial role during the San Francisco conference; they must again elevate their voice in promoting and protecting human rights on the national and local levels.

Third, the UDHR and international human rights treaties inspired by it have launched an entirely new generation of (third-generation) rights to address emergent obstacles and threats that the drafters of the UDHR could not have foreseen. This subset of rights is known as collective rights that benefit humanity, such as the right to a sustainable environment. These rights, however, are hotly contested because third-generation human rights transcend the rights of the individual, which is what the UDHR is based on, and grants rights to the collective.

The creation of the right to a sustainable environment started in 1972 at the United Nations Conference on the Environment in Stockholm.[84] In 2022, the U.N. General Assembly declared in Resolution A/RES/76/300 that there is a human right to a

---

[82] Schabas (ed) (2013, p. 868).

[83] Lindhardt and Strandby (2022, p. 8).

[84] UN Conference on the Human Environment, Declaration of the United Nations Conference on the Human Environment, UN Doc A/Conf.48/14/Rev.1 (16 June 1972), p. 3.

sustainable environment and that direct and indirect environmental damage affects every individual regardless of sovereign boundaries.[85] The resolution supports a growing number of international and regional declarations that recognize a sustainable environment as a human right. They all point to the need for greater openness in interpreting human rights treaties requiring states to mitigate environmental damage based on human rights protections. National courts, too, are slowly beginning to recognize this approach.[86]

Only by acknowledging the current state of human rights and fundamental freedoms—successes and failures—can the human rights systems and instruments be reinforced and, if needed, reinvented to advance human rights for coming generations. The U.N. Charter has been and will remain the aspirational cornerstone of fundamental human rights for all peoples. However, we are also the guardians of those rights, and we must commit ourselves to the core principles enshrined in the Charter to create a more just and peaceful world. The great American civil rights writer James Baldwin put it best when he wrote: "We are responsible for the world in which we find ourselves, if only because we are the only sentient force which can change it."[87]

References

American Law Institute (2018) The statement of essential human rights. https://www.ali.org/news/articles/statement-essential-human-rights/. Accessed 25 Nov 2024

Baldwin J (1972) No name in the street. Dial Press, New York

Bassiouni MC (ed) (2010) The pursuit of international criminal justice: a world study on conflicts, victimization, and post-conflict justice. Intersentia, Antwerp, Portland

Commission to Study the Organization of Peace (1943) Third report. Int Concil 389:201–385

Commission to Study the Organization of Peace (1944) Fourth report. Int Concil 22(5):3–110

Council of Europe Treaty Office (2024) Chart of signatures and ratifications of treaty: convention for the Protection of Human Rights and Fundamental Freedoms (ETS No. 005). https://www.coe.int/en/web/conventions/full-list?module=signatures-by-treaty&treatynum=005. Accessed 21 Nov 2024

Directorate-General for External Policies of the European Union (2010) The role of regional human rights mechanisms. https://www.europarl.europa.eu/RegData/etudes/etudes/join/2010/410206/EXPO-DROI_ET(2010)410206_EN.pdf. Accessed 25 Nov 2024

Eichelberger CM (1943) Third report of the commission to study the organization of peace. Free World 5:365

Ellingston JR (ed) (1945) State of essential human rights. Americans United for World Organization, New York

[85] UNGA, Resolution 76/300 The human right to a clean, healthy and sustainable environment, UN Doc A/Res/76/300 (28 July 2022).

[86] HR Nederlanden (Supreme Court of the Netherlands) December 20, 2019, ECLI:NL:2019:2006 (Urgenda/Staat der Nederlanden), unofficial English translation 59 ILM 814 (2020) (Neth.) [hereinafter *Urgenda* (HR)]. Urgenda Foundation v. State of the Netherlands, Supreme Court of the Netherlands, (December 20, 2019) Urgenda Foundation v. the Netherlands, No. 19/00135, ECLI:NL:HR:2019:2006 (Dutch Supreme Court, December 20, 2019).

[87] Baldwin (1972, p. 65).

Engel JA (2015) The four freedoms: Franklin D. Roosevelt and the evolution of an American idea. Oxford University Press, New York

European Court of Human Rights (2011) Annual Report 2010. https://www.echr.coe.int/documents/d/echr/annual_report_2010_eng. Accessed 25 Nov 2024.

Fella S, Walker N (2023) Work of the Council of Europe. https://researchbriefings.files.parliament.uk/documents/CDP-2023-0119/CDP-2023-0119.pdf. Accessed 25 Nov 2024

Finch GA (1941) The international rights of man. AJIL 35:662–665

Glendon MA (2002) A world made new: Eleanor Roosevelt and the Universal Declaration of Human Rights. Random House, New York

Hathaway O, Shapiro S (2017) The internationalists: how a radical plan to outlaw war remade the world. Simon & Schuster, New York

Henig R (2010) The peace that never was: a history of the league of nations. Haus Publishing, London

Hillman RP (1998) Quincy wright and the commission to study the organization of peace. Glob Gov 4(4):485–499

Hobe S (2012) Article 71. In: Simma B et al (eds) The Charter of the United Nations: a commentary, vol II, 3rd edn. Oxford University Press, pp 1788–1815

Human Rights Committee (2004) General Comment No. 31 [80]: the nature of the general legal obligation imposed on states parties to the covenant. https://digitallibrary.un.org/record/533996?ln=en&v=pdf. Accessed 25 Nov 2024

Meisler S (1995) United Nations—the first fifty years. Atlantic Monthly Press, New York

Lindhardt E, Strandby KH (2022) Guide on human rights curriculum in teacher education. https://www.humanrights.dk/files/media/document/Guide%20on%20Human%20Rights%20Curriculum%20in%20Teacher%20Education_2022.pdf. Accessed 25 Nov 2024

Repucci S, Slipowitz A (2021) Freedom in the world 2021. https://freedomhouse.org/report/freedom-world/2021/democracy-under-siege. Accessed 23 May 2024

Reus-Smit C (2013) Individual rights and the making of the international system. Cambridge University Press, New York

Riedel E, Arend J (2012) Article 55 (c). In: Simma B et al (eds) The Charter of the United Nations: a commentary, vol II, 3rd edn. Oxford University Press, pp 1565–1602

Roosevelt E (1948) The promise of human rights. Foreign Affairs

Schabas WA (ed) (2013) The Universal Declaration of Human Rights: The Travaux Préparatoires, vol I. Cambridge University Press, New York

United Nations (2024a) The San Francisco conference. https://www.un.org/en/about-us/history-of-the-un/san-francisco-conference. Accessed 5 May 2024

United Nations (2024b) Preparatory years: UN Charter history. https://www.un.org/en/about-us/history-of-the-un/preparatory-years. Accessed 5 May 2024

United Nations Conference on International Organization (1945a) Documents of the United Nations Conference on International Organization, San Francisco, 1945, Volume I: General. United Nations Information Organizations, London, New York

United Nations Conference on International Organization (1945b) Documents of the United Nations Conference on International Organization, San Francisco, 1945, Volume III: Dumbarton Oaks Proposals Comments and Proposed Amendments. United Nations Information Organizations, London, New York

United Nations Department of Economic and Social Affairs NGO Branch (2024) Consultative status with ECOSOC and other accreditations. https://esango.un.org/civilsociety/displayConsultativeStatusSearch.do?method=search. Accessed 31 May 2024

United Nations Sustainable Development Group (2024) UN Charter-based institutions including special procedures. https://unsdg.un.org/2030-agenda/strengthening-international-human-rights/un-special-procedures. Accessed 21 Nov 2024

United States Office of the Historian (2016) Milestones: 1937–1945: the Atlantic Conference & Charter, 1941. https://history.state.gov/milestones/1937-1945/atlantic-conf#:~:text=Churchill's%20primary%20goal%20in%20attending,aggressive%20actions%20in%20the%20Pacific. Accessed 5 May 2024

V-Dem Institute (2024) Democracy Report 2024. https://www.v-dem.net/documents/44/v-dem_dr2024_highres.pdf. Accessed 24 May 2024

Waltz S (2002) Reclaiming and rebuilding the history of the Universal Declaration of Human Rights. Third World Q 23(3):437–448

Wolfrum R (2012a) Preamble. In: Simma B et al (eds) The Charter of the United Nations: a commentary, vol I, 3rd edn. Oxford University Press, pp 101–106

Wolfrum R (2012b) Article 1. In: Simma B et al (eds) The Charter of the United Nations: a commentary, vol I, 3rd edn. Oxford University Press, pp 107–120

Chapter 3
Respect International Law

> The Charter is a living document, whose high principles still define the aspirations of people everywhere for lives of peace, dignity and development.
>
> Kofi A. Annan[1]

This chapter examines the U.N. Charter and its nexus to the expansive lens of international law, the driving force behind its creation. The Charter's preamble states that the United Nations is determined "to establish conditions under which justice and respect for the delegations arising from treaties and other sources of international law can be maintained." As such, it codifies conduct among nations that reflect the tenets of international law; it sets forth the means to enforce these tenets and establishes the authority through U.N. institutions and practices to implement a rules-based international order. In establishing this goal, the Charter acts as the "framework constitution of the international community."[2] As U.S. President Harry Truman, the first to compare the Charter to a constitution, stated,

> The Constitution of my own country came from a Convention which—like this one—was made up of delegates with many different views. Like this Charter, our Constitution came from a free and sometimes bitter exchange of conflicting opinions. When it was adopted, no one regarded it as a perfect document. But it grew and developed and expanded. And upon it there was built a bigger, a better, a more perfect union.[3]

Truman also talked about the ebb and flow of the Charter's development:

> This Charter, like our own Constitution, will be expanded and improved as time goes on. No one claims that it is now a final or a perfect instrument. It has not been poured into any fixed mold. Changing world conditions will require readjustments—but they will be the readjustments of peace and not of war.[4]

---

[1] United Nations (1999).

[2] Fassbender (2009, p. 170).

[3] United Nations Conference on International Organization (1945a, p. 715).

[4] *Id.*

D. J. Scheffer and M. S. Ellis, *The UN Charter*,
https://doi.org/10.1007/978-3-031-94866-4_3

The Charter mirroring a constitutional framework was important because it gave the Charter legitimacy and structure and helped establish it as a "supreme" legal text covering all member states. The constitutional nature of the Charter also meant that it would be flexible in its expanding interpretation. Dag Hammarskjöld, the second U.N. secretary-general, expressed similar views and stated that the United Nations "is and should be a living, growing, and experimental institution. If it stops being one, it should either be revolutionized or swept aside in favor of another concept."[5]

To remain flexible and achieve these objectives, the Charter relies on multilateralism—an idea novel at its creation but now entrenched in the very concept of international law. Thus, the Charter's aspiration of being the world's constitution required an organization that gave voice to *all* member states. In doing so, international law would develop (and continue to develop) through a process of democratization involving all member states, regardless of their territorial boundaries or military capabilities.

The declaration of the Syrian delegation at the San Francisco Conference articulated this vision best. They knew that without this democratic governance of the newfound world organization, the U.N. Charter would be a dead letter:

> Human sense of justice, Ladies and Gentlemen, is a living thing. No one can seek to quench it forever. It is a mighty force luminous enough to indicate the path and strong enough to set us on it. Human sense of justice can help to establish right. Order and right can make the world what it ought to be and what we want it to be. It is not, of course, by some miraculous feat of an international meeting like ours. It is not by some magic declaration of principles implemented by international machinery that order and right will reign paramount in our tormented world; it is through faith, universal faith, in what was set before us to do, through democratic governing, through long and sustained efforts that make for a wholesome and continuous evolution. It is by muddling through difficulties and doubts and overcoming them that at last order and right will reign, and above all, by learning from past experience and trials to do better than before that we can avoid such past mistakes and look with hope for the settlement of what is better.[6]

The reference to "past experiences" and "past mistakes" is poignant. It reminds us that international law has deep historical roots dating back to some of the great philosophers, such as Cicero and Plato.[7] And what is called public international law today has its origins as far back as 1625, when the famous legal scholar and jurist Hugo Grotius published *The Law of War and Peace*, which gave birth to the concept of the "law of nations."[8] And the treaties that were the basis for the Peace of Westphalia in 1648,[9] which ended the Thirty Years' War, also influenced the codification of international legal norms.[10]

However, it was only after World War II, with the establishment of the United Nations, that the most comprehensive framework of international law was created.

[5] Månsson (2007, p. 237).

[6] United Nations Conference on International Organization (1945a, p. 570).

[7] Harris (1955, p. 150).

[8] Bull, Kingsbury, and Roberts (1992).

[9] Fassbender (2011).

[10] Foster (1909, p. 152).

This is supported by the fact that member states are required to register each international agreement entered into, which, in turn, forms a mosaic of international legal norms.[11] Since 1945, the United Nations has registered international legal agreements representing every conceivable area of law and deposited over 550 multilateral treaties.[12] This process has permanently established the modern-day system of international legal norms, ranging from the Law of the Sea to Human Rights Law, Space Law, the Law on Treaties, and domestic laws and norms from all states. The mosaic is indeed rich.

During the final drafting of the U.N. Charter at the San Francisco Conference, attendees passionately believed that the United Nations should bring about a world order that would strengthen *peace and security*. Ambassador Celso Velásquez of Peru, the Rapporteur of the Third Commission, captured this sentiment at the conference by asserting that "[t]he future alone will disclose whether we have buil[t] wisely and well, but it is the hope, and, I believe, the conviction, . . . that the labors of these committees viewed in the perspective of time will represent historic contribution to the future peace of all mankind."[13] However, this aspiration could only be achieved by strengthening and codifying *international law*. Law and justice were essential to ensuring lasting peace.

The historical records detect this realization among the delegates, including those representing China (as it was governed in 1945):

> We are glad to see in the completed instrument [the Charter] today many new features. Provisions have been added which emphasize that the adjustment or settlement of international disputes should be in conformity with the principles of justice and international law…[14]

From the League to the Charter—The Enforcement of International Law

Chapter 2 briefly alluded to the League of Nations as a catalyst for the structure of the U.N. Charter, which owes its existence to the League in many critical respects. Before U.S. President Franklin D. Roosevelt played an indispensable role in the creation of the U.N. Charter, another American president, Woodrow Wilson, had set the stage for the creation of the League of Nations, which in its demise subsequently laid the groundwork for a new international legal order on which the U.N. Charter is based.

Like Roosevelt's "Four Freedoms" speech discussed in Chapter 2, Wilson also gave an iconic speech on January 8, 1918. He set out fourteen points that ultimately acted as the blueprint for negotiating the end of World War I and establishing

---

[11] "Every treaty and every international agreement entered into by any Member of the United Nations ... shall as soon as possible be registered with the Secretariat and published by it" Charter of the United Nations 1 UNTS XVI (26 June 1945), Art. 102.

[12] United Nations Treaty Collection (2024).

[13] United Nations Conference on International Organization (1945a, p. 625).

[14] *Id*., p. 693.

the League of Nations. Wilson and Roosevelt shared the same vision—ensuring a stable and just international order. Whereas Wilson failed to secure the support for the League from the U.S. Senate, which refused to ratify the Versailles Treaty, Roosevelt and Truman learned from that defeat and labored hard to secure popular support, hence Senate support for the Charter. They did so, in part, because the U.S. Constitution inspired the wording chosen for the Charter.

The period shortly following World War II also was a time in history when there existed a favorable impression of multilateralism. It was not a time stymied by the desire for political isolationism. As stated earlier, the newly formed United Nations relied on multilateralism through the drafting process. However, this period of optimism would change. By February 1946, Soviet Premier Joseph Stalin had declared the world divided, British Prime Minister Winston Churchill had announced that an Iron Curtain had descended across Europe,[15] and Truman unveiled the "Truman Doctrine" based on containing Soviet expansion.[16] The Cold War had arrived. However, the groundwork for a new international legal order had been laid.

One of the most consequential elements of the modernized legal order and international law itself was the creation of an overarching international court. The League of Nations had created the Permanent Court of International Justice (PCIJ), which operated from 1922 to 1945. The International Court of Justice (ICJ), created under the legal authority of the U.N. Charter, succeeded it in 1946.

The creation of both the PCIJ and the ICJ was premised on shared values, including, most importantly, promoting the resolution of international disputes through a legal rather than a military process. If justice and peace were to prevail, there had to be a binding entity to interpret and enforce international law, provide authoritative rulings, and offer advisory (non-binding) opinions. The Carnegie Endowment for International Peace made it clear that "in any planning for a post-war world based on law and order, an *international court of justice* must be part of the proposed structure"[17] [emphasis added].

The failure of the League of Nations and, in its wake, the precarious existence of the PCIJ required a fresh start with the ICJ constitutionally bonded with the U.N. Charter and operating as the court of the newly conceived United Nations. The Statute of the ICJ[18] would draw upon that of its predecessor but would improve upon it. The understanding that there needed to be an arbiter of law never wavered. The ICJ would have a more expansive jurisdiction than the PCIJ partly because of the greater number of U.N. members. The ICJ also was meant to repudiate the notion that "might is right" and to ensure equality under the law.[19] However, the Court was not established to merely chip away at the "might is right" doctrine but to dismantle it and make international law the guiding engine for dispute resolution. Consequently, the ICJ stands as the preeminent authoritative legal body on international law.

[15] British Information Services (1946).

[16] Hanhimäki (2015, p. 18).

[17] Carnegie Endowment for International Peace (1943), Statement by George Finch.

[18] Statute of the International Court of Justice 33 UNTS 993 (18 April 1946).

[19] See Morris (2021).

Yet, there was no parity among those countries emerging from the horrors of World War II. Because of the scourge of colonial rule, many countries in Asia and Africa were not directly represented during the Charter's creation, and, of course, the Axis Powers were not at the negotiation table. Nonetheless, the victorious allied countries recognized the need to adhere to a new form of equality among states in relation to international law. President Truman recognized this requirement when he stated in San Francisco that:

> [o]ut of this conflict have come powerful military nations, now fully trained and equipped for war. But they have no right to dominate the world. It is rather the duty of these powerful nations to assume the responsibility for leadership toward a world of peace. That is why we have here resolved that power and strength shall be used not to wage war, but to keep the world at peace, and free from the fear of war.
>
> By their own example the strong nations of the world should lead the way to international justice. That principle of justice is the foundation stone. ...[20]

As with the U.N. Charter, the development of the ICJ was the work of several committees. The initial discussions during the war occurred within the Informal Inter-Allied Committee on the Future of the Permanent Court of International Justice in 1943. This committee was created to set the plan for the post-World War II court. It was established at the request of the United Kingdom and published its first report in the *American Journal of International Law* in 1943.[21]

The committee held nineteen meetings and created proposals highlighting the differences the new court should have from the PCIJ to ensure its fullest success. The committee ultimately desired to create a new court with the PCIJ statute as its cornerstone. Interestingly, the committee disfavored compulsory jurisdiction membership to the new court. It also did not see the ICJ as a primary organ of the United Nations. However, as often happens, the initial concept was dramatically altered at a later stage. This alteration also happened with human rights, as discussed in Chapter 2.

By the time of the Dumbarton Oaks Conference (1944), the four allied powers wanted the proposed court to be a *primary organ* of the organization.[22] Chapter 7 of the Dumbarton Oaks Proposals provided the articles for the statute of the ICJ within the U.N. Charter:

1. There should be an international court of justice which should constitute the *principal* judicial organ of the Organization [emphasis added].
2. The court should be constituted and should function in accordance with a statute which should be annexed to and be a part of the Charter of the Organization.
3. The statute of the court of international justice should be either (a) the Statute of the Permanent Court of International Justice, continued in force with such modifications as may be desirable or (b) a new statute in the preparation of which the Statute of the Permanent Court of International Justice should be used as a basis.

---

[20] United Nations Conference on International Organization (1945a, p. 728).

[21] The Department of State to the British Embassy (1943).

[22] See Rosenne (2004, pp. 22–61).

4. All members of the Organization should *ipso facto* be parties to the statute of the international court of justice.
5. Conditions under which states not members of the Organization may become parties to the statute of the international court of justice should be determined in each case by the General Assembly upon recommendation of the Security Council.[23]

But would the position of the four powers be upheld at the San Francisco Conference in 1945 among a much larger cast of countries? Would the new court be the principal judicial organ of the United Nations, and would all UN members agree to be a party to the jurisdiction of the new court?

Although several nations feared that compulsory jurisdiction would erode state sovereignty, more answered in the affirmative for the court's jurisdiction. The Syrian delegation expressed a strong desire for the court to retain significant power:

> The court should work in close cooperation with the Assembly and Council, but the more power we give to the court, the more we can feel sure that differences of that kind will be justly arbitrated and not solved by some arbitrary arrangement.[24]

The ICJ would be compulsory and create an obligation of accountability on *all* nations party to the U.N. Charter. The court would ensure the inclusion of the world's major judicial systems by its composition of 15 judges from diverse jurisdictions. The principal agreement would be that international law should trump national sovereignty. Compulsory jurisdiction would also improve the court's credibility and create a more sustainable foundation of international law. Panama's delegation said it best:

> [T]he sovereign nations of the world must recognize that above their national sovereignty is the sovereignty of the law; and must, therefore, abide by international law and submit their disputes to the mandates of international law as interpreted and applied by a competent court of obligatory jurisdiction.[25]

To achieve this objective, it would be critical for the new court to be annexed to the U.N. Charter and function as an integral component of the United Nations. The PCIJ had failed to do so within the League of Nations. The drafters of the ICJ would not repeat the same mistake. Although the ICJ's statute relied on the PCIJ statute, it would include innovations, particularly in the new court's relationship with the United Nations. The ICJ would be incorporated into the United Nations, and its governing statute would form an indispensable part of the U.N. Charter. Article 92 of the Charter enshrines the objective:

> The International Court of Justice shall be the principal judicial organ of the United Nations. It shall function in accordance with the annexed Statute, which is based upon the Statute

---

[23] United Nations Conference on International Organization (1945b, pp. 10–11).

[24] United Nations Conference on International Organization (1945a, p. 571).

[25] The Panamanian delegation asserted this must be a fundamental postulation for them to agree to its terms *in* United Nations Conference on International Organization (1945a, p. 560).

of the Permanent Court of International Justice and forms an integral part of the present Charter.[26]

Article 93 of the Charter ensured that "all member nations of the United Nations are *ipso facto* parties to the statute of the International Court of Justice."[27] Article 94 went further and asserted that "member states of the United Nations undertake to comply with ICJ decisions."[28]

These articles are significant because together they created the universal notion that the ICJ is *the* "world court." This sharply contrasted with the PCIJ, which seemed more like an arbitral tribunal for treaties since it was not a permanent organ of the League of Nations. The ICJ would be the U.N. organ empowered to facilitate judicial settlement of international disputes and establish legal norms that would guide all states. Even non-members of the United Nations could bring cases before the ICJ for resolution.[29] It indeed would be the world court.

From a historical point of view, it is worth noting some of the complexities surrounding the issue of compulsory adjudication. Prominent legal scholars and non-governmental organizations such as the American Bar Association, the American Branch of the International Law Association, and the famous Austrian jurist Hans Kelsen argued that nations should be obliged to settle *all* conflicts "without exception" through the new court.[30] However, a compromise emerged as was often the case with the Charter's negotiations.

For example, the ICJ lacks "automatic" compulsory jurisdiction. States must still consent to the court's jurisdiction. This restriction seems odd for a court deemed the world's court. However, consent can be given through a special agreement where states agree to refer specific disputes to the court. In addition, a state can consent to a treaty that obligates the signatories to submit disputes related to that treaty to the court for resolution.[31] For example, states parties to the Convention on the Prevention and Punishment of the Crime of Genocide agree to the ICJ's jurisdiction over any disputes arising under the treaty.[32] A state may declare that it recognizes the compulsory nature of the ICJ's jurisdiction *when another state does the same*. This is called an optional clause declaration. Once states consent to the court's jurisdiction, its judgment in the case will be binding and require compliance.[33]

The ICJ also can order immediate provisional measures of protection, pursuant to Article 41 of its statute, to prevent or avoid imminent and irreparable harm to the

---

[26] Oellers-Frahm (2012a, pp. 1897–1950).

[27] Oellers-Frahm (2012b, pp. 1951–1956).

[28] Oellers-Frahm (2012c, pp. 1957–1971).

[29] Charter of the United Nations 1 UNTS XVI (26 June 1945), Art. 93(2).

[30] Kelsen (1944, p. 14).

[31] Statute of the International Court of Justice 33 UNTS 993 (18 April 1946), Art. 36(1).

[32] Convention on the Prevention and Punishment of the Crime of Genocide 78 UNTS 277 (9 December 1948), Art. XI.

[33] Statute of the International Court of Justice 33 UNTS 993 (18 April 1946), Art. 36(2); Between 1946 and 2021, "approximately 30% of the applications in contentious cases [before the ICJ] have invoked [optional clause] declarations as the primary title of jurisdiction"; Donoghue (2021, p. 2).

rights of the parties, including the rights of individuals, prior to a final judgment of the Court. Such provisional measures have a binding character, although states are known to ignore the decisions on provisional measures.[34] Recent ICJ cases, including *South Africa v. Israel* and *Ukraine v. Russian Federation*, demonstrate this point.[35]

The ICJ also issues non-binding advisory opinions (discussed below) on legal issues submitted by an array of U.N. entities (for example, the General Assembly and the Security Council) and other international organizations (for example, the International Monetary Fund and the International Bank for Reconstruction and Development are authorized to request advisory opinions, although they have never done so).

An interesting historical fact is that legal scholars and bar associations did not support the notion of the ICJ delivering advisory opinions, arguing that they would be inappropriate for a judicial body.[36] Ultimately, the argument failed at the San Francisco Conference. Advisory opinions have proven instrumental in helping develop the understanding of why international law matters in disputes.

Another intriguing issue emerged in the 1945 drafting process: Would the Statute of the ICJ give individuals standing to litigate before the Court, considering that the international community is one of diversity, including individuals, stateless peoples, and Indigenous groups? There is no denying that a "considerable part of international law directly affects individuals."[37] However, the drafters did not ultimately bestow standing on individuals to lodge complaints—"only states may be parties in cases before the court."[38] This position was similar to the PCIJ, which lacked this personal jurisdiction.[39] The ICJ's exclusive jurisdiction over state conflicts between nations remains well-embedded and will not likely change.

Another unique aspect of the ICJ is its location. International law is more than just words. It incorporates imagery and symbolism that help shape how we perceive and interact with law. Structures are part of this narrative. The location of the ICJ and its predecessor, the PCIJ, is the Peace Palace built in The Hague. It has proven to be an impressive symbol of the permanence of international law. A stunning neo-Renaissance building, the construction of the Peace Palace was funded by Andrew Carnegie, a Scottish-born immigrant industrialist who made his fortune in the steel industry in the United States. Its architectural features—both exterior and interior—symbolize peace and justice. Many of its fixtures were provided by various countries, representing the multinational contribution to the building. In his autobiography, Carnegie referred to the building as a "Temple of Peace—the most holy building in

[34] Alexianu (2023).

[35] Hathaway (2024); Human Rights Watch (2024).

[36] Peaslee (1945).

[37] Cançado Trindade (2014).

[38] Statute of the International Court of Justice 33 UNTS 993 (18 April 1946), Art. 34.

[39] At the time of the drafting and adoption, in 1920, of the PCIJ Statute, a choice was made for only states to exercise this international judicial function in contentious matters.

the world because it has the holiest end in view. ...dedicated to justice and peace for all nations."[40]

The ICJ's expansive jurisdictional reach is reflected in the number of cases it hears and the number of its advisory opinions. Between May 1947, when the first case was entered on the Court's docket, and November 2024, the ICJ delivered 143 case decisions and 28 advisory opinions. Twenty-three pending cases and requests for advisory opinions before the ICJ (as of 28 November 2024) exist.[41]

The key to every judicial institution is whether contesting parties comply with its decisions. This issue is particularly challenging for the ICJ because the parties are states. Thus, inherent national interests and political pressures will influence a state's willingness to adhere to an ICJ ruling. The ICJ has no enforcement mechanism to ensure compliance with its decisions. Consequently, the court is dependent on the political will of states. For example, in 1985, the United States withdrew its acceptance of the court's jurisdiction for future cases involving selected international disputes because it disagreed with the ICJ's judgment in *Nicaragua v. United States.* [42] However, in what might seem unexpected, states have generally complied with ICJ rulings. A "snapshot" study found that between 1987 and 2004, states frequently complied with the court's decisions,[43] although adherence could depend on the sensitivity of the case. In contrast, with the judgements of the PCIJ, states "bypassed [the court] on almost every major occasion."[44]

State Sovereignty

As discussed in Chapter 2, there has always been a debate about the United Nations' interaction with the sovereignty of states and national laws. Human rights provided some room for penetrating the protective veil of state sovereignty. However, within the context of international law, the drafters of the U.N. Charter upheld the sacrosanct principle of non-interference in state affairs. The reluctance to cede sovereign authority to a centralized international body was always present. State sovereignty would be a core, if not *the* principle, of the United Nations. It stood as the common denominator binding the provisions of the U.N. Charter.

However, the prerogative of states over the concept of universality still created tensions. In San Francisco, arguments arose over whether peace and security could be achieved only through a supplemental "police" force. Many believed that the League of Nations and the Kellogg-Briand Pact, both mentioned in Chapter 2, failed because

[40] Andrew (1920, p. 285).

[41] International Court of Justice (2024).

[42] Nicaragua accused the US of supporting and funding contra rebels within Nicaragua's borders; Robinson (1985).

[43] Paulson (2004).

[44] Bloomfield (1957, p. 155).

"it is useless to outlaw war without eliminating the possibility of legally unsettled and unsettable conflicts."[45] The Luxembourg delegation in San Fransisco stated:

> The League of Nations was intended to be armed, but it was born without shield or sword, in other words, it was still-born. The international organization born of our discussions will have the necessary armed forces to insure respect for its decisions. A great French writer once said that a judge is nothing but a poor dreamer unless he is backed by a police force. . . . Still it will have the great advantage of being able to insure the maintenance of order immediately and for as long as we remain faithful to it in the future. Sheltered by the security it will achieve, it will be possible to organize the world on the basis of recognized and ratified international law and to restore the sway of right over might.[46]

As indicated in Chapter 2, individual rights and protections were central to the drafting of the Charter. Protecting state sovereignty could not translate into unfettered actions against the rights of individuals, as that would upend the very notion of international human rights. Many delegates at the San Francisco Conference expressed hope that the Charter's protection of individual rights would be a subject of international law.[47] This view influenced initiatives to advocate accountability for atrocity crimes decades later.[48] However, non-interference in states' domestic affairs prevailed in San Francisco. This position is articulated in Article 2(7) of the Charter, with an attached exception as noted in Article 51. This area is covered later in the book.

Non-State Parties

The historical records of the Charter reveal a fascinating insight into the role of non-state actors. Chapter 2 discussed their role in the development of international human rights law. However, legal scholars played a significant role in creating overall international law and its judicial organs. After the First World War and before the start of the Second, there was a lack of treaties and consolidated state practice to ascertain customary international law; there also was no depository to review treaties. As discussed in Chapter 2, the American Law Institute played a vital role by compiling national laws and constitutions. Legal scholars drew upon such instruments to identify the major sources of international law that are listed in Article 38 of the ICJ's Statute.[49]

---

[45] Kelsen (1944, p. 32).

[46] United Nations Conference on International Organization (1945a, pp. 502–503).

[47] *Id.*, p. 622.

[48] James (2004, p. 118).

[49] Art. 38(1) Statute of the ICJ provides that "[t]he Court, whose function is to decide in accordance with international law such disputes as are submitted to it, shall apply: (a) international conventions, whether general or particular, establishing rules expressly recognized by the contesting states; (b) international custom, as evidence of a general practice accepted as law; (c) the general principles of law recognized by civilized nations; (d) subject to the provisions of Article 59, judicial decisions and the teachings of the most highly qualified publicists of the various nations, as subsidiary means

Although legal scholarship began to be eclipsed by U.N. General Assembly and Security Council resolutions at the United Nations, legal scholars continued to improve the law through the drafting of principles (such as the Nuremberg Principles) and multilateral treaties, including most recently the proposed draft Convention on the Prevention and Punishment of Crimes Against Humanity. These are discussed below.

The International Law Commission (ILC)

The U.N. Charter prioritized adherence to the law **and** equality under the law.[50] However, to ensure long-term stability in the application of international law, there needs to be a mechanism to establish an accepted legal framework. This would require, in part, a process to collect and codify customary international law norms. Article 13 (a) and (b) of the Charter sets out this mission:

The General Assembly shall initiate studies and make recommendations for the purpose of:

a) promoting international co-operation in the political field and encouraging the progressive development of international law and its codification;
b) promoting international co-operation in the economic, social, cultural, educational, and health fields, and assisting in the realization of human rights and fundamental freedoms for all without distinction as to race, sex, language, or religion.

The International Law Commission (ILC) was created two years after the San Francisco Conference to fulfill these goals and promote education about international law. The Chinese delegation at the time said it best, emphasizing the importance of education to ensure that countries faithfully follow the Charter. China believed that the power to research and codify international law was meant to be a preventive mechanism to preserve peace, much like the recognition of fundamental human rights and freedoms, as discussed in Chapter 2. The delegation also maintained that international law was the key to ensuring that the United Nations became an operating machine rather than a mere legal document.[51]

The ILC would compile legal documents worldwide to ascertain universal customs of law and propose codifying these customs to the General Assembly. This process meant identifying areas of law where state practice had already been well established. Perhaps even more importantly, the ILC would identify gaps in the law where principles had not been fully formulated through state practice. Since its earliest days, the ILC has repeatedly made recommendations on key areas of international

for the determination of rules of law." Statute of the International Court of Justice 33 UNTS 993 (18 April 1946), Art. 38(1).

[50] Morris (2021).

[51] United Nations Conference on International Organization (1945c, p. 70).

law. It remains one of the most critical components of the United Nations and has evolved into a vital entity in the development of international law. The Nuremberg Principles and the Vienna Convention on the Law of Treaties (VCLT) were two of its key developments in the early years.

The Nuremberg Principles

One of the most important and far-reaching manifestations of the ILC's authority was its drafting of the Nuremberg Principles. These principles codified international crimes as established by the Nuremberg trials, held in 1945 and 1946, to prosecute the leadership of Nazi Germany for atrocity crimes.

During the war, the Allies had discussed holding the perpetrators responsible for the atrocities they committed. In October 1941, British Prime Minister Winston Churchill and U.S. President Franklin D. Roosevelt condemned the atrocities, which led to the Inter-Allied Commission on the Punishment for War Crimes and the Declaration of St. James's Palace, signed by thirteen countries.[52] The signatories committed to "the punishment, through the channel of organised justice, of those guilty of or responsible for these crimes, whether they have ordered them, perpetrated them, or participated in them."[53] The Moscow Declaration soon followed with a joint statement by Churchill, Roosevelt and Joseph Stalin of the Soviet Union. It provided that those who had committed crimes with "no particular geographical localisation" (in other words, in their respective countries) would be punished by a joint decision of the Allied governments.[54] The plan to prosecute and punish the major Nazi war criminals was set out in the London Charter, signed by the United States, France, Great Britain and the Soviet Union on August 8, 1945 (see Figs. 3.1 and 3.2).

Consistent with the Charter's focus on peace and security, the Nuremberg Principles aimed to codify offences directly bearing on peace and security.[55] Using the authority of Article 13 of the U.N. Charter, the United States and China introduced a resolution that memorialized the judicial rulings of the Nuremberg Tribunal; the United Kingdom also informally agreed to the proposal. On December 11, 1946, the U.N. General Assembly adopted a resolution that affirmed the Nuremberg precedent:

> THE GENERAL ASSEMBLY,
>
> RECOGNIZES the obligation laid upon it by Article 13, paragraph 1, sub-paragraph a, of the Charter, to initiate studies and make recommendations for the purpose of encouraging the progressive development of inter- national law and its codification;

---

52 The thirteen countries that signed the declaration were Canada, Australia, New Zealand, South Africa, Belgium, the United Kingdom, Czechoslovakia, Greece, Luxembourg, The Netherlands, Norway, Poland, and Yugoslavia.

53 *See* Inter-Allied Conference, Punishment for War Crimes: The Inter-Allied Declaration Signed at St. James's Palace London (13 January 1942), Art. 3.

54 *See* Moscow Conference, Joint Fourt-Nation Declaration (30 October 1943), Art. 6.

55 United Nations (1956, p. 136).

Fig. 3.1 Co-author Mark Ellis standing inside the Church House where the London Charter establishing the International Military Tribunal in Nuremberg was signed (*Source* Mark Ellis)

> TAKES NOTE of the Agreement for the establishment of an International Military Tribunal for the prosecution and punishment of the major war criminals of the European Axis signed in London on 8 August 1945, and of the Charter annexed thereto, and of the fact that similar principles have been adopted in the Charter of the International Military Tribunal for the trial of the major war criminals in the Far East, proclaimed at Tokyo on 19 January 1946.
>
> THEREFORE, AFFIRMS the principles of international law recognized by the Charter of the Nürnberg Tribunal and the judgment of the Tribunal;
>
> DIRECTS the Committee on the codification of international law established by the resolution of the General Assembly of 11 December 1946, to treat as a matter of primary importance plans for the formulation, in the context of a general codification of offences against the peace and security of mankind, or of an International Criminal Code, of the principles recognized in the Charter of the Nürnberg Tribunal and in the judgment of the Tribunal.[56]

The subsequent Nuremberg Principles[57] resonate today and are one of the most profound developments in post-World War II law. The principles ensured that "any person who commits an act which constitutes a crime under international law" (for example, crimes against peace (aggression), crimes against humanity, and war crimes) should be brought to justice. Nations could **not** undermine these principles through their national laws.

---

[56] United Nations (1947, p. 254).

[57] *See generally* United Nations (1957, pp. 374–378).

Fig. 3.2 Co-author Mark Ellis in front of the Church House in Westminster where the London Charter for the Nuremberg Tribunal was signed on August 8, 1945 (*Source* Mark Ellis)

Significantly, the principles explicitly directed that heads of state cannot be shielded from accountability for international crimes and that anyone acting pursuant to an order by a superior cannot invoke that order to escape responsibility for an international crime.

As frequently mentioned in this book, state sovereignty remained a paramount issue for U.N. member states. The Soviet Union, for example, believed that creating an international criminal code would undermine states' inherent sovereignty.[58] However, the prevailing view among many states was that the Nuremberg Principles would be codified in subsequent conventions and tribunals resulting in a holistic body of international criminal law. In fact, this occurred with the creation in recent decades of international criminal courts such as the International Criminal Tribunals for the former Yugoslavia and Rwanda and the International Criminal Court, as well as hybrid tribunals like the Special Court for Sierra Leone and the Extraordinary Chambers in the Courts of Cambodia. They stand as a monument to the efforts to fortify international law as set forth in the Charter.

[58] Graefrath (1990, p. 74).

The Vienna Convention on the Law of Treaties (VCLT)

One of the ILC's early priorities was to address the need for consistent rules governing treaties. In its first session in 1949, the ILC selected the law of treaties as a subject suitable for codification due to "its importance and [...] its political implications".[59] Treaties are the backbone of international relations, yet their regulation was previously fragmented, relying on a mix of customary law and disparate practices. This recognition set the stage for nearly two decades of debate, drafting, and consultation. Between 1949 and 1959, the ILC aimed to produce "an expository code, setting out what the ILC considered to be the customary international law on the subject."[60]

The drafting of the Vienna Convention on the Law of Treaties (VCLT) proceeded with the appointment of special rapporteurs on the law of treaties. From 1952 to 1966, several drafts were prepared, and Sir Hersch Lauterpacht, Sir Gerald Fitzmaurice, and Sir Humphrey Waldock served successively, each contributing to the evolution of the draft articles. In 1966, the ILC adopted the Draft Articles on the Law of Treaties ("Draft Articles") after a final five years of intensive work.[61]

However, feedback from states to the ILC's draft revealed significant divergences. Reservations to treaties were particularly contentious, with states insisting on the right to opt out of specific provisions without undermining the treaty. The ILC had to incorporate numerous modifications to accommodate these concerns, balancing flexibility with maintaining treaty integrity. The draft articles formed the basis for negotiations at the United Nations Conference on the Law of Treaties, held in Vienna from 1968 to 1969. Key issues like the impact of coercion on the legal validity of a treaty and the conditions for withdrawal from a treaty required considerable negotiations and compromise to create the VCLT. In its second session in 1969, the Conference adopted the VCLT based on the Draft Articles, with 79 votes in favor, 1 against, and 19 abstentions.[62] It entered into force on 27 January 1980 upon ratification by 35 states and today 116 countries are party to the convention.[63]

Since the adoption of the VCLT, the ILC has remained actively involved in interpreting and clarifying the convention's principles in response to evolving global challenges.[64] A number of provisions of the VCLT are recognized as comprising customary international law and confirmed as such by the ICJ.[65] One of the most important is the rule of interpreting treaties (Articles 31 and 32 of the VCLT), which

[59] United Nations (1949, paras 90–92).

[60] Aust (2006, para 3).

[61] United Nations (1967, pp. 112–124).

[62] Sinclair (1970, p. 47).

[63] Vierdag (1982, p. 779).

[64] For example, the ILC adopted the Guide to Practice on Reservations to Treaties in 2011 upon its concern with "the number of reservations that appear incompatible with the limits imposed by the law of treaties, in particular article 19 of the Vienna Conventions on the Law of Treaties"; United Nations (2018, pp. 26–38).

[65] Bordin (2014, p. 543).

the ICJ has held to be an expression of customary international law on multiple occasions.[66]

The VCLT's importance to international law cannot be overestimated. It governs the validity of all treaties and has been described as "the constitutional law of the international community."[67] It serves as an essential cornerstone of the global framework of international law. The VCLT's legitimacy is also highlighted in a very practical way, as noted by Sir Ian Sinclair: "No legal adviser to a foreign ministry, whether his government is a party to the convention or not, can afford to ignore the impact of the [VCLT]."[68]

The Convention on the Prevention and Punishment of the Crime of Genocide (Genocide Convention)

The prohibition against the crime of genocide was one of the most important developments of international law in the immediate post-World War II period. U.N. member states perceived the Nuremberg Principles as just that—*principles*. Subsequent conventions would crystallize these principles into binding international law, and courts would interpret and adjudicate such law. An early focus on the crime of genocide led to an early convention-drafting exercise.

Polish lawyer Raphael Lemkin, who settled in the United States during the war, created the term "genocide" as the Holocaust unfolded. But he first described the crime in 1933 during a conference in Madrid. A description of the speech noted that

> [i]n this report to an international conference held in Madrid, Raphael Lemkin (1900-1959) first proposed the creation of a multilateral convention making the extermination of human groups an international crime, paralleling slavery, piracy and other universally recognized "offences against the law of nations." In 1933 he called the crime "Acts of Barbarity." Ten years later, in 1943, he would coin a new word for this crime: "genocide."[69]

Lemkin's work gave impetus to a more nuanced understanding of the acts' uniqueness and severity. For instance, records show that Winston Churchill, in 1941, understood that the atrocities being committed by Nazi Germany were unlike "regular" war crimes. In a radio broadcast on BBC, he acknowledged that they did not have a name. He was not talking specifically about the destruction of Jews but about how Nazi Germany waged its war. He stated this in a speech:

> This frightful business is now unfolding day by day before our eyes. Here is a devil who, in a mere spasm of his pride and lust for domination, can condemn two or three millions, perhaps it may be many more, of human beings to speedy and violent death. Let Russia be blotted out. Let Russia be destroyed. Order the armies to advance. Such were his decrees.

---

66 *Kasikili/Sedudu Island (Botswana/Namibia)*, Judgment, ICJ Reports 1999, 1045, para 18.

67 Daniel (1972, p. 369).

68 Sinclair (1984, p. 275).

69 Lemkin (1933).

> Accordingly, from the Arctic Ocean to the Black Sea, six or seven millions of soldiers are locked in mortal struggle.
>
> […]
>
> He retaliates by the most frightful cruelties. As his armies advance, whole districts are being exterminated. Scores of thousands, literally scores of thousands of executions in cold blood are being perpetrated by the German police troops upon the Russian patriots who defend their native soil. . . . Famine and pestilence have yet to follow in the bloody ruts of Hitler's tanks.
>
> *We are in the presence of a crime without a name.*[70] [emphasis added]

The term "genocide" focuses on the destruction of a group based on its ethnicity, race, religion or nationality. The Greek word "genos" means race and tribe, and the Latin suffix "cide" means killing. Lemkin was far ahead of his time in proposing a multilateral treaty to prevent and punish genocide. Certainly, the convention would not have been created without his advocacy.

Even though the crime of genocide was not prosecuted as a stand-alone crime during the Nuremberg trials ("genocidal" crimes were tried as crimes against humanity), its significance was already eternally embedded in the horrors of the Holocaust. It would become an early manifestation of *jus cogens* norms, which means compelling law where no derogation is permitted.

Thus, a major effort ensued to codify genocide as an "international crime" and to do so through an international treaty. As mentioned earlier in the chapter, the Charter was drafted through the lens of a constitutional framework. In the same way, the Genocide Convention would become "part of the constitutional foundation of the international community."[71] The challenge, however, was deciding how the crime should be viewed within the context of international law. Again, the issue centered around the responsibility of nations. The U.N. General Assembly would go on to adopt the following resolution:

> The Crime of Genocide
>
> Genocide is a denial of the right of existence of entire human groups, as homicide is the denial of the right to live of individual human beings; such denial of the right of existence shocks the conscience of mankind, results in great losses to humanity in the form of cultural and other contributions represented by these human groups, and is contrary to moral law and to the spirit and aims of the United Nations.
>
> Many instances of such crimes of genocide have occurred, when racial, religious, political and other groups have been destroyed, entirely or in part.
>
> The punishment of the crime of genocide is a matter of international concern.
>
> *The General Assembly, therefore,*
>
> *Affirms* that genocide is a crime under international law which the civilized world condemns, and for the commission of which principals and accomplices — whether private individuals, public officials or statesmen, and whether the crime is committed on religious, racial, political or any other grounds — are punishable;
>
> *Invites* the Member States to enact the necessary legislation for the prevention and punishment of this crime;

[70] British Library of Information (1941).

[71] Fassbender (2009, p. 122).

> *Recommends* that international co-operation be organized between States with a view to facilitating the speedy prevention and punishment of the crime of genocide, and, to this end,
>
> *Requests* the Economic and Social Council to undertake the necessary studies, with a view to drawing up a draft convention on the crime of genocide to be submitted to the next regular session of the General Assembly.[72]

The resolution encompassed a more expansive definition of the crime of genocide than did the eventual convention, such as including "political groups", but its purpose was to establish a baseline for negotiations. Drafting the Genocide Convention was the first major test of whether the newly energized idea of "multilateralism" was viable for improving and codifying international law.

Once the General Assembly recognized genocide as a crime under international law, attention turned to drafting the convention that would prohibit the crime. The Secretariat prepared the draft of the convention with Lemkin's assistance. States were invited to submit their observations. The General Assembly continued reviewing the draft and established an *ad hoc* Committee on Genocide (composed of representatives from the United States, the Soviet Union, Lebanon, China, France, Poland and Venezuela) to prepare a second draft.

One of the paramount issues of debate about the Genocide Convention would be whether to define genocide separately or as one among other crimes against humanity, the category of crimes prosecuted at the Nuremberg trials. When the final text of the convention was presented[73] and adopted by the General Assembly in December 1948, the crime of genocide stood alone.

During the earlier drafting process, other contentious issues would emerge. For example, the United Kingdom proposed an amendment that would punish states rather than individuals for genocide. [74] France rejected this amendment because French law did not recognize state responsibility. Instead, France proposed focusing on genocide as an international crime for which "the principal authors and accomplices, whether statesmen or private individuals, should be punished."[75] The emphasis would be on the individual, not the state. However, that singular focus was rejected, and the Genocide Convention would include both individual and state responsibility.

Poland wanted *incitement to commit genocide* included as an international crime, which was also adopted and remains a critical component of the Genocide Convention. It reflects that words can play a powerful catalyst in the execution of the crime of genocide. These and other issues illustrate the complexity of the matter. What was not controversial, however, was that prosecution would be a matter of international concern,[76] even if a state committed the crime in its sovereign territory against its own people. Genocide was a crime that could happen during "peace," but the world had a collective responsibility to prevent it and to punish its perpetrators.

---

[72] UNGA, Resolution 96(I) The Crime of Genocide, UN Doc A/RES/96(I) (11 December 1946).

[73] The final convention draft was completed in the sixth Committee of the General Assembly.

[74] United Nations (1947, p. 255).

[75] *Id.*

[76] *Id.*

A fascinating aspect of the debate on the Convention included the issue of enforcement, a paramount and indispensable aspect of international law. The Genocide Convention is a treaty among states, where states are responsible for prosecuting the crime as an obligation under the Convention and enacting national laws criminalizing genocide. However, the drafters already knew that the strength and credibility of international law depend on voluntary compliance or enforced adherence. Thus, historical records indicate that when drafting the convention, the debate also centered around whether an *international tribunal* should be established to prosecute the crime of genocide. The secretarial draft initially set out that idea:

> …National courts will be called upon to play a part in the punishment of genocide, but in the more serious cases it would appear to be highly desirable that it should be punished by an international tribunal. Such a tribunal might be an international criminal court with general jurisdiction; in the absence of such a court, a special court with jurisdiction limited to genocide would have to be provided for. The question of the establishment of an international criminal court with general jurisdiction exceeds the scope of the question of genocide. It is not for us to deal with this question, but the bodies entrusted with the preparation of the Convention on the punishment of genocide may consider the question in liaison with the other bodies dealing with international criminal law and the codification of international law.[77]

During the drafting process in 1947, the United States signalled its support for an international criminal tribunal to prosecute genocide cases. It suggested creating an *ad hoc* tribunal first, referencing the success of the Nuremberg Tribunal, and then moving to a permanent tribunal. The American delegation asserted:

> {I]t would be preferable to provide for the establishment of ad hoc tribunals to be superseded by a permanent international penal tribunal with appropriate jurisdiction at such time as this may be possible. That this is feasible, is demonstrated by the fact that the Nürnberg Tribunal was an ad hoc tribunal. While it would probably have been preferable for the nations to have had a previously established international penal tribunal to which those cases could have been referred, it is submitted that the problem of the institution of such a tribunal, competent to try international crimes generally, is of such a magnitude as to necessitate a separate project, having the most careful consideration, and inviting the largest number of States possible to become party thereto.[78]

Not all states agreed. Venezuela opposed any international accountability mechanism, only wishing for states to hold their citizens accountable for genocide.[79] The Soviet Union, too, supported the protection of state sovereignty and wanted states rather than an international tribunal to hold perpetrators accountable for the crime of genocide.[80]

The United States' support of an international criminal tribunal and the Soviet Union's opposition to it exemplified disagreement throughout the process. China

---

[77] Abtahi and Webb (2008, p. 225).

[78] *Id.*, p. 379.

[79] Mr. PEREZ-PEROZO (Venezuela), objecting to any reference to an International Court, opposed the whole Article. The Convention should contain only specific obligations on the part of States; UN ECOSOC, Ad Hoc Committee on Genocide Summary Record of the Fourth Meeting, Un Doc E/AC.25/Br.4 (15 April 1948).

[80] *Id.*

seemed to walk the middle line between the two major powers, finding it desirable to set up a tribunal solely focused on the crime of genocide and the need to separate the Nuremberg Principles from the Genocide Convention. It argued that the Nuremberg Principles "related solely to acts committed either during a war of aggression or in connexion with the preparation of such a war."[81]

The final draft of the Genocide Convention omitted a separate international tribunal for the crime of genocide. However, the absence of an international court was rectified with the creation of several *ad hoc* international tribunals in the 1990s, including the ICTY and the ICTR, and the International Criminal Court (ICC) in 2002, the world's first permanent international criminal court. The jurisdiction of these vanguard courts would all cover the crime of genocide.

In addition to promoting the idea of an international tribunal, debate ensued about whether the crime of genocide should fall under the principle of *universal jurisdiction*, which would allow national courts to punish perpetrators of any nationality regardless of where the genocidal act was committed. For example, India advocated that the crime of genocide should fall under universal jurisdiction:

> The General Assembly requests Members to call upon their Governments to ensure that national laws treat the crime of genocide on an equal footing with piracy, traffic in women, children and slaves, and other crimes which have always been recognized as violating the dignity of human beings.[82]

However, powerful states like the United States "did not consider universal jurisdiction of national courts desirable."[83] Decades later, however, universal jurisdiction over the crime of genocide has become widely recognized.[84]

Finally, on December 9, 1948, the *Convention on the Punishment of the Crime of Genocide* was adopted by the General Assembly with a unanimous vote of the 56 member states.[85] The treaty entered into force with sufficient ratifications in 1951.

It is worth noting the ILC's involvement with the drafting of the Genocide Convention did not stop with its adoption. In 1996, the ILC approved the Draft Code of Crimes Against the Peace and Security of Mankind, further developing the legal framework for prosecuting *crimes against humanity*.[86] Then, in August 2019, the ILC "recommended the elaboration of a convention by the General Assembly or by an international conference of plenipotentiaries on the basis of [its Draft Articles on the Prevention and Punishment of Crimes Against Humanity]."[87] Just as the crime of genocide was newly discovered and defined by Raphael Lemkin during the Holocaust, Sir Hersch Lauterpacht pressed forward the legal term "crimes against

---

81 *Id.*

82 United Nations (1947, p. 255).

83 *See* UN ECOSOC, Ad Doc Committee on Genocide Draft Article for the Inclusion in the Convention on Genocide Proposed by the Delegation of China, UN DOC E/AC.25/9 (16 April 1948).

84 Hovell (2018, pp. 434–446).

85 United Nations Audiovisual Library of International Law (2008).

86 United Nations (1998, pp. 15–54).

87 United Nations General Assembly (2019, para 42).

humanity" at roughly the same time and ensured its application in the London Charter of the Nuremberg Tribunal in 1945.[88] The Nuremberg trials marked the first occasion when individuals were prosecuted for crimes against humanity.[89] In approving the Nuremberg Principles, the U.N. General Assembly confirmed crimes against humanity as international crimes.[90] Decades later, crimes against humanity would be defined by the *ad hoc* international criminal tribunals and the Rome Statute of the ICC; the crimes had become well-established under customary international law.[91]

Since the Nuremberg trials, crimes against humanity have been prosecuted widely in both international and domestic contexts despite not being based on a treaty like the Genocide Convention. Nonetheless, the ongoing evolution of the treatment of these crimes exemplifies the breathing and dynamic force of international law and meets the General Assembly's mandate under Article 13 of the Charter of "encouraging the progressive development of international law and its codification."

Yet, international law is never uncontentious. Its development and advancement depend on compromise among the states. After years of debate, progress on creating a treaty for crimes against humanity is accelerating. Recently (as of November 28, 2024), the Sixth Committee of the General Assembly, following the ILC's earlier recommendation, approved a resolution to convene the United Nations Conference of Plenipotentiaries on Prevention and Punishment of Crimes against Humanity to elaborate and conclude a treaty on crimes against humanity.[92] This is a reminder of the arduous journey taken when attempting to codify international law through a treaty mechanism.

Codifying legal tenets such as the Nuremberg Principles, genocide, and crimes against humanity has significantly bolstered the meaning and impact of international law.

---

[88] Art. 6(c) of the London Charter provides that "[t]he following acts, or any of them, are crimes coming within the jurisdiction of the Tribunal for which there shall be individual responsibility: ... Crimes against humanity: namely, murder, extermination, enslavement, deportation, and other inhumane acts committed against any civilian population, before or during the war, or persecutions on political, racial or religious grounds in execution of or in connection with any crime within the jurisdiction of the Tribunal, whether or not in violation of the domestic law of the country where perpetrated." Agreement for the prosecution and punishment of the major war criminals of the European Axis 280 UNTS 1951 (8 August 1945).

[89] *Id.*, Art. 6(c).

[90] UNGA, Resolution 95(I) Affirmation of the Principles of International Law recognized by the Charter of the Nürnberg Tribunal, UN Doc A/RES/95(I) (11 December 1946).

[91] Crimes against humanity are explicitly criminalized in the Rome Statute of the ICC (Article 7), the International Criminal Tribunal for the former Yugoslavia (Article 5), the International Criminal Tribunal for Rwanda (Article 3), the Extraordinary Chambers in the Courts of Cambodia (Article 5), the Special Court for Sierra Leone (Article 2), and the Extraordinary African Chambers (Article 4(ii)).

[92] UNGA, Sixth Committee, United Nations Conference of Plenipotentiaries on Prevention and Punishment of Crimes against Humanity, UN Doc A/C.6/79/L.2/Rev.1 (15 November 2024).

The Future of International Law as Part of the Charter

The United Nations is truly the most prominent "global" organization. Its state membership has grown from 51 countries in 1945 to 193 today. Yet, because of its global membership, unrealistic expectations are often thrust upon it. As the former U.N. Secretary-General Dag Hammarskjöld said: "This organization is created to prevent you from going to hell. It isn't created to take you to heaven."[93] This is a poignant statement because, ultimately, the goals embedded in the Charter rely on member states for fulfillment. Political willingness is the foundation for upholding the Charter's aspirations. Benjamin Cohen said it best: "World law to be effective must be backed by world opinion and the conscience of mankind. If—and only if—we develop a universal conscience, we can have universal law."[94]

However, this universal conscience is often absent. The U.N. Charter, with its 111 articles grouped into 19 chapters, seems utopian considering today's reality of armed conflicts, dysfunctionality, economic disparities, and growing dissatisfaction among nations. It is hard to ignore that states often summarily disregard the principles outlined in the Charter. The Middle East conflict, Sudan's civil war, and Russia's war against Ukraine are just a few of the situations that give the impression of international legal disorder. The divide between the theory of international law and practice seems more significant than at any time since 1945. The Charter appears weak.

In 2008, the late Cherif Bassiouni, a renowned international law scholar, painted a depressing picture of the state of world affairs in his seminal publication, *The Pursuit of International Criminal Justice: A World Study on Conflicts, Victimization, and Post-Conflict Justice.*[95] Between 1945 and 2008, there were 253 distinct armed conflicts in which an estimated minimum of 7.8 million people lost their lives. If victims of repressive authoritarian state regimes were included, the total might have been as high as 101 million victims. During the same period, only 823 persons were indicted by international and regional courts for violations of international humanitarian law. The disparity between these numbers is staggering.

The United Nations must adapt its principles and mechanisms or retreat into irrelevance. The same can be said about the international community at large. Do states want this genuinely global organization to be relevant, and are they willing to support it and abide by its principles? Or do they want to exist in a world fragmented into ideologically defined alliances?

We believe that the key to pursuing the Charter's goal of maintaining peace and security is to modernize and improve the international legal order, not to obliterate it. Thus, making international law relevant for future generations requires adapting it to emerging challenges. As articulated in this chapter, the very nature of international law requires multilateralism and cooperation. Supporting with "tough love" international bodies like the ICJ, the World Trade Organization, and the ICC is critical. So is strengthening the role of regional and domestic entities in actively implementing and

[93] Bryant (2015).

[94] Cohen (1949).

[95] Bassiouni (2010, p. 3).

enforcing international law. This is particularly relevant for global challenges that the drafters of the Charter never imagined. New and robust international legal instruments are needed to combat climate change, expand states' support and compliance with international law, and enhance enforcement mechanisms.

Strengthening the network of international, regional, and national mechanisms to hold key states and non-state actors accountable for violating international law should also be prioritized. For instance, key states such as the United States, Israel, China, Iran, Turkey, Pakistan, Russia, Indonesia and India have yet to sign and ratify the Rome Statute. Encouraging universal membership in the ICC would provide more consistent accountability for atrocity crimes.

Reinvigorating adherence to international law requires the active participation of civil society. Since the creation of the Charter, the growth of civil society's engagement with the United Nations in the international community has been nothing less than miraculous. Over 5,500 non-governmental organizations are now registered with and recognized by the United Nations. Their expertise, legitimacy, and engagement are indispensable for the future development of international law.

One of the most revealing historical aspects of the Charter is the role of developing countries in its drafting. As noted in various chapters of this book, the Global South played a leading role in advancing both human rights law and general international law by participating in the creation of the U.N. Charter. Enhancing their role in addressing international law's current challenges will ensure a more equitable and just legal system.

This chapter has allocated considerable space to the ICJ's relevance as an authority in developing international law. The court's role in the development of international law is indispensable. However, states' compliance with its rulings sometimes is lacking. Innovative mechanisms are needed to close this gap. Is it possible to develop a system of automatic, incremental sanctions for states that fail to comply with ICJ rulings? Alternatively, can a dedicated UN body be created to monitor and facilitate compliance with international decisions?

By pursuing additional innovative strategies, international law can be more relevant and effective in addressing the international community's current and future challenges.

General Assembly resolutions are largely non-binding, which limits their effectiveness. Reforming the Charter to allow some resolutions passed by a qualified majority to have binding legal force, at least in certain global issues such as international environmental law, pandemics, atrocity crimes, and transnational crime, could enhance the General Assembly's role as a lawmaking body.

Expanding U.N. programs to promote education in international law, particularly in developing countries, could help foster a culture of respect for legal norms. Promoting legal literacy about international law - such as curricula in human rights and environmental law - could build greater domestic support for compliance.

Allocating resources to developing nations to strengthen their legal systems and align them with international standards can significantly enhance domestic support for international law. This effort should include providing targeted support to national NGOs specializing in legal reform and capacity building to leverage their expertise.

A more robust utilization of the U.N. Charter's Article 34, which we examine in Chapter 6, could enhance the relevance of international law by enabling the UN Security Council to undertake early investigation of disputes to prevent escalation. To minimize the influence of political decision-making, the Security Council should establish a periodic review process that engages directly with non-political organizations, providing unbiased input on emerging disputes and potential conflicts. This approach would strengthen the Security Council's credibility by fostering a more unified and impartial decision-making process while ensuring focused attention on disputes that threaten international peace and security.

Corruption within states is a growing global phenomenon that significantly undermines international law by weakening regulatory mechanisms, destabilizing financial systems, obstructing the enforcement of criminal laws, and facilitating human rights violations. Notable international efforts to combat corruption include the United Nations Convention against Corruption (UNCAC), which has 191 state parties. The UNCAC obliges member states to implement legislative measures to criminalize various forms of domestic corruption. Similarly, regional institutions like the European Union require member states to establish national anti-corruption agencies. Despite these initiatives, efforts to combat corruption are often deemed insufficient. One proposed solution is the establishment of an International Anti-Corruption Court (IACC) to investigate and prosecute corruption cases when member states are unwilling or unable to do so.[96] Such a court could address the current accountability gap in kleptocratic regimes while incentivizing states to develop effective domestic frameworks to combat corruption, thus enhancing international law.

States must exercise political will to build the common interest forged through adherence to international legal norms. The U.N. Charter offers us that path. As former American diplomat Lincoln Bloomberg once said, within the Charter "there is international law for anyone to see who will."[97] If states can understand that the greatest strength of international law exists when it is accepted as binding by the international community, [98] then we can advance universal adherence to it. In 1946, the U.N. General Assembly pronounced this fundamental tenet:

> International law is based on the assumption that there exists an international community embracing all independent States and constituting a legally organized society. From this assumption there necessarily follows the acknowledgement of a body of rules of a fundamental character universally binding upon all the members of that society.[99]

When all else is said, this should be our mission.

---

[96] Mark L. Wolf, 'The Case for an International Anti-Corruption Court' *Governance Studies at Brookings* (July 2014), 9

[97] Bloomfield (1957, p. 174).

[98] *Id.*, p. 158.

[99] UNGA, Resolution 94 (I) Progressive Development of International Law and its Codification, UN Doc A/64/Add. 1 (11 December 1946).

References

Abtahi H, Webb P (2008) The genocide convention: The Travaux Préparatoires. Martinus Nijhoff, Leiden

Alexianu M (2023) Provisional, but Not (Always) Pointless: Compliance with ICJ provisional measures. EJIL:Talk! https://www.ejiltalk.org/provisional-but-not-always-pointless-compliance-with-icj-provisional-measures/. Accessed 26 November 2024

Aust A (2006) Vienna convention on the law of treaties (1969). In: Max Planck Encyclopedias of Public International Law. Oxford University Press

Bassiouni M C (2010) Assessing conflict outcomes: Accountability and Impunity. In: Bassiouni M C (ed) The Pursuit of International Criminal Justice: A World Study on Conflicts, Victimization, and Post-Conflict Justice. Intersentia, Antwerp, Portland, pp 3–40

Ben Aharon E (2019) Recognition of the Armenian Genocide after its Centenary: a comparative analysis of changing parliamentary positions. Israel Journal of Foreign Affairs 13(3):339–352

Bloomfield LP (1957) Evolution or revolution?: The united nations and the problem of peaceful territorial change. Harvard University Press, Cambridge, Massachusetts

Bordin F L (2014) Reflections of customary international law: The authority of codification conventions and ILC Draft Articles in International Law. ICLQ 63(3) ICLQ: 535–567

British Information Services (1946) Transcript of Text of an address prepared for delivery by The Right Honorable Winston Churchill, M.P., at Westminster College, Fulton, Missouri, Tuesday, March 5, 1946. https://www.nationalarchives.gov.uk/education/resources/cold-war-on-file/iron-curtain-speech/#:~:text=It%20is%20my%20duty%20however,has%20descended%20across%20the%20Continent. Accessed 28 November 2024

British Library of Information (1941) Prime Minister Winston Churchill's broadcast to the world about the meeting with president Roosevelt. https://www.ibiblio.org/pha/timeline/410824awp.html. Accessed 27 November 2024

Bryant N (2015) UN: Seventy years of changing the world. https://www.bbc.co.uk/news/world-us-canada-34310354. Accessed 28 November 2024

Bull H, Kingsbury B, Roberts A (eds) (1992) Hugo Grotius and international relations. Clarendon Press, Oxford

Cançado Trindade A A (2014) Statute of the international court of justice: Introductory Note. https://legal.un.org/avl/ha/sicj/sicj.html. Accessed 26 November 2024

Carnegie A (1920) Autobiography of Andrew Carnegie. Constable & Co., London

Carnegie endowment for international peace (1943) Year Book. The Endowment, Washington DC

Cohen BV (1949) Human rights under the united nations charter. Law Contemp Probl 14:430–437

Daniel J (1972) The Vienna convention of 1969 on the law of treaties and humanitarian law. International Review of the Red Cross 12(136):367–380

Donoghue J E (2021) Consent by states to the jurisdiction of the international court of justice. https://rm.coe.int/presentation-h-e-joan-e-donoghue-president-of-the-international-court-/1680a401df. Accessed 27 November 2024

Fassbender B (2009) The united nations charter as the constitution of the international community. Brill Nijhoff, Leiden

Fassbender B (2011) Westphalia, Peace of (1648). In: Max Planck Encyclopedias of International Law, Max Planck Institute for Comparative Public Law and International Law

Foster JW (1909) The evolution of international law. Yale Law Journal 18(3):149–164

Graefrath B (1990) Universal criminal jurisdiction and an international criminal court. EJIL 1(1):67–88

Hanhimäki JM (2015) The united nations: a very short introduction, 2nd edn. Oxford University Press, New York

Harris CW (1955) The Stoics' "Universal Community" and its relation to modern international organization. Social Science 30(3):150–156

Hathaway O A (2024) Taking stock of ICJ decisions in the 'Ukraine v. Russia' cases—and implications for South Africa's case against Israel. https://www.justsecurity.org/91781/taking-stock-of-icj-decisions-in-ukraine-v-russia-cases-and-implications-for-south-africas-case-against-israel/. Accessed 26 November 2024

Hovell D (2018) The authority of Universal Jurisdiction. EJIL 29(2): 427–456

Human Rights Watch (2024) Israel not complying with world court order in Genocide case. https://www.hrw.org/news/2024/02/26/israel-not-complying-world-court-order-genocide-case. Accessed 26 November 2024

International Court of Justice (2024) Pending Cases. https://www.icj-cij.org/pending-cases. Accessed 28 November 2024

James RA (2004) The San Francisco conference and the evitable UN Vetoes. Journal of National Security Law & Policy 14(97):97–119

Kelsen H (1944) Peace through law. University of California Press, Van Rees Press, New York

Lemkin R (1933) Acts constituting a general (Transnational) danger considered as offences against the law of nations. http://www.preventgenocide.org/lemkin/madrid1933-english.htm. Accessed 27 November 2024

Månsson K (2007) Reviving the 'Spirit of San Francisco': the lost proposals on human rights, justice and international law to the UN Charter. Nordic Journal of International Law 76(2–3):217–239

Morris PS (2021) The League of Nations and the Development of International Law: A New Intellectual History of the Advisory Committee of Jurists, 1st edn. Routledge, Oxford, New York

Oellers-Frahm K (2012) Article 92. In: Simma et al. (eds), The Charter of the United Nations: A Commentary, Volume II, 3rd edn. Oxford University Press, pp 1897-1950 ("Oellers-Frahm (2012a)")

Oellers-Frahm K (2012) Article 93. In: Simma et al. (eds), The Charter of the United Nations: A Commentary, Volume II, 3rd edn. Oxford University Press, pp 1951-1956 ("Oellers-Frahm (2012b)")

Oellers-Frahm K (2012) Article 94. In: Simma et al. (eds), The Charter of the United Nations: A Commentary, Volume II, 3rd edn. Oxford University Press, pp 1957-1971 ("Oellers-Frahm (2012c)")

Paulson C (2004) Compliance with Final Judgments of the International Court of Justice since 1987. AJIL 98(3):434–461

Peaslee AJ (1945) The Dumbarton Oaks Proposal. Forham Law Review 14(1):55–58

Robinson DR (1985) Observations on the International Court of Justice's November 26, 1984 Judgment on Jurisdiction and Admissibility in the Case of Nicaragua v. United States of America. AJIL 79(2):423–430

Rosenne S (2004) Provisional Measures in International Law: The International Court of Justice and the International Tribunal for the Law of the Sea. Oxford University Press, Oxford

Sinclair I M (1970) Vienna Conference on the Law of Treaties. ICLQ 19(1): 47-69

Sinclair IM (1984) The Vienna Convention on the Law of Treaties: The Consequences of Participation and Nonparticipation. Proceedings of the ASIL Annual Meeting 78:271–275

Stalin J (1946) Speech Delivered by J. V. Stalin at a Meeting of Voters of the Stalin Electoral District, Moscow. https://digitalarchive.wilsoncenter.org/document/speech-delivered-stalin-meeting-voters-stalin-electoral-district-moscow. Accessed 28 November 2024

The Department of State to the British Embassy (1943) Document 500.C114/1939. In: Noble G B, Perkins E R (eds). Foreign Relations of the United States: Diplomatic Papers, 1942, General; the British Commonwealth; the Far East, Volume I. United States Government Printing Office, Washington

United Nations (1947) Yearbook of the United Nations 1946-47. https://www.un-ilibrary.org/content/books/9789210602228. Accessed 27 November 2024

United Nations (1949) Survey of International Law in Relation to the Work of Codification of the International Law Commission Preparatory Work Within the Purview of Article 18, Paragraph

1, of the Statute of the International Law Commission. https://legal.un.org/ilc/documentation/english/a_cn4_1_rev1.pdf. Accessed 27 November 2024
United Nations (1956) Yearbook of the International Law Commission 1949. https://legal.un.org/ilc/publications/yearbooks/english/ilc_1949_v1.pdf. Accessed 27 November 2024
United Nations (1957) Yearbook of the International Law Commission 1950 Volume II. https://legal.un.org/ilc/publications/yearbooks/english/ilc_1950_v2.pdf. Accessed 27 November 2024
United Nations (1967) Yearbook of the International Law Commission 1966 Volume II. https://legal.un.org/ilc/publications/yearbooks/english/ilc_1966_v2.pdf. Accessed 27 November 2024
United Nations (1998) Yearbook of the International Law Commission 1966 Volume II Part Two. https://legal.un.org/ilc/publications/yearbooks/english/ilc_1996_v2_p2.pdf. Accessed 28 November 2024
United Nations (1999) Press Release SG/SM/7136 GA/9596 Secretary-general Presents His Annual Report to General Assembly. https://press.un.org/en/1999/19990920.sgsm7136.html. Accessed 26 November 2024
United Nations (2018) Yearbook of the International Law Commission 2011, Vol. II, Part 2. https://www.un-ilibrary.org/content/books/9789210577168. Accessed 27 November 2024
United Nations Audiovisual Library of International Law (2008) Convention on the Prevention and Punishment of the Crimes of Genocide. https://legal.un.org/avl/pdf/ha/cppcg/cppcg_ph_e.pdf. Accessed 28 November 2024
United Nations Conference on International Organization (1945) Documents of the United Nations Conference on International Organization, San Francisco, 1945, Volume I: General. United Nations Information Organizations, London, New York ("United Nations Conference on International Organization (1945a)")
United Nations Conference on International Organization (1945) Documents of the United Nations Conference on International Organization, San Francisco, 1945, Volume III: Dumbarton Oaks Proposals Comments and Proposed Amendments. United Nations Information Organizations, London, New York ("United Nations Conference on International Organization (1945b)")
United Nations Conference on International Organization (1945) Documents of the United Nations Conference on International Organization, San Francisco, 1945, Volume XII: Commission III Security Council. United Nations Information Organizations, London, New York ("United Nations Conference on International Organization (1945c)")
United Nations General Assembly (2019) Report of the International Law Commission. https://documents.un.org/doc/undoc/gen/g19/243/93/pdf/g1924393.pdf. Accessed 28 November 2024
United Nations Treaty Collection (2024) Overview. https://treaties.un.org/pages/overview.aspx?path=overview/overview/page1_en.xml. Accessed 4 October 2024
Vierdag EW (1982) The Law Governing Treaty Relations between Parties to the Vienna Convention on the Law of Treaties and States not Party to the Convention. AJIL 76(4):779–801

Chapter 4
Maintain International Peace and Security

The genesis of the U.N. Charter during the carnage of World War II was grounded in a determination, stated in the Preamble, "to save succeeding generations from the scourge of war, which twice in our lifetime has brought untold sorrow to mankind." Setting aside the convoluted wording of the Covenant of the League of Nations, negotiators who toiled through drafting sessions at Dumbarton Oaks in 1944 and San Francisco in 1945 focused on the noble quest to prevent war (Fig. 4.1). These opening words of the Charter, framed under the mantra, "We the peoples of the United Nations," signaled a notable purpose that the Preamble then amplified. The "peoples" aimed "to unite our strength to maintain international peace and security" and "to ensure, by the acceptance of principles and the institution of methods, that armed force shall not be used, save in the common interest…" The embrace of "principles" pointed to international law that governs warfare, including the determination of just war (what lawyers describe in Latin as *jus ad bellum*). The use of "methods" envisaged the United Nations as an organization dedicated to the pursuit of peace but also to the management of armed force as a collective enterprise of member states. No longer would tyrannical men wield indiscriminate firepower without a strong response by member states of the United Nations determined to save humanity from the scourge of war. Wishful thinking? No, not for anyone who had survived World War II.

The long history of armed conflicts since the Charter's inception reveals both the violation and the enforcement of the Charter provisions focusing on international peace and security. The Founders would be greatly disappointed with the bloody record of the Charter's seeming underperformance during the last 80 years. Chapter VII of the Charter empowers the Security Council to act, including with military force, when international peace and security are at risk. And it has done so, repeatedly, but the Security Council also has fallen victim to the power of the veto, which the Charter permits in Article 27. Resolutions of enforcement under Chapter VII have a haphazard history of compliance (compare the Gulf War of 1990–1991 v. the Anglo-American war beginning in 2003, each being against Iraq) and the innovative

D. J. Scheffer and M. S. Ellis, *The UN Charter*,
https://doi.org/10.1007/978-3-031-94866-4_4

Fig. 4.1 Diplomats negotiating peace and security provisions of the U.N. Charter in San Francisco in 1945 (*Source* UN Photo/Lundquist)

"Chapter VI and a half" peacekeeping operations sometimes worked (Cyprus and Cambodia) and sometimes failed spectacularly (Rwanda and Srebrenica).[1] Two non-military weapons—economic sanctions and war crimes tribunals—have been part of the Chapter VII arsenal binding all nations while attracting their fair share of criticism and denial. The Charter unleashed a whole new paradigm for international peace and security which to this day remains precariously trapped between success and failure.

Following the Preamble of the Charter, Chapter I (Purposes and Principles) brings more clarity to the peace and security mandate of the United Nations. In Article 1, the first purpose of the United Nations is to "maintain international peace and security, and to that end: to take effective collective measures for the prevention and removal of threats to the peace, and for the suppression of acts of aggression or other breaches of the peace, and to bring about by peaceful means, and in conformity with the principles of justice and international law, adjustment of settlement of international disputes or situations which might lead to a breach of the peace."[2]

The terms "war" and "warfare" are absent in this Charter language. Rather, the far more expansive agenda of "international peace and security" is the cornerstone of the Charter. And contrary to the Covenant of the League of Nations, there is no explicit suggestion of unilateral action as a response. Rather, "collective measures" are designated as the means of action by the United Nations, and that action is directed at preventing as well as removing, namely ending, "threats to the peace." Bearing in mind that aggression was an egregious manifestation of warfare during World War

[1] Williamson (1998); Murphy (2004); Bothe (2012), pp. 1171–1199; United Nations Peacekeeping Force in Cyprus (2024); Findlay (1995), p. 155; United Nations Peacekeeping (1999); Human Rights Watch (1995).

[2] Wolfrum (2012a), pp. 107–120.

II, Article 1 singles out "the suppression of acts of aggression" as a primary purpose, leaving wide open what actions might constitute "suppression." The same objective, "suppression," is applied to "other breaches of the peace," which invites an almost infinite range of circumstances that could be regarded as "breaches of the peace." There is no constraint that limits "suppression" of either aggression or breaches of peace to conventional warfare or uses of armed force. In the same vein, there are infinite ways to imagine "suppression" as a weapon of choice for the United Nations to use in the realm of peace and security.

The Dumbarton Oaks Proposals did not require that "conformity with the principles of justice and international law" would condition the "peaceful means" to be used for the "adjustment or settlement of international disputes or situations which might lead to a breach of the peace." Yet those words of justice and law were logical add-ons in San Francisco, for they removed concern that might arise whether the means, though peaceful, might still run counter to rule of law precepts. With that guardrail in place—justice and international law—the United Nations could focus its attention on the wide range of peaceful means available to confront "disputes or situations" that could disrupt the peace. No specific terms describe "peaceful means," so one's imagination can run free over what could be possible in any number of circumstances threatening the peace.

A good part of Article 2 of the U.N. Charter establishes the normative framework for managing international peace and security.[3] Both the United Nations as an international organization and all of its member states must adhere to this article's fundamental principles. Article 2(3) requires all member states to "settle their international disputes by peaceful means in such a manner that international peace and security, and justice, are not endangered."[4] This wording reaches beyond that approved at Dumbarton Oaks, which did not specify disputes as "international" in character and omitted "justice" entirely from the provision. In the Charter, not only must nations ensure that their *international* disputes are settled peacefully and without violence, they need to employ the long view that in their actions international peace and security will prevail alongside *justice*, and thus that the settlement is not endangering peace, security, or justice. That demands considerable foresight as well as perspective. Thus, settling a dispute peacefully that leaves a border between two nations still hotly contested fails both the peace and security test—as it leaves the future unstable—and the justice test, as there would be no lasting justice until the border is demarcated beyond any realistic challenge. Peacefully ending a transnational reign of atrocity crimes but failing to achieve accountability of the perpetrators of such crimes would not meet the requirements of justice, which the victims typically would demand be fulfilled. Further, letting impunity for atrocity crimes stand would undermine deterrence and the prospects for peace and security, particularly between two or more countries, where the failure of justice can generate continued warfare and atrocities.

[3] Paulus (2012a), pp. 121–132.

[4] Tomuschat (2012), pp. 181–199.

Article 2(4) of the Charter ranks as the document's most significant and publicized provision: "All Members shall refrain in their international relations from the threat or use of force against the territorial integrity or political independence of any state, or in any other manner inconsistent with the Purposes of the United Nations."[5] The "international relations" that member states engage in operate on countless levels of inter-state conduct. The term encompasses bilateral and multilateral diplomacy and deal-making, negotiated ad hoc agreements and treaty-making, cultural exchanges, international trade, and even the waging of every type of armed conflict and wars and the peace negotiations that sometimes achieve a measure of stability in the aftermath.

The Charter offers no explanation or description of "force" and does not require that "armed force" must be the only type of force prohibited by the Charter. One could apply any modern understanding of the character of "force" to the provision. For example, the use of cyber weapons or disinformation or diplomatic subterfuge or malign artificial intelligence or even malicious environmental distortions can be understood to be "force" in today's world. Both Dumbarton Oaks and San Francisco drafts used the broadest of terms–force–so the potential of numerous types of "force" existed in the founders' thinking from an early stage. In modern times, the options of "force" in the conduct of international relations is essentially unlimited.

The Dumbarton Oaks Proposals lacked reference to the use of force "against the territorial integrity or political independence of any state," as those words were added to the draft Charter in San Francisco. The Charter's final wording thus articulates three, rather than just one, platform upon which to prohibit the use of force. The first entails "territorial integrity." The integrity of a nation's territory can be undermined or decimated today with assaults of military power, cyberattacks on the internet, mass refugee migration, transborder environmental damage, space-based targeting of infrastructure networks, and whatever other insidious weapon of choice leaps across the national border or descends from the heavens to wreak havoc on a nation's sovereign territory. The second concerns using force against the "political independence" of a nation. This could entail situations where force, of any type, seeks to change or threaten or manipulate the government of a nation in such a way as to deny its government and its populace of their freedom of deliberation, governance, and political ideology or persuasion. Given the end of the Cold War and the collapse of rigid ideological carve-outs of blocs of nations (East v. West, democracy v. communism), the world is a mosaic of sovereign nations confidently promoting their own independent political identities even if they are allied or aligned with one of the major military powers or if strictly non-aligned and sometimes playing one mega-power against another.[6] The struggle between the nations of NATO, including the United States, and the Russia/China/North Korea/Iran cluster of totalitarian states continues to fester.[7] The most prominent division today, though, might be viewed as North v. South.[8] Even in that expanding sphere of international politics, the political

---

[5] Randelzhofer and Dörr (2012), pp. 200–234.

[6] Gheboianu and Popescu (2023); Keohane et al. (1993).

[7] Kendall-Taylor and Fontaine (2024).

[8] Shidore (2023).

independence of each rising power remains a paramount feature of their advocacy and projection of influence and clout on the world scene. When national leaders speak from the podium of the U.N. General Assembly each September at the launch of a new annual session, most proudly assert their politically independent views of world affairs even if some invoke the righteousness of the camp they identify with in a turbulent world.[9]

Thus, the importance and sensitivity of what a nation would consider "its political independence" is only amplified in contemporary times. Prohibiting any use of the manifold means of "force" against that independence is of singular importance for most nations. With the exceptions of Georgia and Ukraine—both invaded by Russian forces—in recent years, nations fear not the threat of a military invasion but of interference with their political independence. The Charter stands as a bulwark, now more than ever before, against that threat.

The third prohibition on the "threat or use of force" articulated in both the Dumbarton Oaks Proposals and Article 2(4) of the Charter arises "in any other manner inconsistent with the Purposes of the United Nations." Those purposes create a large field upon which "force" in its manifold characterizations is denied any legitimacy by the Charter. Implementing unilateral measures to maintain international peace and security would contradict the requirement of collective measures and peaceful means of dispute resolution to achieve this purpose expressed in Article 1(1). The threat or use of force is prohibited for the purposes set forth in Article 1(2), which include developing friendly relations among nations while respecting the "principle of equal rights and self-determination of peoples…". The Article 2(4) admonition sends a powerful signal *not* to use force to *deny* self-determination of peoples, which was and remains a powerful principle of international law most vividly played out in the vast de-colonization era following World War II and recognized in the Charter as a key task for the United Nations to fulfill. Whether in modern times armed force, in particular, can be legitimately used to *achieve* self-determination is another matter entirely, given the largely decolonized world we now live in and the strong Charter invocation against the use of armed force.[10] However, the plight of a minority population deprived of fundamental rights and under armed assault by a repressive regime might still legitimize the right to use armed force to achieve not only the self-defense of such a population but also its right of self determination.

A further purpose of the Charter, expressed in Article 1(2), is "to take other appropriate measures to strengthen universal peace," which we examine in Chapter 6 when we discuss the Charter's dedication to peacemaking. Here we stress that Article 2(4) prohibits the use of force as an "appropriate" measure to "strengthen universal peace." Often belligerents claim that conducting warfare or initiating military interventions serve the purpose of achieving peace itself, and if the cause is just that indeed may be the result. But the Charter tries to quash that line of advocacy or propaganda by nations. The Charter's emphasis lies in achieving and maintaining peace through peaceful means and not to unleash "force" as a readily available excuse

[9] United Nations General Debate (2024).
[10] Oeter (2012), pp. 313–333.

to wreck violence and havoc and atrocities while deceptively invoking the aim of strengthening universal peace.

Article 2(4) also prohibits the threat or use of force in any manner inconsistent with the purpose set forth in Article 1(3), namely for the United Nations to forge ahead solving a wide range of societal problems and promoting human rights and fundamental freedoms. Of course, one can seek to rationalize the use of force, including armed force, as a means to an end for any of these elements of international cooperation. But the Charter clearly rejects such strategies in the wording of Article 2(4), which creates a global commitment to achieve the Charter's purposes without resort to force—of whatever character—not only in the world of 1945 but in the modern world of our own lives. The exception to Article 2(4) will arise in the Charter's mandate of collective security and enforcing the Charter with armed force under Chapter VII, as well as the inherent right to self-defense recognized in Article 51, all to which we return shortly.

In the meantime, however, the Charter recognizes in Article 2(5) that the United Nations can only operate effectively in accordance with the Charter if nations assist it in doing so and refrain from giving assistance to those nations "against which the United Nations is taking preventive or enforcement action."[11] This powerful mandate binds U.N. member states to the organization's daily work across the globe, in effect requiring nations to meet the colossal challenge of having the U.N.'s back and empowering the organization with nations' collective fortitude to achieve missions for humanity. In the same vein, Article 2(5) blocks nations from assisting any country that the United Nations is essentially disciplining with preventive or enforcement action. There are no words explaining the precise meaning of "preventive or enforcement action," but it certainly encompasses the many different types of actions (non-military and military and those yet to be conceived) that the Security Council could take under the Charter's Chapter VII authority against a recalcitrant nation. Also, when the General Assembly highlights under Article 11(3), particularly for preventive purposes, a situation "likely to endanger international peace and security," that sends a signal to member states not to risk violating Article 2(5) by rendering assistance to any nation aggravating that situation.

There are very few territorial patches of Earth that are not identified as a member state of the United Nations or as a non-self-governing territory (see Chapter 6). Three "nations" have not achieved membership in the United Nations: Kosovo has been denied membership since it declared its independence in 2008 and attracted the opposition of Russia and China in the Security Council. As of this writing over 110 governments have recognized Kosovo as a sovereign country.[12] Vatican City State, governed by The Holy See of the Catholic Church, is diplomatically recognized across the globe but remains detached from U.N. membership aside from an observer mission and that appears to be its preference.[13] The State of Palestine, which is recognized by more than 145 countries and is a "non-member Observer State" at the

[11] Aust (2012), pp. 235–251.

[12] Republic of Kosovo Ministry of Foreign Affairs and Diaspora (2022).

[13] World Population Review (2024).

United Nations, remains outside the membership club due to repeated opposition by the United States in the Security Council, which ostensibly will not be lifted until Israel signs a peace agreement with Palestinian authorities recognizing a Palestinian nation.[14]

Article 2(6) of the Charter, drawn directly from the Dumbarton Oaks Proposals, empowers the United Nations "to ensure that states which are not Members of the United Nations [currently including Kosovo, Palestine, and the Vatican] act in accordance with these [Charter] Principles so far as may be necessary for the maintenance of international peace and security."[15] Though this act of self-preservation in the face of tyranny and murderous threats from a non-member state may seem confusing (Should the United Nations exercise jurisdiction over a non-member state?), the drafters of the Charter could not leave bare a major gap in the document that would enable non-member states to threaten the peace and security of all nations. This power is manifest in how the United Nations has engaged significantly in the affairs of both Kosovo and Palestine in recent decades in order to manage peace and security challenges.[16] That doubtless will continue under, at a minimum, the authority of this lesser known provision in the Charter.

The final prominent Principle set forth in the Charter is Article 2(7), which governments frequently reference to contest the purported interference by the United Nations in their domestic affairs.[17] It is the first and final refuge for leaders and governments to evade scrutiny by the United Nations and its agencies of policies and actions undertaken within and situations arising inside their national borders. Article 2(7) is the Charter's salute to the staying power of sovereignty after Adolf Hitler, Benito Mussolini, and Hirohito blew apart that cardinal rule of international law to wage World War II. Importantly, however, the provision is rather narrow in its sweep of application, prohibiting only the United Nations from interference in the internal affairs of a nation. The Charter, on its face, does not purport to prohibit one or more sovereign nations, acting outside of the authority of the United Nations, from interfering in the domestic affairs of another sovereign nation. This contrasts with the usual argument for non-interference directed towards a nation, such as the United States, taking action that targets or criticizes something that, like a major human rights violation, occurs domestically in another country. Article 2(7) *denies only the United Nations* from intervening "in matters which are essentially within the domestic jurisdiction of any state…" while green lighting a single nation or group of nations outside of the Organization to engage in such intervention at their own risk, legally and otherwise. Nor does Article 2(7) limit the principle of non-interference only to Member States of the United Nations, but protects "any state" from such U.N. intervention.

---

[14] United Nations Human Rights Office of the High Commissioner (2024); United Nations Meetings Coverage and Press Releases (2024).

[15] Talmon (2012), pp. 252–279.

[16] United Nations Peacekeeping (2024); United Nations Relief and Works Agency for Palestine Refugees in the Near East (2024).

[17] Nolte (2012), pp. 280–311.

The Dumbarton Oaks Proposals had prohibited General Assembly, Security Council, or International Court of Justice interference in "situations or disputes arising out of matters which *by international law are solely* within the domestic jurisdiction of the state concerned." (Emphasis added).[18] John Foster Dulles, who was on the U.S. delegation at San Francisco, thought the Dumbarton language using "international law" to define the boundaries of domestic jurisdiction left far too many uncertainties for the future, as it might end up delineating a narrow domain for internal affairs as international law increasingly intruded into sovereign space over the years. Dulles was determined to leave the judgment of what constituted American sovereignty, and thus the hands-off domain of the country, strictly to Americans. So he excised "international law" from the text.[19] Instead of the highly dubious proposition of what, in each instance, is "solely" within the internal affairs of a country, the constraint on U.N. interference emerged in San Francisco as the far more flexible standard of what is "*essentially* within the domestic jurisdiction of any state…". [emphasis added] Even if a matter had some application or relevance to a nation's foreign policy or engagement, for example, the fact that the activity was grounded primarily inside the country's borders would bring into play Article 2(7) and its prohibition on U.N. conduct. The fact that some politically repressed minority members escaped or were driven from a country may not, in the eyes of that government, create an international situation exceeding the constraints of Article 2(7). Dulles may have worried about what the United Nations might try to do about the plight of Native Americans or the civil rights of African-Americans or Asian-Americans or even crackdowns on members of the Communist Party in the United States, given the Soviet Union's clout in the United Nations.

Despite the broad landscape of what "essentially" constitutes domestic jurisdiction, or internal affairs, of a nation, Article 2(7) of the Charter empowers the United Nations to require member states "to submit such [domestic] matters to settlement under the present Charter…" That largely would mean pacific settlement of disputes, which is governed by Chapter VI of the Charter, but it also can be seen as settlement through enforcement actions authorized by the Security Council under Chapter VII of the Charter. Thus a nation that unilaterally intervenes in the domestic matters of another nation might find the United Nations in some way, through the General Assembly or Security Council or through its judicial organ, the International Court of Justice, redirecting that nation's actions towards a U.N.-orchestrated settlement.

The final caveat about the principle of non-interference in the internal affairs of any state, as mandated by Article 2(7), is essential to the viability of the entire Charter and the United Nations: "…[T]his principle shall not prejudice the application of enforcement measures under Chapter VII." The Dumbarton Oaks Proposals lacked this caveat. The Security Council can authorize, under a Chapter VII enforcement resolution, any intervention it may wish into the domestic jurisdiction, or internal affairs, of any nation. The Responsibility to Protect (R2P) principle, approved by the General Assembly in 2005, was designed to take advantage of the Security

[18] United Nations Conference on International Organization (1945), p. 13.

[19] Schlesinger (2003), p. 238.

Council's power to override Article 2(7)'s shield of domestic jurisdiction and act as a critical deterrence mechanism to protect populations from massive human rights violations, specifically atrocity crimes.[20] However, R2P's implementation has been disappointing and reflects flaws in the Charter's grant of veto power to the five permanent members, any one of which can block effective action.[21] The disunity in the Security Council has been and remains the case among the major powers, meaning that the opportunities for the Security Council to override the sanctity of "domestic jurisdiction" under Article 2(7) are exceptionally limited. The General Assembly stepped into the breach with new procedures recently, but the end result still renders R2P a toothless tiger in too many instances where atrocity crimes need to be confronted.[22]

While the Security Council is the Charter's major engine behind international peace and security, the General Assembly, as shown with the adoption of the R2P principle, still plays a critical role as the world's legislative body of all member states. Chapter VI of the Charter focuses on the General Assembly. Article 10 opens the door widely for the General Assembly to "discuss any questions or any matters within the scope of the present Charter or relating to the powers and functions of any organs" in the Charter and to make recommendations to member states or the Security Council on such questions or matters. Article 11 offers more detail, authorizing the General Assembly to "consider the general principles of co-operation in the maintenance of international peace and security, including the principles governing disarmament and the regulation of armaments, and may make recommendations with regard to such principles to the Members or to the Security Council or to both." Note the repeated emphasis on "principles," pointing to the general character of this General Assembly function that would elaborate the theory of maintaining international peace and security but not the actual implementation which would be left to the Security Council (see below).

Article 11(2) of the Charter invites the General Assembly to "discuss any questions relating to the maintenance of international peace and security brought before it by any Member of the United Nations, or by the Security Council," or by a non-member state and to make recommendations to nations or the Security Council or both.[23] The General Assembly also, under Article 11(3), "may call the attention of the Security Council to situations which are likely to endanger international peace and security." This affords the General Assembly the power to be an engine of prevention at the United Nations, which is always critical to pursue in order to short circuit actual disputes that endanger international peace and security.

Article 14 empowers the General Assembly to "recommend measures for the peaceful adjustment of any situation, regardless of origin, which it deems likely to impair the general welfare or friendly relations among nations, including situations

---

[20] Global Centre for the Responsibility to Protect (2024); Vashakmadze (2012), pp. 1201–1236.

[21] Lepard (2021); Scheffer and Walker (2018), pp. 495–499.

[22] UNGA, Resolution 76/L.52 Standing mandate for a General Assembly debate when a veto is cast in the Security Council, UN Doc A/76/L.52 (20 Apr 2022).

[23] Klein and Schmahl (2012a), pp. 498–502.

resulting from a violation of the provisions of the present Charter setting forth the Purposes and Principles of the United Nations [namely, Articles 1 and 2]."[24] The provision was barely developed at Dumbarton Oaks where diplomats described the General Assembly's task "to make recommendations with regard to any such principles or questions." At San Francisco, the delegates focused again, in Article 14, on the capacity of the General Assembly to prevent dangerous situations from spiraling out of control.

The major exception to these "free speech" and "shout out" provisions in Articles 10, 11, and 14 of the Charter is found in Article 12, which blocks the General Assembly from making any recommendations on a dispute or situation that the Security Council is *already handling* unless the Council so requests.[25] Article 12 does not prevent the General Assembly from diving into debate about international peace and security issues being addressed by the Security Council; the General Assembly simply cannot recommend any actions about such issues to Member States or to the Security Council if the Council is seized with the issue. This conforms to what emerged from Dumbarton Oaks where the major powers controlled the entire process and ensured the primacy of the Security Council on which they planned to sit. The delegations from the United States, United Kingdom, and Soviet Union exercised overriding influence at Dumbarton Oaks, so for them there were no minefields to navigate in their determination to deny the General Assembly the right to make recommendations on international peace and security issues to the Security Council, which, even if General Assembly recommendations had been permitted in the drafting of the Charter, the Council could simply take alternative action while nonetheless benefitting from the General Assembly's input.

This specific denial of the power of recommendations is amplified in Article 12(2) where the Secretary-General must notify the General Assembly periodically of the international peace and security issues being dealt with by the Security Council so that the Assembly knows unmistakably when to forego making any such recommendations.[26] In addition, Article 15(1) empowers the General Assembly to "receive and consider annual and special reports from the Security Council; these reports shall include an account of the measures that the Security Council has decided upon or taken to maintain international peace and security."[27] This reporting requirement reinforces the dominant power of the Security Council once it is seized with a situation concerning international peace and security.

Any General Assembly recommendations regarding the maintenance of international peace and security—that are not otherwise blocked by Article 12—require a two-thirds majority of the members present and voting in order to be adopted.[28] This rule in Article 18(2) of the Charter applies as well to certain other issues acted upon by the General Assembly, but it is a potent reminder of how the successful launch

---

[24] Zöckler and Riznik (2012), pp. 552–566.

[25] Klein and Schmahl (2012b), pp. 507–524.

[26] *Id.*, pp. 520–523.

[27] Hilger, Tichy, and Bittner (2012), pp. 567–570.

[28] Wolfrum (2012b), p. 625.

of any action on international peace and security in the General Assembly remains a high bar.

The Charter provisions on the powers of the Security Council focus almost exclusively on international peace and security. At Dumbarton Oaks, the delegates firmly pronounced this when drafting, "In order to ensure prompt and effective action by the Organization, members of the Organization should by the Charter confer on the Security Council primary responsibility for the maintenance of international peace and security and should agree that in carrying out these duties under this responsibility it should act on their behalf." Article 24(1) of the Charter replicates this wording.[29] Additional Dumbarton Oaks text was preserved in Articles 24(2) and (3), 25, and 26 of the Charter.

The Security Council's specific powers to discharge its duties are found in Chapters V, VI, VII, VIII, and XII of the Charter. In Chapter V, Article 24(2) requires the Security Council to discharge its duties on maintaining international peace and security "in accordance with the Purposes and Principles of the United Nations."[30] Article 25 obligates all Member States of the United Nations "to accept and carry out the decisions of the Security Council in accordance with the present Charter."[31] This was a huge leap beyond the far weaker provisions of the Covenant of the League of Nations and reflects a core provision that had been drafted into the Dumbarton Oaks Proposals, particularly with respect to Security Council enforcement decisions adopted under Chapter VII authority.

Another fresh provision that appeared at Dumbarton Oaks and then in Article 26 of the Charter takes into account the societal price of dealing with the Council's purpose: "In order to promote the establishment and maintenance of international peace and security with the least diversion of armaments of the world's human and economic resources, the Security Council shall be responsible for formulating, with the assistance of the Military Staff Committee referred to in Article 47, plans to be submitted to the Members of the United Nations for the establishment of a system for the regulation of armaments."[32] This regulatory system of armaments never came to pass as the Cold War sidelined much of the Charter's implementation and the Military Staff Committee, rendered impotent by the superpower standoff, has remained an empty vessel during the post-Cold War decades. But Article 26 places a marker on an aspirational goal that still merits the highest priority among governments: how to limit the stockpiling of armaments in the face of the critical need for governments to expend financial resources on the human agenda, which includes economic growth and stability in every country. The Charter explicitly recognizes that objective. Recent wars, particularly in Ukraine, have thrown a wrench into this goal as the dire need to manufacture and deliver munitions and weapons to Ukraine for its defense against a Russian war of aggression has revitalized the armaments industry in defense of freedom and democracy not only in Ukraine but elsewhere,

---

[29] Peters (2012a), pp. 761–786.

[30] *Id.*, pp. 780–781.

[31] Peters (2012b), pp. 787–854.

[32] Schütz (2012), pp. 855–870.

such as in Taiwan.[33] Nonetheless, the Charter stands available as a codified means to reach a more reasonable balance between armaments and the needs of human populations.

Contrary to the erratic procedures set out in the Covenant of the League of Nations, the Charter established the Security Council as a body that is able to function continuously, which means not only periodically but also any other time, including holidays, weekends and nights (New York time) if necessary. Article 28 so provides and requires each member of the Council to be represented at all times at the seat of the Organization, which is in New York City.[34] The Council also can hold meetings elsewhere if it so decides, and has occasionally done so in such cities as Addis Ababa (1972), Panama City (1973), Geneva (1990), and Nairobi (2004).[35] This is a vastly underutilized option that could enhance the image of the Council, a U.N. organ distained by much of the world because of the Charter's grant of unyielding power and veto privilege to its narrow band of permanent members: China, France, Russia, United Kingdom, and United States.

Reflecting the Dumbarton Oaks Proposals, Article 29 of the Charter empowers the Security Council to "establish such subsidiary organs as it deems necessary for the performance of its functions."[36] In the realm of international peace and security, the Security Council has used this power to establish various types of subsidiary bodies covering peacekeeping operations, special political missions and offices, the International Criminal Tribunals for the former Yugoslavia and Rwanda and the International Residual Mechanism for Criminal Tribunals, admission of new member states, peacebuilding commission, counter-terrorism committee, weapons of mass destruction committee, and various working groups and sanctions committees.

Article 31 of the Charter permits the Security Council to invite into Council discussions, without the right to vote, any member state that is not sitting on the Security Council as a non-permanent member provided "the interests of that Member are specially affected."[37] Article 32 further mandates that any Member of the United Nations or any non-Member state that is a party to a dispute under consideration by the Security Council "shall be invited to participate, without vote, in the discussion relating to the dispute."[38] These procedural opportunities were set forth in the Dumbarton Oaks Proposals, where the Security Council's grip on how deliberations would be managed was firmly established. The participation of member states that are not normally sitting on the Security Council as permanent or non-permanent members is a frequent feature of Council meetings. For example, in meetings concerning the Russia/Ukraine war, an official from Ukraine's Mission to the United Nations attends. For discussions about Israel/Palestinian matters, diplomats from Israel's Mission

33 Nicastro et al. (2024), p. 1.

34 Bühler (2012), pp. 943–967.

35 *Id.*, pp. 977–981.

36 Paulus (2012b), pp. 985–1027.

37 Dolzer and Kreuter-Kirchhof (2012a), pp. 1050–1063.

38 Dolzer and Kreuter-Kirchhof (2012b), pp. 1064–1067.

to the United Nations and from the non-Member Permanent Observer Mission of Palestine to the United Nations typically appear in the Security Council chamber.

The Security Council's role in peaceful ("pacific") settlement of disputes is covered in Articles 33–38 of the Charter and will be examined in the sixth chapter of this book. It is in the Charter's Chapter VII, titled as "Action with Respect to Threats to the Peace, Breaches of the Peace, and Acts of Aggression" and consisting of Articles 39–51, that the Charter's most critical provisions on international peace and security are embedded, with the Security Council wielding all of the power of the United Nations. Indeed, there is not a single mention in Chapter VII of either the General Assembly or the International Court of Justice.

Chapter VII of the Charter remains largely faithful to what was worked out at Dumbarton Oaks for activating the Security Council to take action to maintain or restore international peace and security. In many respects, the powers and procedures in this part of the Charter were the core tasks to be deliberated on at Dumbarton Oaks, and there was little tolerance among the negotiating powers at the Washington estate for the follow-on San Francisco conference to perform open heart surgery on this part of the Charter.

We will walk through the twelve articles of Chapter VII sequentially as the way each element of the Charter appears has a preceding and subsequent procedure to understand. Activating Article 39 would follow the efforts spelled out in Chapter VI of the Charter to try to harness a dispute with peaceful means of dispute settlement. In theory and usually in practice, the Security Council reaches Article 39 authority when peaceful measures under Chapter VI have failed. Under Article 39, which sets the table for the following ten articles of the Charter, the Security Council "shall determine the existence of any threat to the peace, breach of the peace, or act of aggression and shall make recommendations, or decide what measures shall be taken in accordance with Articles 41 and 42, to maintain or restore international peace and security."[39] The Council is empowered to define and identify a situation of war-like conditions (threat to or breach of the peace or act of aggression) and recommend or, more powerfully, literally decide how to deal with that situation. The view of any particular leader or government as to whether any of the three prongs of Article 39 have been triggered is inconsequential under the Charter; the Security Council makes that determination and can exercise any or all of the potentially awesome powers of Chapter VII. The negotiators at Dumbarton Oaks had zero interest in a paper tiger organization, so long as they could control it through the Security Council.

Article 40 of the Charter takes one step back before the Security Council unleashes the full power that Article 39 mandates. Missing entirely from the Dumbarton Oaks Proposals, Article 40 was drafted in San Francisco and introduces the option of "provisional measures." The text of Article 40 reads, "In order to prevent an aggravation of the situation, the Security Council may, before making the recommendations or deciding upon the measures provided for in Article 39, call upon the parties concerned to comply with such provisional measures as it deems necessary or desirable. Such provisional measures shall be without prejudice to the rights, claims, or position of

[39] Krisch (2012a), pp. 1272–1296.

the parties concerned. The Security Council shall duly take account of failure to comply with such provisional measures."[40]

The option of pressing the "parties" in a volatile situation to comply with provisional measures could mean calling upon them to implement a ceasefire or enable humanitarian and medical access to civilians trapped in the fighting or engage in direct talks immediately to defuse the conflict or even just comply with international humanitarian law in all respects. These can all be immediate steps which, depending on how the parties react to the Council's call for implementation, set up a decision whether to advance to an Article 39 recommendation or decision for Council action. Article 40 affords the parties which, for example, could be nations, factions of governments, liberation groups, insurgent militia, or even terrorist organizations, to act in a manner that avoids further Chapter VII action by the Security Council. However, a party's failure to comply with Article 40 provisional measures would be taken into account by the Council in deciding on further action that might severely impact that party.

The Security Council enters the world of tangible pro-active operations to achieve peace and security when it activates Article 41 authority. This toolbox entitles the Security Council to "decide what measures not involving the use of armed force are to be employed to give effect to its decisions, and it may call upon the Members of the United Nations to apply such measures. These may include complete or partial interruption of economic relations and of rail, sea, air, postal, telegraphic, radio, and other means of communication, and the severance of diplomatic relations."[41] Thus, short of the use of armed force the Council has a wide range of means to disrupt a party engaged in, as highlighted by Article 39, "any threat to the peace, breach of the peace, or act of aggression…" The most common action under Article 41 authority is the imposition of economic sanctions by the Security Council on a recalcitrant nation or designated citizens.[42] The Council has called on countries to impose diplomatic sanctions on violating countries.[43]

The list appearing in Article 41 is not all-inclusive of non-military measures of enforcement. The creation of the International Criminal Tribunals for the former Yugoslavia (1993) and Rwanda (1994) occurred under Article 41 authority. One could envisage the Council in the future authorizing cyberspace interventions that disrupt a nation's military or cyber operations responsible for violating the peace or committing aggression. The Council could deny a country access to cultural or

[40] Krisch (2012b), pp. 1297–1304.

[41] Krisch (2012c), pp. 1305–1329.

[42] The following are examples of resolutions from various UN Security Council sanctions regimes. UN Security Council, Resolution 2253, UN Doc S/RES/2253 (17 Dec 2015); UN Security Council, Resolution 2733, UN Doc S/RES/2733 (31 May 2024); UN Security Council, Resolution 2750, UN Doc S/RES/2750 (11 Sep 2024); UN Security Council, Resolution 2758 (2024), UN Doc S/RES/2758 (13 Nov 2024).

[43] The following are examples of UN Security Council resolutions calling upon nations to impose diplomatic sanctions on violating countries. UN Security Council, Resolution 1044, UN Doc S/RES/1044 (31 Jan 1996); UN Security Council, Resolution 1054, UN Doc S/RES/1054 (26 Apr 1996); UN Security Council, Resolution 2094, UN Doc S/RES/2094 (7 Mar 2013).

sports events, such as the Olympics. Musicians and scholars could even be prohibited from traveling to the uncooperative country and all airlines could be denied access to its airports. Use of the SWIFT system of financial transactions could be denied to a country violating the Council's decision under Chapter VII authority.

The particular situation confronting the Security Council may suggest that Article 41 measures will not work or if employed have been ineffective. In either case, the Security Council can step up to the most powerful provision of the Charter, one that authorizes the Security Council to use military means to confront dangers to peace and security. Article 42, drawn from the Dumbarton Oaks Proposals, reads: "Should the Security Council consider that measures provided for in Article 41 would be inadequate or have proved to be inadequate, it may take such action by air, sea, or land forces as may be necessary to maintain or restore international peace and security. Such action may include demonstrations, blockade, and other operations by air, sea, or land forces of Members of the United Nations."[44]

Throughout the history of the United Nations, the Security Council has invoked Article 42 many times and demonstrated its will to take decisive military action.[45] However, during the Cold War and in recent years the fractured political character of the Permanent Five (P-5) has diminished their resort to Article 42, thus weakening the influence of the United Nations when Article 39 situations arise.

As the means of threatening the peace and waging war become increasingly shaped by technological developments, particularly in cyberspace and with reliance on artificial intelligence, the text of Article 42 may appear antiquated. Yet the provision's wording is elastic enough to rise to the challenge in coming years. The modern techniques of warfare are developing within the domains of "air, sea, and land forces" and, importantly, reference to "air" forces certainly encompasses outer space and what can be deployed and used there. Further, the use of cyber weapons entails technology and internet communications employed by all such forces. The range of operations available to military forces are left open-ended in the final sentence of Article 42.

The fact that Article 42 measures are to be preceded by Article 41's non-military options remains as logical and critical to world peace today as it did in 1945. The issue is one of timing and whether there is enough time to invoke Article 41 measures before concluding that only the use of force under Article 42 will resolve the threat to or disruption of international peace and security. The nanosecond speed of cyber weapons and the 80-year threat of the imminent impact of nuclear weapons since the inception of the United Nations shows how tenuous is the dividing line between Articles 41 and 42. The real issue is not the wording, relevance, or utility of these Charter provisions but rather how the Members of the Security Council, particularly the P-5 that are well-stocked with the most modern weapons systems, manage their decision-making when the threat environment becomes so precariously dangerous.

---

[44] Krisch (2012d), pp. 1330–1350.

[45] The following are examples of decisions involving Article 42. UN Security Council, Resolution 1484, UN Doc S/RES/1484 (30 Mar 2003); UN Security Council, Resolution 1563, UN Doc S/RES/1563 (17 Sep 2004); UN Security Council, Resolution 1551, UN Doc S/RES/1551 (9 Jul 2004).

The most powerful Charter provision, Article 42, is followed by perhaps the Charter's weakest provision, lengthy Article 43.[46] While paved with good intentions in 1944 at Dumbarton Oaks and set in stone in San Francisco in 1945, the concept and wording of Article 43 never stood a chance of implementation once the Cold War disrupted the Security Council's cohesion and will to combine military forces under the same U.N. tent of authority. Nonetheless, Article 43 has a logic behind it in order to ensure that armed forces are available to rapidly respond to maintain international peace and security under Security Council authority. When the concept was ironed out at Dumbarton Oaks, the drafters hailed from the United States (led by Roosevelt), United Kingdom (led by Churchill), and Soviet Union (led by Stalin). It remains instructive to see what these founders envisaged under Article 43 as it is entirely possible, perhaps in the distant future, to activate the provision in a new world of political realignments and an expanded cast of permanent members of the Security Council.

Article 43 contains three clauses:

1. All Members of the United Nations, in order to contribute to the maintenance of international peace and security, undertake to make available to the Security Council, on its call and in accordance with a special agreement or agreements, armed forces, assistance, and facilities, including rights of passage, necessary for the purpose of maintaining international peace and security.
2. Such agreement or agreements shall govern the numbers and types of forces, their degree of readiness and general location, and the nature of the facilities and assistance to be provided.
3. The agreement or agreements shall be negotiated as soon as possible on the initiative of the Security Council. They shall be concluded between the Security Council and Members or between the Security Council and groups of Members and shall be subject to ratification by the signatory states in accordance with their respective constitutional processes.[47]

The actual text of the Charter relies heavily on a presumption, which proved completely mistaken following the creation of the Charter and the end of World War II, that the Article 43 agreements would flourish among Member States and create a sizable military force for purposes designed by the Security Council. Several of the succeeding articles in the Charter speak to this presumption.

Article 44 ensures that any country called upon by the Security Council to deploy its armed forces pursuant to its Article 43 agreement with the Security Council shall first "participate in the decisions of the Security Council concerning the employment of contingents of that Member's armed forces."[48] There is no clarification in Article 44 or elsewhere in the Charter whether the contributing Member would have a vote in the Council beyond its right to speak up during the decision-making process. Nor

---

[46] Krisch (2012e), pp. 1351–1356.

[47] Charter of the United Nations 1 UNTS XVI (26 June 1945), Article 43.

[48] Reinisch and Novak (2012a), pp. 1357–1359.

is there any precedent to guide the process as no Article 43 agreements have ever been negotiated and concluded.

Article 45 envisages a rapid response air force capability for U.N. missions where "urgent military measures" are required. The language refers only to "air-force contingents for combined international enforcement action" but ties their availability to "limits laid down in the special agreement or agreements referred to in Article 43…" and then the Security Council would determine their "combined action."[49] The Article 43 agreements must first exist and yet they have never been forged. Article 45 remains, in practice, a hollow vessel of military capability for the Security Council. But like Article 43, that disutility could change if permanent members of the Council adjust politically in ways that unify rather than distance them.

Articles 46 and 47 of the Charter describe the composition and functional responsibilities of the Military Staff Committee, a creature of highly optimistic thinking at Dumbarton Oaks about Allied cooperation and common purpose for the post-war world.[50] While the Military Staff Committee, consisting of the "Chiefs of Staff of the permanent members of the Security Council or their representatives," was established and still exists and meets periodically at U.N. Headquarters in New York City, its practical contribution to international peace and security remains practically nil.

In contrast, Articles 48 and 49 create legal obligations for Member States that are central to the Charter's viability and to the United Nations as an international organization. Article 48(1) ties nations to the Security Council's decisions: "The action required to carry out the decisions of the Security Council for the maintenance of international peace and security shall be taken by all the Members of the United Nations or by some of them, as the Security Council may determine." Article 48(2) further requires that, "Such decisions shall be carried out by the Members of the United Nations directly and through their action in the appropriate international agencies of which they are members."[51]

There are many examples of this obligation being honored by Members, be it in response to economic or financial sanctions mandated by the Security Council or in Chapter VII authorizations in the use of armed force against a non-compliant country. The latter might not order a country to contribute to a U.N.-mandated military action, but it opens the door for Member States to decide to act with armed force directly once the Security Council authorizes such action.[52] Article 49 amplifies the commitment of nations to the decisions of the Security Council: "The Members of the United Nations shall join in affording mutual assistance in carrying out the measures decided upon by the Security Council."[53] These words codify the old-fashioned but fundamental duty of membership: teamwork. When the Security Council calls for action by Member States, they are obligated to work together to provide the "mutual assistance" that signifies their combined contribution to the U.N. operations. The true

[49] Reinisch and Novak (2012b), pp. 1360–1361.

[50] Reinisch and Novak (2012c), pp. 1362–1363; Reinisch and Novak (2012d), pp. 1364–1375.

[51] Reinisch and Novak (2012e), pp. 1376–1384.

[52] UN Security Council, Resolution 678, UN Doc S/RES/678 (29 Nov 1990).

[53] Reinisch and Novak (2012f), pp. 1385–1388.

strength of the Security Council rests on Member States respecting, and complying with, the obligations set forth in Articles 48 and 49.

The second most prominent provision of the U.N. Charter is Article 51, which essentially is the exception to the rule in Article 2(4)'s prohibition on the threat or use of force.[54] The wording of Article 51 did not emerge from Dumbarton Oaks. In San Francisco, Latin American delegations sought to ensure the unrestrained power of their own region to authorize use of force in its own defense. They wanted to uphold regional self-defense and the full strength and commitment of the Monroe Doctrine, under which the United States had long pledged (for 122 years) to repel any foreign invasion of Latin American nations.[55] The Latins rejected any prospect of a veto override, particularly by the Soviets, in the Security Council when it came to their own regional self-defense. In response, the major powers in the P-5, including the United States, were determined not to let there arise a parallel opportunity for regional bodies to ignore the United Nations and act, completely unrestrained, on their own accord to respond to what would still constitute a threat to *international* peace and security—the whole point of the United Nations.[56]

U.S. officials and advisers huddled together in the Fairmont Hotel on May 10, 1945, and on that day drafted what became Article 51 as an antidote to the Latin American demand for full discretion over regional self-defense:

> Nothing in the present Charter shall impair the inherent right of individual or collective self-defence if an armed attack occurs against a Member of the United Nations, until the Security Council has taken measures necessary to maintain international peace and security. Measures taken by the Members in the exercise of this right of self-defence shall be immediately reported to the Security Council and shall not in any way affect the authority and responsibility of the Security Council under the present Charter to take at any time such action as it deems necessary in order to maintain or restore international peace and security.[57]

Key to Article 51 is its acknowledgement, with treaty words, of the "inherent right of individual or collective self-defence." These words are drawn from customary international law which had confirmed, long before 1945, that nations have an independent right to defend themselves, individually or collectively, from armed attacks.[58] The American drafting team created a wide opening for the Latin American nations to exercise self-defense if one or more of them were attacked, which was the independent right that the Latins sought to lock into the Charter. But there would be three caveats: First, once the Security Council steps into the situation and takes necessary measures to maintain international peace and security, that action by the Security Council would control. Second, nations exercising the inherent right of self-defense, either individually or collectively, must immediately report what they are doing to the Security Council. Third, such countries must not interfere with actions taken by the Council "to maintain or restore international peace and security."

---

[54] Randelzhofer and Nolte (2012), pp. 1397–1428.

[55] Monroe J, Seventh Annual Message (Monroe Doctrine) (2 Dec 1823) Miller Center.

[56] Schlesinger (2003), pp. 175–192.

[57] Charter of the United Nations 1 UNTS XVI (26 June 1945), Article 51.

[58] Murphy (2012), pp. 496–507.

Warfare and threats to international peace and security have become far more varied and technologically advanced in their character since World War II. The timing of defensive responses to cyber warfare, advanced nuclear delivery systems, drone warfare, and weapons guided by artificial intelligence may afford only seconds for the country at risk to respond. Thus the identification of "inherent" self-defense can attract new meanings on an almost daily basis, particularly when a fractured Security Council fails to respond, if at all, quickly enough to such rapid assaults. Article 51 is the laboratory where the use of armed force is often at its most dynamic and controversial level, but it occurs on a battlefield that the Charter does not shy away from.

The final provisions of the Charter concerning international peace and security are found in Chapter VIII and its Articles 52–54 ("Regional Arrangements"). The self-defense wording preserved in Article 51 enabled the P-5 to salvage Chapter VIII, which retained in the Security Council the oversight and ultimate control of regional arrangements or agencies regarding enforcement actions. Article 52 permits regional arrangements or agencies to deal with matters relating to international peace and security provided they "and their activities are consistent with the Purposes and Principles of the United Nations."[59] These regional bodies must seek pacific settlement of local disputes before referring them to the Security Council, which must also encourage pacific settlement of regional disputes.

Article 53 authorizes the Security Council to "utilize regional arrangements or agencies for enforcement action under its authority," but the Council must explicitly authorize any enforcement action by such regional bodies.[60] The "enforcement action" would be to enforce compliance with the U.N. Charter but the authorization requirement would not pertain to any self-defense action justified under Article 51 of the Charter. An outdated coda to Article 53 prevents regional bodies from taking unauthorized action against any "enemy state," namely any state that had been an enemy of any signatory of the Charter during World War II. Article 54 requires a regular flow of information to the Security Council about activities taken or contemplated by regional bodies for the maintenance of international peace and security.[61]

The final reference to international peace and security in the Charter arises in Article 106, which was intended to fill the gap in enforcement capabilities until Article 43 special agreements were in place to enable the Security Council to begin exercising its responsibilities under Article 42 (even though such special agreements are not literally required for action under Article 42). During this interim period, Article 106 mandated that the four major Allied nations during World War II, joined by France, and thus the P-5, "shall consult with one another and as occasion requires with other Members of the United Nations with a view to such joint action on behalf of the Organization as may be necessary for the purpose of maintaining international

---

[59] Walter (2012a), pp. 1445–1477.

[60] Walter (2012b), pp. 1478–1505; Ress and Bröhmer (2012), pp. 1506–1524.

[61] Walter (2012c), pp. 1525–1534.

peace and security."[62] The interim period technically continues to this day as no Article 43 special agreements have been negotiated much less finalized and ratified as treaties between the Security Council and Member States. This unanticipated anomaly suggests the P-5 could agree outside of Security Council procedures to take action, and sometimes joint action with other nations, on behalf of the United Nations to maintain international peace and security. In other words, there need be no Security Council meeting or vote under Council rules or authorizing resolution in order to launch authorized military action "on behalf of the United Nations."

The P-5 have never claimed to act under Article 106, but the potential for it to occur in a turbulent world remains. Most likely the provision will remain dormant as disunity among the P-5 makes any such consultation arriving at a common plan highly unlikely. But the obligation only to consult is a very low bar for legal authority to act and one can still imagine future situations beckoning Article 106 to the fore.

Article 107 is a relic of World War II removing the Charter from the war's sphere of action entirely: "Nothing in the present Charter shall invalidate or preclude action, in relation to any state which during the Second World War has been an enemy or any signatory to the present Charter, taken or authorized as a result of that war by the Governments having responsibility for such action." This essentially meant that what happened in World War II stays in World War II and the Charter has nothing to do with any action taken or authorized as a result of that war. Article 107 separated the Charter from World War II and whatever was good or bad during it. There would be a fresh start in world affairs.

The pillar of international peace and security in the Charter must embrace a new understanding of what constitutes its core principles under modern conditions. What, for example, defines the right of inherent self-defense, particularly in a world increasingly threatened by drones and cyber warfare, and how can nations exercise a new responsibility to rescue civilian populations from humanitarian catastrophe without fearing allegations about violating the Charter? In that vein, the Responsibility to Protect principle demands a new interpretation of how nations may legitimately use military force in response to atrocity crimes decimating a civilian population, and not be derailed by anemic Charter procedures.

References

Aust HP (2012) Article 2 (5). In: Simma B, Khan D, Nolte G, Paulus A (eds) The charter of the United Nations: A commentary, vol 1, 3rd edn. Oxford University Press, pp 235–251

Bothe M (2012) Peacekeeping. In: Simma B, Khan D, Nolte G, Paulus A (eds) The charter of the United Nations: A commentary, vol 1, 3rd edn. Oxford University Press, pp 1171–1199

Bühler K (2012) Article 28. In: Simma B, Khan D, Nolte G, Paulus A (eds) The charter of the United Nations: A commentary, vol 1, 3rd edn. Oxford University Press, pp 939–981

[62] Geiger (2012), pp. 2179–2182.

Dolzer R, Kreuter-Kirchhof C (2012) Article 31. In: Simma B, Khan D, Nolte G, Paulus A (eds) The charter of the United Nations: a commentary, vol 1, 3rd edn. Oxford University Press, pp 1050–1063 ("Dolzer and Kreuter-Kirchhof (2012a)")

Dolzer R, Kreuter-Kirchhof C (2012) Article 32. In: Simma B, Khan D, Nolte G, Paulus A (eds) The charter of the United Nations: a commentary, vol 1, 3rd edn. Oxford University Press, pp 1064–1067 ("Dolzer and Kreuter-Kirchhof (2012b)")

Findlay T (1995) SIPRI research report no. 9: Cambodia: the legacy and lessons of UNTAC. Oxford University Press, New York

Geiger R (2012) Article 106. In: Simma B, Khan D, Nolte G, Paulus A (eds) The charter of the United Nations: a commentary, vol 2, 3rd edn. Oxford University Press, pp 2179–2182

Gheboianu M, Popescu D (eds) (2023) Post-communism, Democracy, and Illiberalism in Central and Eastern Europe after the fall of the Soviet Union. Lexington Books

Global Centre for the Responsibility to Protect (2024) What is R2P? https://www.globalr2p.org/what-is-r2p/. Accessed 4 Dec 2024

Hilger R, Tichy H, Bittner P (2012) Article 15. In: Simma B, Khan D, Nolte G, Paulus A (eds) The charter of the United Nations: a commentary, vol 1, 3rd edn. Oxford University Press, pp 567–574

Human Rights Watch (1995) Bosnia-Hercegovina: the fall of Srebrenica and the failure of U.N. Peacekeeping. https://www.hrw.org/legacy/summaries/s.bosnia9510.html. Accessed 4 Dec 2024

Kendall-Taylor A, Fontaine R (2024) The axis of upheaval. Foreign Aff 103(3):50–63

Keohane R O, Nye J S, Hoffmann S (eds.) (1993) After the cold war: International Institutions and State Strategies in Europe, 1989–1991. Center for International Affairs

Klein E, Schmahl S (2012) Article 11. In: Simma B, Khan D, Nolte G, Paulus A (eds) The charter of the United Nations: a commentary, vol 1, 3rd edn. Oxford University Press, pp 491–506 ("Klein and Schmahl (2012a)")

Klein E, Schmahl S (2012) Article 12. In: Simma B, Khan D, Nolte G, Paulus A (eds) The charter of the United Nations: a commentary, vol 1, 3rd edn. Oxford University Press, pp 507–524 ("Klein and Schmahl (2012b)")

Krisch N (2012) Article 39. In: Simma B, Khan D, Nolte G, Paulus A (eds) The charter of the United Nations: a commentary, vol 2, 3rd edn. Oxford University Press, pp 1272–1296 ("Kirsch (2012a)")

Krisch N (2012) Article 40. In: Simma B, Khan D, Nolte G, Paulus A (eds) The charter of the United Nations: a commentary, vol 2, 3rd edn. Oxford University Press, pp 1297–1304 ("Kirsch (2012b)")

Krisch N (2012) Article 41. In: Simma B, Khan D, Nolte G, Paulus A (eds) The charter of the United Nations: a commentary, vol 2, 3rd edn. Oxford University Press, pp 1305–1329 ("Kirsch (2012c)")

Krisch N (2012) Article 42. In: Simma B, Khan D, Nolte G, Paulus A (eds) The charter of the United Nations: a commentary, vol 2, 3rd edn. Oxford University Press, pp 1330–1350 ("Kirsch (2012d)")

Krisch N (2012) Article 43. In: Simma B, Khan D, Nolte G, Paulus A (eds) The charter of the United Nations: a commentary, vol 2, 3rd edn. Oxford University Press, pp 1351–1356 ("Kirsch (2012e)")

Lepard BD (2021) Challenges in implementing the responsibility to protect: the security council veto and the need for a common ethical approach. J Ethics 25:223–246

Murphy SD (2004) Assessing the legality of invading Iraq. Georgetown Law Journal 92(2):173–257

Murphy S D (2012) Principles of International Law, 2nd edn. West Academic Publishing

Nicastro LA, Bowen AS, McGarry BW, Gettinger DM, DiMascio J, Arabia C L (2024) Defense production for Ukraine: background and issues for congress. https://crsreports.congress.gov/product/pdf/R/R48182. Accessed 4 Dec 2024

Nolte G (2012) Article 2 (7). In: Simma B, Khan D, Nolte G, Paulus A (eds) (2012) The charter of the United Nations: a commentary, vol 1, 3rd edn. Oxford University Press, pp 280–311

Oeter S (2012) Self-Determination. In: Simma B, Khan D, Nolte G, Paulus A (eds) The charter of the United Nations: a commentary, vol 1, 3rd edn. Oxford University Press, pp 313–333
Paulus A (2012) Article 2. In: Simma B, Khan D, Nolte G, Paulus A (eds) The charter of the United Nations: a commentary, vol 1, 3rd edn. Oxford University Press, pp 121–132 ("Paulus (2012a)")
Paulus A (2012) Article 29. In: Simma B, Khan D, Nolte G, Paulus A (eds) The charter of the United Nations: a commentary, vol 1, 3rd edn. Oxford University Press, pp 983–1027 ("Paulus (2012b)")
Peters A (2012) Article 24. In: Simma B, Khan D, Nolte G, Paulus A (eds) The charter of the United Nations: a commentary, vol 1, 3rd edn. Oxford University Press, pp 761–786 ("Peters (2012a)")
Peters A (2012) Article 25. In: Simma B, Khan D, Nolte G, Paulus A (eds) The charter of the United Nations: a commentary, vol 1, 3rd edn. Oxford University Press, pp 787–854 ("Peters (2012b)")
Randelzhofer A, Dörr O (2012) Article 2 (4). In: Simma B, Khan D, Nolte G, Paulus A (eds) The charter of the United Nations: a commentary, vol 1, 3rd edn. Oxford University Press, pp 200–234
Randelzhofer A, Nolte G (2012) Article 51. In: Simma B, Khan D, Nolte G, Paulus A (eds) The charter of the United Nations: a commentary, vol 2, 3rd edn. Oxford University Press, pp 1397–1428
Reinisch A, Novak G (2012) Article 44. In: Simma B, Khan D, Nolte G, Paulus A (eds) The charter of the United Nations: a commentary, vol 2, 3rd edn. Oxford University Press, pp 1357–1359 ("Reinisch and Novak (2012a)")
Reinisch A, Novak G (2012) Article 45. In: Simma B, Khan D, Nolte G, Paulus A (eds) The charter of the United Nations: a commentary, vol 2, 3rd edn. Oxford University Press, pp 1360–1361 ("Reinisch and Novak (2012b)")
Reinisch A, Novak G (2012) Article 46. In: Simma B, Khan D, Nolte G, Paulus A (eds) The charter of the United Nations: a commentary, vol 2, 3rd edn. Oxford University Press, pp 1362–1363 ("Reinisch and Novak (2012c)")
Reinisch A, Novak G (2012) Article 47. In: Simma B, Khan D, Nolte G, Paulus A (eds) The charter of the United Nations: a commentary, vol 2, 3rd edn. Oxford University Press, pp 1364–1375 ("Reinisch and Novak (2012d)")
Reinisch A, Novak G (2012) Article 48. In: Simma B, Khan D, Nolte G, Paulus A (eds) The charter of the United Nations: a commentary, vol 2, 3rd edn. Oxford University Press, pp 1376–1384 ("Reinisch and Novak (2012e)")
Reinisch A, Novak G (2012) Article 49. In: Simma B, Khan D, Nolte G, Paulus A (eds) The charter of the United Nations: a commentary, vol 2, 3rd edn. Oxford University Press, pp 1385–1388 ("Reinisch and Novak (2012f)")
Republic of Kosovo Ministry of Foreign Affairs and Diaspora (2022) List of acquaintances. https://mfa-ks.net/lista-e-njohjeve/. Accessed 4 Dec 2024
Ress G, Bröhmer J (2012) Article 53 (Enemy State Clause). In: Simma B, Khan D, Nolte G, Paulus A (eds) The charter of the United Nations: a commentary, vol 2, 3rd edn. Oxford University Press, pp 1506–1524
Scheffer D, Walker A (2018) Twenty-first century paradigms on military force for humane purposes. In: Sadat LN (ed) Seeking accountability for the unlawful use of force. Cambridge University Press, pp 493–525
Schlesinger S (2003) Act of creation: the founding of the United Nations. Westview Press
Schütz H (2012) Article 26. In: Simma B, Khan D, Nolte G, Paulus A (eds) The charter of the United Nations: a commentary, vol 1, 3rd edn. Oxford University Press, pp 855–870
Shidore S (2023) The return of the global south. https://www.foreignaffairs.com/world/return-global-south-critique-western-power. Accessed 4 Dec 2024
Talmon S (2012) Article 2 (6). In: Simma B, Khan D, Nolte G, Paulus A (eds) The charter of the United Nations: a commentary, vol 1, 3rd edn. Oxford University Press, pp 252–279
Tomuschat C (2012) Article 2 (3). In: Simma B, Khan D, Nolte G, Paulus A (eds) The charter of the United Nations: a commentary, vol 1, 3rd edn. Oxford University Press, pp 181–199

United Nations Conference on International Organization (1945) Documents of the United Nations Conference on International Organization, San Francisco, 1945, Volume III: Dumbarton Oaks Proposals Comments and Proposed Amendments. United Nations Information Organizations, London

United Nations General Debate (2024) General Debate of the 79th Session. https://gadebate.un.org/en. Accessed 4 Dec 2024

United Nations Human Rights Office of the High Commissioner (2024) UN experts urge all States to recognise State of Palestine. https://www.ohchr.org/en/press-releases/2024/06/un-experts-urge-all-states-recognise-state-palestine. Accessed 4 Dec 2024

United Nations Meetings Coverage and Press Releases (2024) Security Council Fails to Recommend Full United Nations Membership for State of Palestine, Owing to Veto Cast by United States. https://press.un.org/en/2024/sc15670.doc.htm. Accessed 4 Dec 2024

United Nations Peacekeeping (1999) Rwanda – UNAMIR background. https://peacekeeping.un.org/mission/past/unamirS.htm. Accessed 4 Dec 2024

United Nations Peacekeeping (2024) UNMIK fact sheet. https://peacekeeping.un.org/en/mission/unmik Accessed 4 Dec 2024

United Nations Peacekeeping Force in Cyprus (2024) About. https://unficyp.unmissions.org/about. Accessed 4 Dec 2024

United Nations Relief and Works Agency for Palestine Refugees in the Near East (2024) UNRWA. https://www.unrwa.org/ Accessed 4 Dec 2024

Vashakmadze M (2012) Responsibility to Protect. In: Simma B, Khan D, Nolte G, Paulus A (eds) The charter of the United Nations: a commentary, vol 1, 3rd edn. Oxford University Press, pp 1201–1236

Walter C (2012) Article 52. In: Simma B, Khan D, Nolte G, Paulus A (eds) The charter of the United Nations: a commentary, vol 2, 3rd edn. Oxford University Press, pp 1445–1477 ("Walter (2012a)")

Walter C (2012) Article 53. In: Simma B, Khan D, Nolte G, Paulus A (eds) The charter of the United Nations: a commentary, vol 2, 3rd edn. Oxford University Press, pp 1478–1505 ("Walter (2012b)")

Walter C (2012) Article 54. In: Simma B, Khan D, Nolte G, Paulus A (eds) The charter of the United Nations: a commentary, vol 2, 3rd edn. Oxford University Press, pp 1525–1534 ("Walter (2012c)")

Williamson E D (1998) The legal background on the use of force to induce Iraq to comply with security council resolutions. https://www.asil.org/insights/volume/2/issue/1/legal-background-use-force-induce-iraq-comply-security-council-resolutions. Accessed 4 Dec 2024

Wolfrum R (2012) Article 1. In: Simma B, Khan D, Nolte G, Paulus A (eds) The charter of the United Nations: a commentary, vol 1, 3rd edn. Oxford University Press, pp 107–120 ("Wolfrum (2012a)")

Wolfrum R (2012) Article 18. In: Simma B, Khan D, Nolte G, Paulus A (eds) The charter of the United Nations: a commentary, vol 1, 3rd edn. Oxford University Press, pp 621–636 ("Wolfrum (2012b)")

World Population Review (2024) Countries not in the United Nations 2024. https://worldpopulationreview.com/country-rankings/countries-not-in-the-un. Accessed 4 Dec 2024

Zöckler M, Riznik D (2012) Article 14. In: Simma B, Khan D, Nolte G, Paulus A (eds) The charter of the United Nations: a commentary, vol 1, 3rd edn. Oxford University Press, pp 552–566

Chapter 5
Promote Economic and Social Progress

The world was slowly emerging from the Depression when World War II arrived, spurring war-related industrial production but also devastating wide swaths of populated lands in Europe and Asia and smashing cultural heritages. The U.N. Charter's founders confronted enormous societal problems but did not hesitate to articulate essential goals for the future. As the leading Founder of the U.N. Charter, President Franklin D. Roosevelt instilled the document with the priority of economic and social well-being alongside that of international security. His State of the Union messages to the U.S. Congress in 1944 and 1945 highlighted these societal goals, which found expression at Dumbarton Oaks and during the Charter drafting at San Francisco.[1]

In its Preamble, the Charter promises "to promote social progress and better standards of life in larger freedom" and tasks the United Nations "to employ international machinery for the promotion of the economic and social advancement of all peoples."[2] The third Purpose of the United Nations, expressed in Article 1(3), is "[t]o achieve international cooperation in solving international problems of an economic, social, cultural or humanitarian character…"[3] These are among the most difficult aspirations of the Charter and the United Nations to this day. While maintaining international peace and security is often seen as the primary mission of the United Nations as mandated by the Charter, the often far more challenging and long-term purpose is to defeat poverty, eliminate societal barriers to human progress, promote and protect cultural attributes and differences among nations and peoples, and prevent humanitarian catastrophes (natural or man-made) from denying any populace of its right to survive humanely on Planet Earth. Most nations, and thus most Members of the United Nations, are part of the "South" and regard economic and social issues as the paramount challenge for the United Nations.

---

[1] Roosevelt F D, State of the Union Message to Congress (11 Jan 1944) The American Presidency Project; Roosevelt F D, State of the Union Address (6 Jan 1945) The American Presidency Project.

[2] Wolfrum (2012a, pp. 101–106).

[3] Wolfrum (2012b, pp. 107–120).

D. J. Scheffer and M. S. Ellis, *The UN Charter*,
https://doi.org/10.1007/978-3-031-94866-4_5

Chapters X and XI of the Charter focus on economic and social co-operation and the Economic and Social Council tasked to do something about it. Article 55 reads in part:

> With a view to the creation of conditions of stability and well-being which are necessary for peaceful and friendly relations among nations based on respect for the principle of equal rights and self-determination of peoples, the United Nations shall promote:

a. Higher standards of living, full employment, and conditions of economic and social progress and development;
b. Solutions of international economic, social, health, and related problems; and international cultural and educational co-operation; and
c. Universal respect for, and observance of, human rights and fundamental freedoms for all without distinction as to race, sex, language, or religion.[4]

One can understand the "conditions of stability and well-being" to encompass these three elements that the United Nations, through its Economic and Social Council, is tasked to promote. These words also echo Franklin Roosevelt's aims set out in his State of the Union addresses to the U.S. Congress. (We examined the third category of human rights and fundamental freedoms listed in Article 55(c) in Chapter 2.)

The Dumbarton Oaks negotiators inserted an early version of these societal aims into their draft of the Charter but with sparse wording: "With a view to the creation of conditions of stability and well-being, which are necessary for peaceful and friendly relations among nations, the Organization should facilitate solutions of international economic, social and other humanitarian problems and promote respect for human rights and fundamental freedoms." The Dumbarton Oaks Proposals also proposed establishment of the Economic and Social Council and the idea that the "specialized agencies in economic, social and other organizations and agencies" be brought into "relationships," namely, agreements with the United Nations.

The additional wording crafted into Article 55 arose during the San Francisco conference and elevated, explicitly, the importance of "equal rights" and "self-determination" in the work of the soon-to-be-established United Nations. After all, a large number of delegations from Latin America, Africa, and Asia attended the San Francisco Conference and clearly had more on their minds that international peace and security, which had been the wartime focus of the Allied powers sitting at Dumbarton Oaks. The new references to "higher standards of living" and "full employment" were controversial in San Francisco, in part because the United States delegation did not believe that in any market economy, full employment could be guaranteed. Their proposal to reference instead "adequate employment" proved unacceptable to other delegations.[5] Nonetheless, Article 55 softens the task at hand by limiting the United Nations to promoting (not ensuring) the three baskets of objectives, including full employment and higher standards of living. The concept of "promotion" can be, and

---

[4] Charter of the United Nations 1 UNTS XVI (26 June 1945), Art. 55; Stoll (2012a, pp. 1535–1564); Riedel and Arend (2012, pp. 1565–1602).

[5] Schlesinger (2003, pp. 240–241).

has been, structured in many innovative ways to address the Article 55 objectives while not requiring mandatory actions to achieve any of them.

Under Article 56 all Member States "pledge to take joint and separate action in cooperation" with the United Nations to achieve the purposes (economic, social, health, cultural, educational, human rights and fundamental freedoms) set out in Article 55.[6] A major step in forging joint action follows in Article 57 of the Charter, which requires that "various specialized agencies, established by intergovernmental agreement and having wide international responsibilities, as defined in their basic instruments, in economic, social, cultural, educational, health, and related fields, shall be brought into relationship with the United Nations in accordance with the provisions of Article 63."[7] The latter provision empowers the Economic and Social Council to enter into agreements with the specialized agencies and with the approval of the General Assembly, and then "co-ordinate the activities of the specialized agencies through consultation with and recommendations to such agencies and through recommendations to the General Assembly and to the Members of the United Nations."[8]

What are the[9] "specialized agencies?" [10]They are the most impactful[11] operations deployed[12] globally under the[13] authority of the United Nations[14] and mean more to the future of the world[15] than any other[16] function mandated by the Charter, including international peace and security outside its ceaseless vigil to avoid nuclear Armageddon. Once one reads the list of the specialized agencies below, one begins to grasp the enormous range and depth of these organizations, which remain quasi-independent but also deeply tied in law and practice to the United Nations in treaties binding the Economic and Social Council to each of the specialized agencies. Recall that not a single Article 43 agreement between the Security Council and any Member State has been forged to provide forces for any Security Council enforcement action authorized by Article 42. But on the economic, social, cultural, health, and educational fronts of human endeavor, there is an impressive body of specialized agencies linked to the Economic and Social Council and thus the interests and global presence of the United Nations.

The specialized agencies (and their headquarters cities) of the United Nations comprise these international organizations:

---

[6] Stoll (2012b, pp. 1603–1610).

[7] Meng (2012a, pp. 1611–1649).

[8] Meng (2012d, pp. 1697–1708).

[9] Food and Agriculture Organization (2024).

[10] International Civil Aviation Organization (2024).

[11] International Fund for Agricultural Development (2024).

[12] International Labour Orgnization (2024).

[13] International Maritime Organization (2024).

[14] International Monetary Fund (2024).

[15] International Telecommunication Union (2024).

[16] United Nations World Tourism Organization (2024).

- Food and Agriculture Organization (FAO) (Rome)
- International Civil Aviation Organization (ICAO) (Montreal)
- International Fund for Agricultural Development (IFAD) (Rome)
- International Labour Organization (ILO) (Geneva)
- International Maritime Organization (IMO) (London)
- International Monetary Fund (IMF) (Washington, D.C.)
- International Telecommunication Union (ITU) (Geneva)
- United Nations Educational, Scientific, and Cultural Organization (UNESCO) (Paris)[17]
- United Nations Industrial Development Organization (UNIDO) (Geneva)[18]
- Universal Postal Union (UPU) (Bern)[19]
- United Nations World Tourism Organization (UNWTO) (Madrid)
- World Bank Group (WBG) (Washington, D.C.), of five legally separate but affiliated institutions:
  - International Bank for Reconstruction and Development (IBRD)
  - International Centre for Settlement of Investment Disputes (ICSID)
  - International Development Association (IDA)
  - International Finance Corporation (IFC)
  - Multilateral Investment Guarantee Agency (MIGA)
- World Health Organization (WHO) (Geneva)
- World Intellectual Property Organization (WIPO) (Geneva)
- World Meteorological Organization (WMO) (Geneva).

There is scarcely[20] any field of human[21] endeavor that[22] is not touched in some way by at least[23] one of these specialized[24] agencies tied to the[25] United Nations under Charter authority.[26] Every day some part of your life[27] connects to the purposes and operations of the specialized agencies and thus to the United Nations and the Charter that governs it.

Article 58 of the Charter provides that the United Nations "shall make recommendations for the co-ordination of the policies and activities of the specialized agencies."[28] The Economic and Social Council performs that function. Under Article

17 United Nations Educational, Social, and Culture Organization (2024).

18 United Nations Industrial Development Organization (2024).

19 Universal Postal Union (2024).

20 World Bank Group (2024).

21 World Bank Group International Centre for Settlement of Investment Disputes (2024).

22 World Bank Group International Development Association (2024).

23 International Finance Corporation (2024).

24 Multilateral Investment Guarantee Agency (2024).

25 World Health Organization (2024).

26 World Intellectual Property Organization (2024).

27 World Meteorological Organization (2024).

28 Meng (2012b, pp. 1650–1655).

60, "Responsibility for the discharge of the functions of the Organization set forth in this Chapter [International Economic and Social Co-operation] shall be vested in the General Assembly and, under the authority of the General Assembly, in the Economic and Social Council, which shall have for this purpose the powers set forth in Chapter X."[29]

The Economic and Social Council, vastly overshadowed by the Security Council in popular awareness, is governed by Articles 61–72 and, since 1971, has had 54 Member States elected by the General Assembly in batches of 18 Members each year for three-year terms that are renewable by re-election.[30] (The membership was 18 in 1945 and raised to 27 in 1963.)[31] Its influence has risen steadily since the mid-1950's as decolonization took hold and statistical data became more readily available to gauge the state of national economies and their development needs. Unlike the Security Council, the Economic and Social Council wields no enforcement power to compel compliance from Member States or even the specialized agencies. Each member of the Economic and Social Council casts one vote and no nation has a veto power. Not surprisingly, everything in the Economic and Social Council's field of oversight and operations is prefaced with the word "may" and consequently the Council seeks and is reliant upon the voluntary attention and cooperation of Member States and the specialized agencies.

In this vein, Article 62 sets out four functions and powers for the Economic and Social Council that the body "may" seek to fulfill:

1. Make or initiate studies and reports with respect to international economic, social, cultural, educational, health, and related matters and may make recommendations to the General Assembly, Member States, and the specialized agencies.
2. Make recommendations promoting respect for, and observance of, human rights and fundamental freedoms for all.
3. Prepare draft conventions for the General Assembly on matters falling within the Council's competence.
4. Call international conferences on matters falling within its competence.[32]

Articles 64, 65, and 66 spell out how the Economic and Social Council can make its views and influence known at the United Nations, the specialized agencies, and among Member States.[33] These would appear highly bureaucratic paper-pushing functions at first glance, but they provide the forum and platform on which the United Nations intervenes in a vast array of societal issues. If it were otherwise, we would be writing about a world government that controls the lives of people globally with mandatory edicts of regulation and oversight.

---

[29] Meng (2012c, pp. 1658–1665).

[30] United Nations Dag Hammarskjöld Library (2024).

[31] *Id.*

[32] Röben (2012), pp. 1678–1696.

[33] Kunig and Tietje (2012a, pp. 1709–1717); Kunig and Tietje (2012b, pp. 1718–1722); Kunig and Tietje (2012c, pp. 1723–1727).

The United Nations, despite the occasional fear-mongering levied upon it by cynics, is an organization that nudges and persuades in line with the aspirations of the General Assembly and the Economic and Social Council and only rarely unleashes the Chapter VII power of the Security Council to compel performance by nations in response to the imperatives of peace and security.[34] In one sense, the individual person and the sovereign national government stand independent from the Charter and the United Nations, waiting to be persuaded to act upon the utterance of U.N. recommendations and authorizations. In another sense, individuals and governments are not blind to the reality that the world simply will not survive as habitable or enjoyable unless there is respect for and confidence in the U.N.'s overall guidance, including from the specialized agencies.

The General Assembly, the Economic and Social Council, and the specialized agency of UNESCO veered into intensely controversial ideological proposals, such as for a "New International Economic Order (NIEO)," and the "New World Information Order," and other politically-charged initiatives during the 1970's and 1980's.[35] The NIEO even had a comeback moment in 2018 when the General Assembly adopted a resolution reaffirming "the need to continue working towards a new international economic order based on the principles of equity, sovereign equality, interdependence, common interest, cooperation and solidarity among all States."[36] Environmental issues, unmentioned in the Charter, have surged forward throughout the U.N. system since the 1990's as climate change dramatically alters the world's environmental stability, particularly as a consequence of global warming.[37]

The eminent scholar, Paul Kennedy, recorded in his masterful survey of the United Nations, *The Parliament of Man* (2006), this reflection about the objectives of the Charter:

> When the Charter was written, there were fewer than two billion humans on the planet. In the following half-century or so, and most probably unforeseen by those present at the creation, that number trebled, to six billion (2000). Those four billion additional mouths represent the greatest absolute increase of humankind, and in the shortest time, in all of history. Their need for food, clothing, habitats, health care, education, and jobs placed stupendous and unprecedented demands upon our society and our environment. Many of those demands are still unmet, at least among the poorest in the world; and others are only half-met. But it is difficult to imagine how much more riven and ruinous our world of six billion people would be today had there been no UN social, environmental, and cultural agendas—and no institutions to attempt, sometimes well and sometimes poorly, to put them into practice on the ground. It is a mixed record, but it is difficult to see how it could be otherwise.[38]

As of this writing, the world's population has grown to 8.2 billion.

<u>Something other than nations</u>

[34] Schaefer (2023).

[35] Franczak (2019); Shamsuddin (1987, p. 80); New York Times (1981).

[36] UNGA, Resolution 73/240 Towards a New International Economic Order, UN Doc A/RES/73/240 (20 Dec 2018).

[37] United Nations (2024a).

[38] Kennedy (2006, p. 176).

A critical feature of the principle of equal rights and self-determination that Article 55 prioritizes lies in Chapters XI (Articles 73 and 74) and XII (Articles 75–85).[39] The entire issue of non-state territories was not addressed at Dumbarton Oaks but it roared forward at the San Francisco conference. These articles were added to the Charter in order to address the post-World War II reality of "non-self-governing territories" and the creation of an international trusteeship system to guide such territories "towards self-government or independence." Such result mostly occurred over the span of several decades. These components of the Charter were in large part overtaken, fortunately and as proof of their worth, by the decolonization era.[40]

The United Nations identified 72 "non-self-governing territories" in the immediate aftermath of World War II.[41] The world was still an untidy collection of territorial domains over which the victorious Allies maintained or seized control. Among such territories were lands called Alaska, French Somaliland, Indo-China, Morocco, Martinique, French Guiana, Fiji, Mauritius, Hawaii, Greenland, Brunei, British Honduras, Cyprus, Grenada, Singapore, Trinidad and Tobago, and the Uganda Protectorate. Under Article 73 of the Charter, these and other lands were "territories whose peoples have not yet attained a full measure of self-government." But these were not abandoned patches of Earth. Victorious U.N. Member States of World War II, like France, the United Kingdom, and the United States, assumed responsibilities under the Charter for the administration of such territories—albeit often having served as long-time colonial masters.

Under Article 73, the administering powers were to "recognize the principle that the interests of the inhabitants of these territories are paramount and accept as a sacred trust the obligation to promote to the utmost, within the system of international peace and security established by the present Charter, the well-being of the inhabitants of these territories..."[42] The meanings of "international peace and security" and "well-being" in the Article 73 architecture of non-self-governing territories point to five duties of the administrating powers:

a. to ensure, with due respect for the culture of the peoples concerned, their political, economic, social, and educational advancement, their just treatment, and their protection against abuses;
b. to develop self-government, to take due account of the political aspirations of the peoples, and to assist them in the progressive development of their free political institutions, according to the particular circumstances of each territory and its peoples and their varying stages of advancement;
c. to further international peace and security;

[39] Fastenrath (2012a), pp. 1829–1839; Fastenrath (2012b, p. 1840); Rauschning (2012a, pp. 1841–1848); Rauschning (2012b, pp. 1849–1860); Rauschning (2012c, pp. 1861–1866); Rauschning (2012d, p. 1867); Rauschning (2012e, pp. 1868–1870); Rauschning (2012f, pp. 1871–1872); Rauschning (2012g, pp. 1873–1874); Rauschning (2012h, pp. 1875–1877); Rauschning (2012i, pp. 1878–1880); Rauschning (2012j, p. 1881); Rauschning (2012k, p. 1882).

[40] United Nations (2024b).

[41] United Nations (2024c).

[42] Fastenrath (2012a, pp. 1829–1839).

d. to promote constructive measures of development, to encourage research, and to co-operate with one another and, when and where appropriate, with specialized international bodies with a view to the practical achievement of the social, economic, and scientific purposes set forth in this Article; and
e. to transmit regularly to the Secretary-General for information purposes, subject to such limitation as security and constitutional considerations may require, statistical and other information of a technical nature relating to economic, social, and educational conditions in the territories for which they are respectively responsible other than [trust territories].[43]

Members of the United Nations agreed under Article 74 "that their policy in respect of the [non-self-governing territories], no less than in respect of their metropolitan areas, must be based on the general principles of good-neighbourliness, due account being taken of the interests and well-being of the rest of the world, in social, economic, and commercial matters."[44] The fact that the Framers of the Charter thought to remind sovereign nations to behave properly in their relations with non-self-governing territories may seem quaint, but the world had just emerged from a global war of devastating character and sought civility among all nations and scores of territories.

Ultimately, these objectives translated into statehood or incorporation into existing nations for most of the non-self-governing territories, which was achieved largely before the end of the 20th Century. However, seventeen of the original non-self-governing territories remain so designated today and each one is administered by France, the United Kingdom, the United States, or New Zealand. Spain relinquished its responsibilities over Western Sahara in 1975 but the General Assembly left its fate uncertain by tasking the territory's people to pursue decolonization of their land, a continuing task due to contentious regional politics.[45] Aside from Gibraltar, the other non-self-governing territories are islands: Anguilla, Bermuda, British Virgin Islands, Cayman Islands, Montserrat, Saint Helena, Turks and Caicos Islands, United States Virgin Islands, American Samoa, French Polynesia, Guam, New Caledonia, Pitcairn, Tokelau, and Falkland Islands (Malvinas). The latter territory is contested by the United Kingdom and Argentina, which led to war between the two countries in 1982 with British control remaining intact in the aftermath.[46]

Articles 73 and 74 continue to resonate to the present day as representing both the Charter's historical landmark of decolonization and as guideposts for well managed governance of lands that have remained at peace for several decades. The potential for independent statehood remains alive for the 17 non-self-governing territories if and when the populace of any of them chooses to seek it.

---

[43] Charter of the United Nations 1 UNTS XVI (26 June 1945), Art. 73.

[44] Fastenrath (2012b, p. 1840).

[45] UNGA, Resolution 2072 (XX) Question of Ifni and Spanish Sahara, UN Doc A/RES/2072/XX (16 Dec 1965); UNGA, Resolution 2229 (XXI) Question of Ifni and Spanish Sahara, UN Doc A/RES/2229/XXI (20 Dec 1966); UNGA, Resolution 34/37 Question of Western Sahara, UN Doc A/RES/34/37 (21 Nov 1979).

[46] Royal British Legion (2024).

The international trusteeship system, which does not include the non-self-governing territories but represents a separate category of "trust territories" under Articles 75–91 of the Charter, has long been an anomaly as every trust territory has achieved independent statehood.[47] The initial purpose behind this part of the Charter, which actually has been its most successful undertaking by working itself out of a job, was to transfer each of the former League of Nations mandates that had been under the rule of Germany or Japan prior to 1945 into the control of the United Kingdom, France, Australia, New Zealand, Belgium, or the United States under individual agreements. Italy, which had surrendered to the Allied Powers in September 1943, retained its jurisdiction over the Territory of Somaliland until its independence.

The 11 trust territories and the nations they transitioned into (in the years listed) are British Cameroon (Nigeria and Republic of Cameroon 1961), French Cameroon (Republic of Cameroon 1960), Territory of Nauru (Nauru 1968), Territory of New Guinea (Papua New Guinea 1975), Ruanda-Urundi (Republic of Rwanda and Republic of Burundi 1962), Tanganyika Territory (United Republic of Tanzania 1961), French Togoland (Togo 1960), British Togoland (Ghana 1957), Western Samoa (Independent State of Samoa 1962), Trust Territory of the Pacific Islands (Northern Mariana Islands, Marshall Islands, and Federated States of Micronesia 1986, and Palau 1994), and, as noted above, the Territory of Somaliland (Somalia 1960).

The Charter set a high bar in Article 76, just like Article 73 did for the non-self-governing territories, for the objectives of the trusteeship system. They included "progressive development towards self-government or independence…respect for human rights and for fundamental freedoms for all…equal treatment in social, economic, and commercial matters…"[48] The trusteeship system was guided by the now defunct Trusteeship Council, governed by Articles 86–91.[49] Its membership included Member States administering the trust territories, Security Council Members (some also being in the first group), and a certain number of additional Members elected by the General Assembly. The basic function of the Trusteeship Council was to monitor the trusteeship system through a reporting system, deploy its diplomats on periodic visits to the trust territories, and implement the individual trusteeship agreements.[50] For several decades, this oversight proceeded as trust territories transformed into independent nations.

---

[47] Rauschning (2012a, pp. 1841–1848); Rauschning (2012b, pp. 1849–1860); Rauschning (2012c, pp. 1861–1866); Rauschning (2012d, p. 1867); Rauschning (2012e, pp. 1868–1870); Rauschning (2012f, pp. 1871–1872); Rauschning (2012g, pp. 1873–1874); Rauschning (2012h, pp. 1875–1877); Rauschning (2012i, pp. 1878–1880); Rauschning (2012j, p. 1881); Rauschning (2012k, p. 1882); Geiger (2012a, pp. 1883–1886); Geiger (2012b, pp. 1887–1889); Geiger (2012c, pp. 1890–1891); Geiger (2012d, p. 1892); Geiger (2012e, pp. 1893–1894); Geiger (2012f, pp. 1895–1896).

[48] Rauschning (2012b, pp. 1849–1860).

[49] Geiger (2012a), pp. 1883–1886; Geiger (2012b, pp. 1887–1889); Geiger (2012c, pp. 1890–1891); Geiger (2012d, p. 1892); Geiger (2012e, pp. 1893–1894); Geiger (2012f, pp. 1895–1896).

[50] Lüdert et al. (2023).

With the end of the trusteeship system, Articles 75–91 of the Charter have expired. If a realistic opportunity arises to amend the Charter, these provisions could be deleted entirely from the document. That being said, the trusteeship system governed by the Charter succeeded, alongside the administration of non-self-governing territories, in transforming the world map into a largely decolonized global society.

References

Fastenrath U (2012a) Article 73. In: Simma B, Khan D, Nolte G, Paulus A (eds) The charter of the United Nations: a commentary, vol 2, 3rd edn. Oxford University Press, pp 1829–1839

Fastenrath U (2012b) Article 74. In: Simma B, Khan D, Nolte G, Paulus A (eds) The charter of the United Nations: a commentary, vol 2, 3rd edn. Oxford University Press, p 1840

Food and Agriculture Organization (2024) FAO: Food and agriculture organization of the United Nations. Retrieved from https://www.fao.org/home/en. Accessed on 6 Dec 2024

Franczak M (2019) Losing the battle, winning the war: neoconservatives versus the new international economic order, 1974–82. Dipl Hist 43(5):867–889

Geiger R (2012a) Article 86. In: Simma B, Khan D, Nolte G, Paulus A (eds) The charter of the United Nations: a commentary, vol 2, 3rd edn. Oxford University Press, pp 1883–1886

Geiger R (2012b) Article 87. In: Simma B, Khan D, Nolte G, Paulus A (eds) The charter of the United Nations: a commentary, vol 2, 3rd edn. Oxford University Press, pp 1887–1889

Geiger R (2012c) Article 88. In: Simma B, Khan D, Nolte G, Paulus A (eds) The charter of the United Nations: a commentary, vol 2, 3rd edn. Oxford University Press, pp 1890–1891

Geiger R (2012d) Article 89. In: Simma B, Khan D, Nolte G, Paulus A (eds) The charter of the United Nations: a commentary, vol 2, 3rd edn. Oxford University Press, p 1892

Geiger R (2012e) Article 90. In: Simma B, Khan D, Nolte G, Paulus A (eds) The charter of the United Nations: a commentary, vol 2, 3rd edn. Oxford University Press, pp 1893–1894

Geiger R (2012f) Article 91. In: Simma B, Khan D, Nolte G, Paulus A (eds) The charter of the United Nations: a commentary, vol 2, 3rd edn. Oxford University Press, pp 1895–1896

International Civil Aviation Organization (2024) ICAO. Retrieved from https://www.icao.int/Pages/default.aspx. Accessed on 6 Dec 2024

International Finance Corporation (2024) IFC: International Finance Corporation. Retrieved from https://www.ifc.org/en/home. Accessed on 6 Dec 2024

International Fund for Agricultural Development (2024) IFAD. Retrieved from https://www.ifad.org/en/. Accessed on 6 Dec 2024

International Labour Organization (2024) ILO: International labour organization. Retrieved from https://www.ilo.org/. Accessed on 6 Dec 2024

International Maritime Organization (2024) IMO: International maritime organization. Retrieved from https://www.imo.org/. Accessed on 6 Dec 2024

International Monetary Fund (2024) International monetary fund. Retrieved from https://www.imf.org/en/Home. Accessed on 6 Dec 2024

International Telecommunication Union (2024) ITU. Retrieved from https://www.itu.int/en/Pages/default.aspx. Accessed on 6 Dec 2024

Kennedy P (2006) The parliament of man. Vintage Books

Kunig P, Tietje C (2012a) Article 64. In: Simma B, Khan D, Nolte G, Paulus A (eds) The charter of the United Nations: a commentary, vol 2, 3rd edn. Oxford University Press, pp 1709–1717

Kunig P, Tietje C (2012b) Article 65. In: Simma B, Khan D, Nolte G, Paulus A (eds) The charter of the United Nations: a commentary, vol 2, 3rd edn. Oxford University Press, pp 1718–1722

Kunig P, Tietje C (2012c) Article 66. In: Simma B, Khan D, Nolte G, Paulus A (eds) The charter of the United Nations: a commentary, vol 2, 3rd edn. Oxford University Press, pp 1723–1727

Lüdert J, Ketzmerick M, Heise J (eds) (2023) The United Nations trusteeship system: legacies, continuities, and change, 1st edn. Routledge
Meng W (2012a) Article 57. In: Simma B, Khan D, Nolte G, Paulus A (eds) The charter of the United Nations: a commentary, vol 2, 3rd edn. Oxford University Press, pp 1611–1649
Meng W (2012b) Article 58. In: Simma B, Khan D, Nolte G, Paulus A (eds) The charter of the United Nations: a commentary, vol 2, 3rd edn. Oxford University Press, pp 1650–1655
Meng W (2012c) Article 60. In: Simma B, Khan D, Nolte G, Paulus A (eds) The charter of the United Nations: a commentary, vol 2, 3rd edn. Oxford University Press, pp 1658–1665
Meng W (2012) Article 63. In: Simma B, Khan D, Nolte G, Paulus A (eds) The charter of the United Nations: a commentary, vol 2, 3rd edn. Oxford University Press, pp 1697–1708
Multilateral Investment Guarantee Agency (2024) World Bank group guarantees: MIGA. Retrieved from https://www.miga.org/. Accessed on 6 Dec 2024
New York Times (1981) The debate sharpens on a new world information order. Retrieved from https://www.nytimes.com/1981/02/15/weekinreview/the-debate-sharpens-on-a-new-world-information-order.html. Accessed on 6 Dec 2024
Rauschning D (2012a) Article 75. In: Simma B, Khan D, Nolte G, Paulus A (eds) The charter of the United Nations: a commentary, vol 2, 3rd edn. Oxford University Press, pp 1841–1848
Rauschning D (2012b) Article 76. In: Simma B, Khan D, Nolte G, Paulus A (eds) The charter of the United Nations: a commentary, vol 2, 3rd edn. Oxford University Press, pp 1849–1860
Rauschning D (2012c) Article 77. In: Simma B, Khan D, Nolte G, Paulus A (eds) The charter of the United Nations: a commentary, vol 2, 3rd edn. Oxford University Press, pp 1861–1866
Rauschning D (2012d) Article 78. In: Simma B, Khan D, Nolte G, Paulus A (eds) The charter of the United Nations: a commentary, vol 2, 3rd edn. Oxford University Press, p 1867
Rauschning D (2012e) Article 79. In: Simma B, Khan D, Nolte G, Paulus A (eds) The charter of the United Nations: a commentary, vol 2, 3rd edn. Oxford University Press, pp 1868–1870
Rauschning D (2012f) Article 80. In: Simma B, Khan D, Nolte G, Paulus A (eds) The charter of the United Nations: a commentary, vol 2, 3rd edn. Oxford University Press, pp 1871–1872
Rauschning D (2012g) Article 81. In: Simma B, Khan D, Nolte G, Paulus A (eds) The charter of the United Nations: a commentary, vol 2, 3rd edn. Oxford University Press, pp 1873–1874
Rauschning D (2012h) Article 82. In: Simma B, Khan D, Nolte G, Paulus A (eds) The charter of the United Nations: a commentary, vol 2, 3rd edn. Oxford University Press, pp 1875–1877
Rauschning D (2012i) Article 83. In: Simma B, Khan D, Nolte G, Paulus A (eds) The charter of the United Nations: a commentary, vol 2, 3rd edn. Oxford University Press, pp 1878–1880
Rauschning D (2012j) Article 84. In: Simma B, Khan D, Nolte G, Paulus A (eds) The charter of the United Nations: A Commentary, vol 2, 3rd edn. Oxford University Press, p 1881
Rauschning D (2012k) Article 85. In: Simma B, Khan D, Nolte G, Paulus A (eds) The charter of the United Nations: a commentary, vol 2, 3rd edn. Oxford University Press, p 1882
Riedel E, Arend J (2012) Article 55 (c). In: Simma B, Khan D, Nolte G, Paulus A (eds) The charter of the United Nations: a commentary, vol 2, 3rd edn. Oxford University Press, pp 1565–1602
Röben V (2012) Article 62. In: Simma B, Khan D, Nolte G, Paulus A (eds) The charter of the United Nations: a commentary, vol 2, 3rd edn. Oxford University Press, pp 1678–1696
Royal British Legion (2024) The falklands war. Retrieved from https://www.britishlegion.org.uk/stories/the-falklands-war. Accessed on 6 Dec 2024
Schaefer B D (2023) The U.N.'s latest proposals would undermine U.S. sovereignty. Retrieved from https://www.heritage.org/global-politics/commentary/the-uns-latest-proposals-would-undermine-us-sovereignty. Accessed on 6 Dec 2024
Schlesinger S (2003) Act of creation: the founding of the United Nations. Westview Press
Shamsuddin M (1987) The new world information order. Pakistan Horizon 40(1):80–94
Stoll T (2012a) Article 55 (a) and (b). In: Simma B, Khan D, Nolte G, Paulus A (eds) The charter of the United Nations: a commentary, vol 2, 3rd edn. Oxford University Press, pp 1535–1564
Stoll T (2012b) Article 56. In: Simma B, Khan D, Nolte G, Paulus A (eds) The charter of the United Nations: a commentary, vol 2, 3rd edn. Oxford University Press, pp 1603–1610

United Nations (2024a) Climate change. Retrieved fromhttps://www.un.org/en/global-issues/climate-change. Accessed on 6 Dec 2024
United Nations (2024b) Decolonization. Retrieved from https://www.un.org/en/global-issues/decolonization. Accessed on 6 Dec 2024
United Nations (2024c) Non-self-governing territories. Retrieved from https://www.un.org/dppa/decolonization/en/nsgt. Accessed on 6 Dec 2024
United Nations Dar Hammarskjöld Library (2024) UN membership: economic and social council membership. Retrieved from https://research.un.org/en/unmembers/ecosocmembers/. Accessed on 6 Dec 2024
United Nations Educational, Social, and Cultural Organization (2024) UNESCO. Retrieved from https://www.unesco.org/en. Accessed on 6 Dec 2024
United Nations Industrial Development Organization (2024) UNIDO: United Nations industrial development organization. Retrieved from https://www.unido.org/. Accessed on 6 Dec 2024
Universal Postal Union (2024) UPU: Universal postal union. Retrieved from https://www.upu.int/en/home. Accessed on 6 Dec 2024
United Nations World Tourism Organization (2024) UN tourism. Retrieved from https://www.unwto.org/. Accessed on 6 Dec 2024
Wolfrum R (2012a) Preamble. In: Simma B, Khan D, Nolte G, Paulus A (eds) The charter of the United Nations: a commentary, vol 1, 3rd edn. Oxford University Press, pp 101–106
Wolfrum R (2012b) Article 1. In: Simma B, Khan D, Nolte G, Paulus A (eds) The charter of the United Nations: a commentary, vol 1, 3rd edn. Oxford University Press, pp 107–120
World Bank Group (2024) International Bank for Reconstruction and Development. Retrieved from https://www.worldbank.org/en/who-we-are/ibrd. Accessed on 6 Dec 2024
World Bank Group International Centre for Settlement of Investment Disputes (2024) ICSID: international centre for settlement of investment disputes world bank group. Retrieved from https://icsid.worldbank.org/. Accessed on 6 Dec 2024
World Bank Group International Development Association (2024) IDA: International development association. Retrieved from https://ida.worldbank.org/en/home. Accessed on 6 Dec 2024
World Health Organization (2024) World health organization. Retrieved from https://www.who.int/. Accessed on 6 Dec 2024
World Intellectual Property Organization (2024) WIPO. Retrieved from https://www.wipo.int/portal/en/index.html. Accessed on 6 Dec 2024
World Meteorological Organization (2024) World meteorological organization. Retrieved from https://wmo.int/. Accessed on 6 Dec 2024

Chapter 6
Enable the Peacemakers

The U.N. Charter emerged from the commitment of Allied leaders (particularly U.S. President Franklin Delano Roosevelt and British Prime Minister Winston Churchill) to convert war into peacemaking, and to keep it that way. Thus, the text of the Charter expresses the aspirational objectives "to practice tolerance and live together in peace with one another as good neighbours" and to settle "international disputes by peaceful means in such a manner that international peace and security, and justice, are not endangered."[1] The Charter reaches beyond the international theater to engage regional opportunities for peacemaking. Article 52 requires Member States to make every effort to achieve pacific settlement of local disputes through regional arrangements or regional agencies before referring them to the Security Council, which still must encourage the same pacific means of resolving local disputes.[2]

The U.N. Secretary-General holds the Charter brief to bring to the Security Council's attention any matter which in his opinion may threaten the maintenance of international peace and security.[3] Throughout the 80-year history of the Charter, the Secretary-General (who as of this writing has always been a man, but surely will be a woman someday soon) has liberally used the position to be chief peacemaker in a turbulent world, sometimes successfully but more often falling far short of the desired peace. The Secretary-General and his special envoys and representatives, acting under the authority of the Charter, have made many key contributions in the search for peace. Dag Hammarskjöld, the second U.N. Secretary-General, perished in a plane crash in 1961 while pursuing peace in central Africa.[4] Sergio Vieira de Mello is one of many special envoys who, with the Charter as their firm backstop, have forged peace with personal brilliance, courage, and commitment, but in his case

[1] Charter of the United Nations 1 UNTS XVI (26 June 1945), Preamble; Charter of the United Nations 1 UNTS XVI (26 June 1945), Art. 2(3); Tomuschat (2012a, pp. 181–199).

[2] Walter (2012, pp. 1445–1447).

[3] Charter of the United Nations 1 UNTS XVI (26 June 1945), Art. 99; Chesterman (2012b, pp. 2009–2021).

[4] United Nations (2024).

D. J. Scheffer and M. S. Ellis, *The UN Charter*,
https://doi.org/10.1007/978-3-031-94866-4_6

also with his life during the bombing of the U.N. mission in Baghdad, Iraq, in August 2003.[5]

The pillar of the Charter that enables peacemakers to practice their diplomacy for the sake of humankind will, in the future, need to embrace the spaces in which peacemakers increasingly work, such as cyber space (social media), international financial institutions, corporations, and the broader private sector.

This chapter focuses on Article 14 (part of *Functions and Powers*), Articles 33–38 (*Pacific Settlement of Disputes*), Article 52 (part of *Regional Arrangements*), and Article 99 (part of *The Secretariat*) of the Charter. These are the primary tenets of the Charter that empower the General Assembly, the Security Council, the International Court of Justice, regional organizations, and the U.N. Secretary-General to act as peacemakers in disputes and situations that endanger the maintenance of international peace and security.

Functions and Powers—The General Assembly

Article 14 of the Charter is one of the document's most meaningful, albeit crippled, provisions as it articulates the power of the General Assembly over a broad range of nations' behavior. Its single sentence reads: "Subject to the provisions of Article 12 [conflicting Security Council action], the General Assembly may recommend measures for the peaceful adjustment of any situation, regardless of origin, which it deems likely to impair the general welfare or friendly relations among nations, including situations resulting from the violation of the provisions of the present Charter setting forth the Purposes and Principles of the United Nations."[6]

The bare language of Article 14 holds enormous potential. But its history is otherwise, as it began with a focus on revising treaties as peaceful change and yet that is not so popular with nations bound to those treaties. And that narrow focus of concern derailed what Article 14 could become. "Peaceful change" can mean so much more, but the opportunity to expand the meaning and interpretation of Article 14 never gained sufficient ground at the United Nations.[7]

In theory at least, Article 14 empowers the General Assembly to intervene roughly on the same level as the Security Council when peaceful change is at stake. An activist General Assembly could express a powerful voice on the world stage under Article 14 powers. In the pursuit of a peaceful path forward, the General Assembly can make recommendations to member States, which is no small power diplomatically or otherwise despite the fact that it is of nonbinding character. What the General Assembly recommends as tangible "measures" for peaceful change could encompass a wide range of options. The "peaceful adjustment of any situation, regardless of

[5] United Nations Human Rights Office of the High Commissioner (2024).

[6] Klein and Schmahl (2012b, pp. 522–524); Fleischhauer and Simma (2012, pp. 525–551); Zöckler and Riznik (2012, pp. 552–566).

[7] Zöckler and Riznik (2012, pp. 553–557).

origin" points to a non-violent solution that would comply with international law. There is no limit to the possibilities of what that "peaceful adjustment" might entail depending on the nations involved and the circumstances of the situation. Nor is there any limit to the nature of the situation, as it can arise from any "origin." Indeed, neither "situation" nor "origin" has any definition that would restrict the General Assembly from focusing on virtually almost any matter confronting humankind.

That openness is reinforced with the following wording, namely that the situation is deemed "likely to impair the general welfare or friendly relations among nations, including situations resulting from a violation of the provisions of the present Charter setting forth the Purposes and Principles of the United Nations." These words in the Charter place the General Assembly on a wide-open playing field of human endeavor and planetary conditions about which to make recommendations for peacefully managing all manner of things. Indeed, the General Assembly can compete with the Security Council in the scope of their respective mandates, with the General Assembly actually holding a considerable advantage extending far beyond the maintenance of international peace and security.[8]

The General Assembly does not usually specify the precise Charter article under which it acts when adopting resolutions. But Article 14 could be viewed as permeating the character of many such resolutions. In the past it was explicitly referenced, such as in early resolutions relating to racial matters in South Africa.[9] More often the authority of Article 14 is at work in General Assembly resolutions as a principle, not as a statutory requirement. In the "Agenda for Peace" in 1992, the Secretary-General called for greater use of Article 14 by the General Assembly.[10] But his proposal never gained traction. While there are many more actors on the world stage today advocating for peaceful change than the negotiators in San Francisco could have imagined, that need not detract from the purpose embedded in Article 14 to galvanize the General Assembly as a major force for peaceful change. Lacking is the political will to so use it.

Pacific Settlement of Disputes

Chapter VI of the U.N. Charter provides the template for seeking peaceful means of resolving disputes and situations that can lead, if unresolved, to actual breakdowns in international peace and security, such as armed conflicts. These are the most optimistic provisions of the U.N. Charter for they set the stage for a truly successful United Nations, an international organization that might staunch the tides of war and ensure peace and stability for global populations if governments appreciated and relied on the aims of Chapter VI in particular. Articles 33, 34, and 35(1) of the Charter mirror a few of the provisions in the Dumbarton Oaks Proposals which also

---

[8] Id., pp. 561–562.

[9] Id., p. 564.

[10] Boutros (1992); Id., p. 565.

gave prominence to making an initial bid for peaceful means of resolving disputes "likely to endanger the maintenance of international peace and security."[11]

Article 33(1), which sets up the peacemaking premise of Chapter VI, is one sentence: "The parties to any dispute, the continuance of which is likely to endanger the maintenance of international peace and security, shall, first of all, seek a solution by negotiation, enquiry, mediation, conciliation, arbitration, judicial settlement, resort to regional agencies or arrangements, or other peaceful means of their own choice."[12] The Charter places the initial responsibility ("first of all") on the parties—which could be nations, non-state actors, or others—and not on any U.N. body to resolve the dispute and to do so through any one of many methods. This can be viewed as a means of encouraging such parties to take the first step and to act responsibly through any of the means described in Article 33(1) and essentially talk their way out of starting a war. The peace-seeking methodology of deterrence has no prioritization of method(s) to use and no mandatory power backing up its request to the parties. But the aim is to impress upon governments, in particular, their own capacity and duty under the Charter, just as the Dumbarton Oaks Proposals had proffered to seek the peaceful resolution of disputes. Pacific efforts by disputing states, for example, can begin diplomatically with bilateral or multilateral talks or leap immediately (or ultimately) to judicial options with tribunals or courts.

The additional power lift arises in Article 33(2), which states, "The Security Council shall, when it deems necessary, call upon the parties to settle their dispute by such means." This language is somewhat stronger than proposed at Dumbarton Oaks, where the comparable sentence was suggestive in tenor: "The Security Council should call upon the parties to settle their dispute by such means."[13] In contrast, the Charter provision invites the Security Council to determine the necessity of a Council (peaceful) intervention and if one is so decided, to direct the parties to act ("…shall, when it deems necessary call upon the parties…") in a manner that settles the dispute and avoids the parties resorting to armed force or other violent means to do so.

Article 34 of the Charter replicates a provision that had been prioritized in the Dumbarton Oaks Proposals as the first provision for peaceful settlement of disputes but in San Francisco was placed immediately after Article 33's responsibility of the parties, "first of all," to settle a dispute.[14] Article 34 speaks to the power of investigation: "The Security Council may investigate any dispute, or any situation which might lead to international friction or give rise to a dispute, in order to determine whether the continuance of the dispute or situation is likely to endanger the maintenance of international peace and security."[15] This places the Security Council squarely in the middle of fact-finding—of searching for the truth—when a dispute erupts between nations or other "parties" but also in situations where a dispute may be absent but there is a possibility of one occurring or of "international friction" being ignited.

[11] United Nations Conference on International Organization (1945, p. 12).

[12] Tomuschat (2012b, pp. 1069–1085).

[13] United Nations Conference on International Organization (1945, p. 12).

[14] Id., p. 11.

[15] Schweisfurth (2012a, pp. 1086–1107).

Given the large number of complex situations and disputes scattered across the globe, Article 34 establishes the platform upon which the Security Council can act quickly, if necessary, to investigate and establish the facts in order to manage misunderstandings, ignorance, or misinformation and establish an action plan based on facts to address the problem. The Council's discretion to act under Article 34 is absolute. It can act before the parties to the dispute seek to settle their differences or following their initial effort. It can act on strictly its own initiative to launch an investigation. A Security Council investigation ultimately could lead to a decision to approve an enforcement action under Chapter VII of the Charter, so investigations can matter.

The vote required to launch an Article 34 investigation is regarded as substantive and not procedural in character.[16] Thus, Security Council investigations require, under the standard of Article 27(3), a majority of the nine non-permanent member affirmative votes as well as the concurring votes (no veto) of the permanent members, or more non-permanent member affirmative votes if one or more permanent members abstain and there is no veto.

An Article 34 investigation by the Security Council requires the cooperation of the relevant member States because of their Article 25 obligation to "accept and carry out the decisions of the Security Council…"[17] Other articles of Chapter VI of the Charter cast the Security Council in a posture of appealing or recommending to member States a particular course of action. But Article 34, coupled with Article 25, effectively mandates member State cooperation if the Security Council decides to investigate a dispute or situation as described in Article 34. The Article 34 power to investigate can place the Security Council in the center of efforts to prevent armed conflicts and atrocities by undertaking investigations that would guide peacemaking initiatives with accurate information and understanding of the dispute or situation that might risk international peace and security.

Despite the potential conveyed by Article 34's wording, in reality the Security Council has only rarely invoked Article 34 explicitly.[18] While it may be only inferentially that the Security Council employs this tool for peace, Article 34 remains the underlying authority for the Council's many efforts to discover the facts. Politically, member States prefer being persuaded or coaxed into cooperating with U.N. investigations rather than being compelled to do so under a pointed Article 34 initiative. In the result, there have been plenty of investigative or fact-finding missions launched by the Security Council over the decades and one might regard these as operating in the shadow of Article 34, even though the Council declined to invoke the provision when creating such missions.[19] Article 34 notably empowers the Security Council to seek the truth and hold out the prospect that by ascertaining the facts, the Council may guide the parties towards diplomatic or other peaceful outcomes to disputes and situations threatening international peace and security. Once a conflict erupts, however,

---

[16] Id., pp. 1100–1101.

[17] Peters (2012, pp. 787–854).

[18] Schweisfurth (2012a, p. 1092).

[19] Id., pp. 1092–1094.

the quest for prevention has failed and Article 34's purpose is largely overtaken by the reality of a war or some other violent outcome.

Any member State of the United Nations, namely any one of the 193 nations that are party to the U.N. Charter, has the right under Article 35(1) to "bring any dispute, or any situation of the nature referred to in Article 34, to the attention of the Security Council or of the General Assembly."[20] This language was drawn from the Dumbarton Oaks Proposals and represents one of the more democratic elements of the Charter: even if not directly or indirectly engaged in a dispute or situation of an Article 34 character (see above), a country that enjoys U.N. membership can seize the opportunity to alert the General Assembly or the Security Council of the matter and to expect either body to deal with it.[21] Under the Rules of the Security Council, a request made under Article 35 requires that the Security Council at least convene a meeting. The Rules of the General Assembly only require that the matter be included in the provisional agenda of the General Assembly, which need not then be accepted as the final agenda by either the Security Council or the General Assembly.[22]

Upon receiving notification under Article 35 of an Article 34 dispute or situation, the Security Council (having called a meeting) or the General Assembly can act on their own discretion and either cast aside the information or take affirmative steps to address the matter. If the General Assembly decides to act, then it must do so in accordance with the procedures set out in Articles 11 and 12 of the Charter, which govern the work of the General Assembly. Article 11 empowers the General Assembly to weigh in with discussion and recommendations on questions relating to the maintenance of international peace and security, but as earlier discussed in Chapter 4, Article 12 denies it the right to make recommendations if the Security Council is already seized with the dispute or situation.[23]

Article 36 of the Charter empowers the Security Council to seek pacific settlement of disputes before the more prominent provisions of Chapter VII of the Charter kick in for the Council to consider. The wording of Article 36(1) suggests flexibility: "The Security Council may, at any stage of a dispute of the nature referred to in Article 33 ('any dispute, the continuance of which is likely to endanger the maintenance of international peace and security') or of a situation of like nature, recommend appropriate procedures or methods of adjustment."[24] This presents a wide-open set of options for the Security Council to consider in order to resolve the dispute or situation before it turns, for example, into violence or armed conflict or the military occupation of foreign territory or claim to territorial seas. The scope for "appropriate procedures" confines the Security Council to non-forcible means aimed at settling a dispute or situation. The meaning of appropriate "methods of adjustment" again points to non-forcible tactics that might lean heavily on compromise of longstanding positions,

---

20 Schweisfurth (2012b, pp. 1111–1114).

21 United Nations Conference on International Organization (1945, pp. 11–12); Id., p. 1113.

22 Schweisfurth (2012b, pp. 1113–1114).

23 Klein and Schmahl (2012a, pp. 491–506).

24 Giegerich (2012a, pp. 1119–1145).

economic incentives or penalties, diplomatic interventions with obstructionist parties, or engagement by civil society in the settlement talks.

Article 36(1) mirrors the language of the Dumbarton Oaks Proposals, except that the Charter also includes "a situation of like nature," words that were added in San Francisco.[25] There is no guidance on what those words mean, but it likely reflects a high degree of seriousness in the nature of the situation at issue. The San Francisco Conference went further by stipulating in Article 36(2) that, "The Security Council should take into consideration any procedures for the settlement of the dispute which have already been adopted by the parties."[26] This additional language reflected the relatively large number of nations in San Francisco and their interest, as sovereign countries, in having the Security Council respect the agreements, including settlements, reached between two or more governments to resolve inter-state problems. That kind of multinational sentiment did not permeate the hallways of Dumbarton Oaks where only a few great powers had convened in 1944. But this caveat represented an early intervention by what much later became labeled the Global South and whose earliest members to the United Nations populated the San Francisco Conference.

The third component of Article 36 is drawn from the Dumbarton Oaks Proposals and reads, "In making recommendations under this Article the Security Council should also take into consideration that legal disputes should as a general rule be referred to the International Court of Justice (ICJ) in accordance with the provisions of the Statute of the Court [which is annexed to the Charter]."[27] Article 36(3) links by inference to two other articles of the Charter. The first is Article 1(1), which recites the first Purpose of the United Nations as being "to bring about by peaceful means, and in conformity with the principles of justice and international law, adjustment or settlement of international disputes or situations which might lead to a breach of the peace." Recommending that the dispute or situation be submitted to the ICJ clearly would fit this Purpose and demonstrate the Security Council's role in seeking pacific settlements within the context of Chapter VI of the Charter. But referencing the Statute of the ICJ in Article 36(3) reminds the Security Council that the jurisdictional hurdles at the ICJ, as set forth in the Statute of the Court, always have to be met before the ICJ would be in a position to engage in the matter.

That said, it is no small matter for the Security Council to garner the necessary votes, particularly among the permanent members, to activate the ICJ into launching a judicial scrutiny of a dispute or situation facing the Council. One might consider the ICJ the Security Council's ultimate adviser given the Court's rigorous legal standards for examining tough problems facing the United Nations and its member States.

With that point in mind, Article 96(1) of the Charter empowers the Security Council, as well as the General Assembly, to "request the International Court of Justice to give an advisory opinion on any legal question."[28] This fits well with Article

[25] United Nations Conference on International Organization (1945, p. 12).

[26] Giegerich (2012a, pp. 1135–1137).

[27] Id., pp. 1137–1141.

[28] Oellers-Frahm (2012, pp. 1975–1986).

36(3)'s guidance that the Security Council "should also take into consideration that legal disputes should as a general rule be referred by the parties" to the ICJ.[29] So if a legal dispute arises, then the Security Council has explicit guidance ("should") short of a duty ("shall") to consider the good offices of the ICJ. There is no jurisdictional hurdle that the Security Council must leap over to activate the ICJ's deliberation for and then delivery of an advisory opinion (which would be non-binding) about a dispute or situation that *may* enhance prospects that the Security Council could seize upon for a peaceful settlement.

However, the Security Council has only once in its 80-year history invoked Article 36(3) to refer a dispute as described in Article 33 or "a situation of like nature" to the ICJ for adjudication. This occurred in connection with a legal dispute between the United Kingdom and Albania in 1947 over innocent passage rights in the Corfu Channel and related reparations claims.[30] Major power rivalry, both during the Cold War and during the last two decades, has made this provision of the Charter a relic of the hopes expressed in San Francisco in 1945. But Article 36(3)'s potential remains largely untapped as a means of settling disputes peacefully, particularly when they involve legal issues which, if addressed by the ICJ following the Security Council's recommendation to the disputing parties, might stand a good chance of being peacefully resolved. Bluntly put, what would the Security Council have to lose by acting under Article 36(3) and coaxing the disputing parties towards a legal resolution before the ICJ? Such a recommendation would demonstrate the Security Council using international law for worthy political aims to maintain international peace and security.

The Charter anticipates failure. So did the Dumbarton Oaks Proposals and their wording was incorporated generously into Chapter VI of the Charter. One example is the failure of parties to resolve a dispute through any one of several means of settlement described in Article 33. That failure may well happen. So Article 37(1) of the Charter, as did the Dumbarton Oaks Proposals, mandates a next step: "they [such parties] shall refer it to the Security Council."[31] Then, once the dispute is referred to the Council, Article 37(2) controls: "If the Security Council deems that the continuance of the dispute is in fact likely to endanger the maintenance of international peace and security, it shall decide whether to take action under Article 36 or to recommend such terms of settlement as it may consider appropriate." The fallback to Article 36 means the Security Council, seized with the matter, can "recommend appropriate procedures or methods of adjustment."[32]

But the Council also may step beyond proposals that essentially plot the search for answers and actually recommend real settlement terms, in other words, decide how the matter should be resolved and recommend their decision to the disputing parties. The fate of international peace and security is emphatically at stake, so the

[29] Giegerich (2012a, pp. 1137–1141).

[30] Corfu Channel (U.K. v. Alb.), Judgment, 1949 I.C.J. 15 (Apr 9).

[31] United Nations Conference on International Organization (1945, p. 13); Giegerich (2012b, pp. 1148–1153).

[32] Giegerich (2012b, pp. 1153–1160).

Security Council must try something, albeit still in the realm of peaceful initiatives rather than war. However, while the text of Article 37(2) mandates that the Security Council must ("shall") act either under Article 36 or recommend terms of settlement, if the necessary Council votes cannot be garnered for action under either option, then neither option can be fulfilled by the Council.

Articles 36 and 37 undergird much of the Security Council's resolutions even if they are not explicitly cited in those resolutions. If the Security Council is not acting under Chapter VII authority to move into enforcement territory, then one can be fairly certain that the Council is looking at the non-forcible means proffered by these two provisions.

Article 38 of the Charter has been described as both a "sleeping beauty" and a "dead letter." The single sentence reads, "Without prejudice to the provisions of Articles 33 to 37, the Security Council may, if all the parties to any dispute so request, make recommendations to the parties with a view to a pacific settlement of the dispute."[33] The Dumbarton Oaks Proposals did not include this provision. It arose in San Francisco from a proposal introduced by the United Kingdom acting on behalf of the Commonwealth States which wanted the Security Council to be empowered to make recommendations for any kind of dispute (including minor disputes) if the parties to that dispute desire such Council intervention. Such dispute could even be outside the field of international peace and security, a fact that holds considerable potential for the Security Council under Charter authority. The Commonwealth nations, which at San Francisco in 1945 consisted of Australia, Canada, India, New Zealand, Pakistan, South Africa, Sri Lanka, and the United Kingdom, wanted to incentivize the Security Council to intervene politically with recommendations at any point during a dispute, provided all of the parties to that dispute so requested and regardless of whether those governments had failed to settle the dispute (the premise of Article 37). This placed in the hands of all governments involved in a dispute the opportunity to engage the Security Council at their collective request as a mediator of sorts making recommendations to peacefully resolve it.

Despite the optimism built into Article 38, it has never been explicitly invoked by any group of parties to a dispute. The reason might lie in what appears now to be the archaic composition of the Security Council which does not reflect the realities of power distribution in the modern world. Many governments, particularly in the Global South, would not be keen to seek the recommendations of five permanent members of the Security Council that remain frozen in the power dynamics of World War II and of the Cold War despite an altered world since then.

Chapter VI of the Charter embodies significant potential for the peaceful settlement of disputes with reliance on the Security Council, the General Assembly, and the International Court of Justice to act, but also highly dependent on the political will of the parties in a dispute or involved in a situation that threatens international peace and security to lean on the United Nations for its assistance.

[33] Giegerich (2012c, pp. 1162–1170).

Regional Arrangements

The purpose of Article 52 is to establish the criticality in United Nations affairs of regional "arrangements or agencies," a description that can be and has been very widely interpreted in the quest to maintain international peace and security.[34] If a dispute can be addressed at a lower level of global governance, then that option is the one to be chosen and pursued.

The Dumbarton Oaks Proposals included most of the language that was incorporated into Article 52, which opens Chapter VIII of the Charter on the subject of "Regional Arrangements." Article 52(1) mirrored the Dumbarton Oaks language and mandates

> Nothing in the present Charter precludes the existence of regional arrangements or agencies for dealing with such matters relating to the maintenance of international peace and security as are appropriate for regional action, provided that such arrangements or agencies and their activities are consistent with the Purposes and Principles of the United Nations.[35]

At Dumbarton Oaks a condensed version of what became Article 52(2)-(3) of the Charter was agreed upon: "The Security Council should encourage settlement of local disputes through such regional arrangements or by such regional agencies, either on the initiative of the states concerned or by reference from the Security Council."[36] The Charter expands upon this language.

Article 52(2)–(3) establishes how, under U.N. Charter authority, regional organizations like the European Union, the Organization of American States, the African Union, the Association of Southeast Asian Nations, and The Organization for Security and Co-operation in Europe should seek peaceful settlement of local disputes. Article 52(2) states: "The Members of the United Nations entering into such [regional] arrangements or constituting such agencies shall make every effort to achieve pacific settlement of local disputes through such regional arrangements or by such regional agencies before referring them to the Security Council." This requires a clear initial responsibility on the part of regional organizations to try to settle "local disputes" locally before bringing the matter to the Security Council. In theory, limiting this provision only to local disputes points to disputes that do not "affect international peace and security in a global dimension."[37] Nonetheless, local disputes can still be inter-state in character or can pertain to strictly internal conflicts that at some point morph into a threat to international peace and security (such as nationwide genocide as occurred in Rwanda in 1994).[38] There thus can be no definitive delineation between "local" and "international." For the members of the Security Council, this dance with regional bodies becomes a matter of discretion and judgment as to when a local dispute crosses the line from being strictly local in character

[34] Walter (2012, pp. 1445–1477).

[35] Id., pp. 1446–1468.

[36] United Nations Conference on International Organization (1945, p. 17).

[37] Walter (2012, p. 1469).

[38] Id.

to becoming an international dispute of concern to the Council, particularly one that threatens international peace and security.

Article 52(3) amplifies the importance of regional efforts at peace settlement and of the Security Council in pressing for such regional endeavors: "The Security Council shall encourage the development of pacific settlement of local disputes through such regional arrangements or by such regional agencies either on the initiative of the states concerned or by reference from the Security Council." The task of "encouragement" is rarely employed in treaty language like the U.N. Charter but it clearly signals how important the regional approach to peacemaking is so as to avoid burdening the Security Council with a local dispute that should first be handled by those nations most directly concerned.

There are several examples in the history of the Charter where Article 52 has underpinned a mixture of regional and Security Council efforts (not always successful) at pacific settlement of local disputes. These include Guatemala (1954), Cuba (1960 and 1962), Haiti (1953), Dominican Republic (1965), Falkland Islands (1982), Nicaragua (1983), and Western Sahara (since 1978).[39]

The Secretariat

Article 99 is another provision in the Charter that can generate peacemaking to resolve disputes and manage situations as well as peace enforcement initiatives if the dispute or situation is so dire as to merit Security Council attention under Chapter VII of the Charter. While the Secretary-General is first and foremost the "chief administrative officer" of the United Nations, Article 99 recites a very simple but potent sentence: "The Secretary-General may bring to the attention of the Security Council any matter which in his opinion may threaten the maintenance of international peace and security."[40] This reflects comparable language in the Dumbarton Oaks Proposals. President Roosevelt had suggested the individual be the "World's Moderator," but that did not fly at Dumbarton Oaks (not least because there already existed the "Moderator of the Church of Scotland").[41] The San Francisco Conference found no reason to spend much time discussing Article 99's final formulation. The Preparatory Commission of the United Nations reported the essence of what was intended by the negotiators at San Francisco:

> The Secretary-General may have an important role to play as a mediator and as an informal adviser of many governments, and will undoubtedly be called upon from time to time, in the exercise of his administrative duties, to take decisions which may justly be called political. Under Art. 99 of the Charter, moreover, he has been given a quite special right which goes

[39] Id., pp. 1471–1474.

[40] Charter of the United Nations 1 UNTS XVI (26 June 1945), Art. 97; Chesterman (2012a, pp. 1991–2001); Chesterman (2012b, pp. 2009–2021).

[41] United Nations Conference on International Organization (1945, p. 21); Chesterman (2012b, p. 2011).

> beyond any power previously accorded to the head of an international organization, viz: to which, in his opinion, may threaten the maintenance of international peace and security. It is impossible to foresee how this Article will be applied: but the responsibility it confers upon the Secretary-General will require the exercise of the highest qualities of political judgement, tact, and integrity.[42]

As one noted scholar of the United Nations, Professor Simon Chesterman, wrote about Article 99: "It is an error to understand Art. 99 as equating the [Secretary-General] with a sixteenth member of the [Security Council], but no exaggeration to say that it represents the most important delegation of political discretion to an international civil servant in the history of international organization."[43]

There have been only four instances when the U.N. Secretary-General explicitly invoked Article 99 in order to put it on the Security Council agenda: Dag Hammarskjold did so regarding the Republic of the Congo in 1960; Kurt Waldheim invoked it regarding the Iran hostage crisis in Iran in 1979; Javier Perez de Ceullar referred to Article 99 when notifying the Security Council of the Lebanese civil war in 1989; and Antonio Guterres used it to bring the war between Israel and Hamas to the attention of the Security Council in December 2023.[44] But successive Secretary-Generals have inferred authority from or been influenced by Article 99 to initiate many types of diplomatic interventions and to use the "good offices" of the Secretary-General over the 80-year history of the United Nations.[45] The implicit exercise of this authority has become a major characteristic of the U.N. Secretary-General's work.

As one example of this power to send emissaries around the globe to help cover the work of the Secretary-General, co-author David Scheffer served at the request of Secretary-General Ban Ki-moon and then Secretary-General Antonio Guterres as the Secretary-General's Special Expert on U.N. Assistance for the Khmer Rouge Trials (2012–2018). Such a "special procedure" utilized by the Secretary-General was not directly tied to the work of the Security Council during those years (as the situation in Cambodia by then had fallen off the Council's agenda of threats to international peace and security), but it can reflect a broad interpretation of the Secretary-General's authority under Article 99 to project himself or herself into matters that engage or have engaged the Security Council. One of the objectives of the Extraordinary Chambers in the Courts of Cambodia, where the trials of Khmer Rouge leaders took place, was to achieve international justice for the atrocity crimes of the Pol Pot regime of 1975–1979 but only after the U.N. peacekeeping operations in Cambodia in the 1990's helped maintain international peace and security and stabilize the overall security of the country.[46] The Secretary-General's Special Expert directly represented the Secretary-General's interest and engagement in the processes of justice, with the full knowledge of, and without any objection from, the Security Council. Future U.N. Secretaries-General will exercise their discretion in how they utilize Article 99

[42] Chesterman (2012b, p. 2010).

[43] Id.

[44] Ewelukwa Ofodile (2024).

[45] Chesterman (2012b, pp. 2016–2021).

[46] Widyono (2008).

authority under the Charter. The force of his or her character, intelligence, courage, diplomacy, and humanity can help maintain the peace or restore it but only if this unique Charter power is actually invoked.

References

Boutros-Ghali B (1992) An Agenda for Peace: Preventive Diplomacy, Peacemaking and Peace-keeping. United Nations, New York

Chesterman S (2012a) Article 97. In: Simma B, Khan D, Paulus A (eds) The Charter of the United Nations: A Commentary, vol 2, 3rd edn. Oxford University Press, pp 1991–2001

Chesterman S (2012b) Article 99. In: Simma B, Khan D, Paulus A (eds) The Charter of the United Nations: A Commentary, vol 2, 3rd edn. Oxford University Press, pp 2009–2021

Ewelukwa Ofodile U (2024) Explainer – Article 99 of the UN Charter: What Is It, Why Did the UN Secretary-General Invoke It, and Is it Effective? https://www.jurist.org/features/2024/02/13/explainer-article-99-of-the-un-charter-what-is-it-why-did-the-un-secretary-general-invoke-it-and-is-it-effective/. Accessed 6 Dec 2024

Fleischhauer C, Simma B (2012) Article 13. In: Simma B, Khan D, Paulus A (eds) The Charter of the United Nations: A Commentary, vol 1, 3rd edn. Oxford University Press, pp 525–551

Giegerich T (2012a) Article 36. Simma B, Khan D, Paulus A (eds) The Charter of the United Nations: A Commentary, vol 1, 3rd edn. Oxford University Press, pp 1119–1145

Giegerich T (2012b) Article 37. Simma B, Khan D, Paulus A (eds) The Charter of the United Nations: A Commentary, vol 1, 3rd edn. Oxford University Press, pp 1146–1160

Giegerich T (2012) Article 38. Simma B, Khan D, Paulus A (eds) The Charter of the United Nations: A Commentary, vol 1, 3rd edn. Oxford University Press, pp 1161–1170 ("Giegerich (2012c)")

Klein E, Schmahl S (2012a) Article 11. In: Simma B, Khan D, Paulus A (eds) The Charter of the United Nations: A Commentary, vol 1, 3rd edn. Oxford University Press, pp 491–506

Klein E, Schmahl S (2012b) Article 12. In: Simma B, Khan D, Paulus A (eds) The Charter of the United Nations: A Commentary, vol 1, 3rd edn. Oxford University Press, pp 507–524

Oellers-Frahm K (2012) Article 96. In: Simma B, Khan D, Paulus A (eds) The Charter of the United Nations: A Commentary, vol 2, 3rd edn. Oxford University Press, pp 1975–1990

Peters A (2012) Article 25. In: Simma B, Khan D, Paulus A (eds) The Charter of the United Nations: A Commentary, vol 1, 3rd edn. Oxford University Press, pp 787–854

Schweisfurth T (2012a) Article 34. In: Simma B, Khan D, Paulus A (eds) The Charter of the United Nations: A Commentary, vol 1, 3rd edn. Oxford University Press, pp 1086–1107

Schweisfurth T (2012b) Article 35. In: Simma B, Khan D, Paulus A (eds) The Charter of the United Nations: A Commentary, vol 1, 3rd edn. Oxford University Press, pp 1108–1118

Tomuschat C (2012a) Article 2 (3). In: Simma B, Khan D, Nolte G, Paulus A (eds) The Charter of the United Nations: A Commentary, vol 1, 3rd edn. Oxford University Press, pp 181–199

Tomuschat C (2012b) Article 33. In: Simma B, Khan D, Nolte G, Paulus A (eds) The Charter of the United Nations: A Commentary, vol 1, 3rd edn. Oxford University Press, pp 1069–1085

United Nations (2024) 63 years later, mystery still surrounds death of Dag Hammarskjöld. https://www.un.org/en/delegate/63-years-later-mystery-still-surrounds-death-dag-hammarskj%C3%B6ld/. Accessed 6 Dec 2024

United Nations Conference on International Organization (1945) Documents of the United Nations Conference on International Organization, San Francisco, 1945, Volume III: Dumbarton Oaks Proposals Comments and Proposed Amendments. United Nations Information Organizations, London, New York

United Nations Human Rights Office of the High Commissioner (2024) Sergio Vieira de Mello. https://www.ohchr.org/en/about-us/high-commissioner/past/sergio-viera-de-mello. Accessed 6 Dec 2024

Walter C (2012) Article 52. In: Simma B, Khan D, Nolte G, Paulus A (eds) The Charter of the United Nations: A Commentary, vol 2, 3rd edn. Oxford University Press, pp 1445–1477
Widyono B (2008) The Spectre of the Khmer Rouge over Cambodia. https://www.un.org/en/chronicle/article/spectre-khmer-rouge-over-cambodia. Accessed 6 Dec 2024
Zöckler M, Riznik D (2012) Article 14. In: Simma B, Khan D, Nolte G, Paulus A (eds) The Charter of the United Nations: A Commentary, vol 1, 3rd edn. Oxford University Press, pp 552–566

Chapter 7
The Modern Charter

The United Nations Charter of the future may *not* reflect modernizing amendments approved, as Article 108 requires, by a two-thirds vote of the General Assembly and then ratified nationally by two thirds of the Members of the United Nations. The political obstacles in today's highly fractured multipolar world would make efforts to amend the Charter exceptionally problematic and difficult. Despite decades of diplomacy, there remains scant hope of even expanding the composition of the Security Council to be more representative of the real world.[1] Faced with. such impediments to change, the Charter should be adapted as a reinterpreted document that is both faithful to the Founders' original intent and tailored to modern realities.

In each chapter we have pointed to how this reinterpretation can nurture a better understanding of the Charter's importance and inspire a revival of its rightful place in global affairs. There is nothing wrong with a fresh interpretation if it is essentially a modernization exercise, fully informed by original intent, to ensure the continuing relevance and power of the Charter's text. The five pillars of humankind amplified by the Charter remain unchanged but our understanding of them requires both knowledge of the original text and a pragmatic understanding that will project the Charter into the future.

Pillar I: Protect Human Rights and Fundamental Freedoms

Human rights and fundamental freedoms are foundational tenets of the Charter. Without these principles that evoke equality and the values of each person's life and well-being on Planet Earth, the Charter would be little more than an aging document of security pledges to preserve the sovereignty of nations. The Charter spawned an impressive amount of codification and institutionalization of a fresh

[1] U.S. Department of State (2024).

D. J. Scheffer and M. S. Ellis, *The UN Charter*,
https://doi.org/10.1007/978-3-031-94866-4_7

human rights agenda in the 20th Century, with a momentum that has prevailed far into the 21st Century without any real prospect of slowing down. There are clear articulations now of what "human rights and fundamental freedoms" actually mean in both word and deeds. Multilateral organizations and civil society groups are deeply invested in and actively ensure the advocacy for such principles as well as compliance and enforcement, when possible. Without the U.N. Charter, there would have been no U.N. General Assembly to debate and approve the Nuremberg Principles, the Universal Declaration of Human Rights, or the Convention on the Prevention and Punishment of the Crime of Genocide immediately following World War II, or then to launch the negotiations leading to the International Covenants on Civil and Political Rights and on Economic, Social and Cultural Rights and many other human rights treaties that followed. Nonetheless, the headwinds confronting this 80-year endeavor to advance human rights and fundamental freedoms have been and remain fierce: authoritarian governments and tyrannies that trample such rights; reservations to treaties that result in shielding nations and peoples from full implementation of the lofty aims of such international agreements; gridlock in the U.N. Security Council to prevent or end gross violations of such principles; and the impact of poverty, unemployment, wars, and ecological disasters that derail the imperatives of individual and group rights.

In Chapter 2 we set forth some ideas, not to amend the Charter but to interpret its prominent commitment to human rights and fundamental freedoms with three key principles: First, these rights and freedoms should be seen as universal and all-inclusive for peoples across the globe. There should be no pockets of denial of such rights and freedoms because of historical, autocratic, or even cultural barriers erected by those who fear the power of the principles at stake. Thus arguments to carve out exceptions should be seen for what they are: tactics to prevent the full realization of human rights and fundamental freedoms in order to preserve a ruler's or regime's political power. Of course, individuals may freely exercise their choice to fully or partially eschew the protection of such rights and freedoms for the sake of their cultural values, but the opening premise of the Charter's emphasis on human rights and fundamental freedoms should be seen as a clarion call to universal compliance. The Charter should be understood as a mandate for continuous education, particularly among the youth, to promote respect for human rights and fundamental freedoms set forth not only in the Charter but in the many treaties that draw from its inspiration.

Second, there are a multitude of civil society organizations focusing on human rights protection across the globe and with a focus on the lives of those at risk in every country. The Charter's commitment to human rights and fundamental freedoms offers legitimacy to these groups, which, however implausible it may seem, merit the respect, understanding, and cooperation of government authorities that are under their scrutiny.

Third, and perhaps most significantly, the Charter needs to expand its reach in the field of human rights by becoming a beacon not only for individual rights, but also for collective human rights that focus on benefiting minority groups and humanity as a whole. That is natural territory for the Charter, born from a world war's assault on the collective rights of the global population. In an age of survival from existential threats, which now defines the plight of humankind, the collective rights of peoples are often the primary human rights challenge. These threats, and the human rights associated with them, include environmental catastrophes, global pandemics, mass atrocity crimes, disinformation or artificial intelligence, and increased risks of nuclear Armageddon. Each gives rise to human rights challenges for the collective group of people most directly impacted by swarming violations of their human rights.

Pillar II: Respect International Law

The U.N. Charter, the foremost treaty among all nations, is the cornerstone of modern international law. Its words and the many multilateral treaties that are inspired by it have created a rich body of international law, birthed under U.N. auspices and offering a global list of obligations nations breach or ignore at their peril. While respect for international law has been bolstered by the Charter and by the United Nations as the implementing agent for eight decades, more needs to be done to strengthen the rule of law in the conduct of foreign policy by all nations.

Additional international treaties, crafted by the experts of the U.N. International Law Commission and negotiated among nations in preparatory commissions convened by the U.N. General Assembly, doubtless will arise in the near future to tame artificial intelligence, overcome the existential threats of climate change, govern outer space, regulate the character of modern warfare and commission of atrocities, and protect the health of billions of individuals. Achieving near universal state party ratification or accession in many key U.N.-generated treaties remains essential and daunting, but not impossible to achieve in the coming years. The role of civil society in negotiating and pressing for the enforcement of international treaties for decades has proven indispensable to upholding the Charter and treaty law and will only grow in future years.

The continued evolution of international law and how and when it should be enforced, particularly by U.N. bodies, will increasingly be influenced by the nations and voices of the "Global South." Everyone can gain from that prospect because international law is no longer dominated by the "West" or the "North." The perspectives emerging from the Global South will be the vanguard of international law in the years ahead. In fact, the negotiations during the final drafting of the Charter in 1945 saw significant influence wielded by diplomats from developing nations in what is now described as the Global South. That influence will continue to grow in the future.

The International Court of Justice (ICJ), a signature component of the Charter and judicial core of the United Nations, is also shaping the content of international law as its jurisprudence increases steadily with contentious inter-state cases and U.N.-generated advisory opinions. Innovative ways to ensure state compliance with the rulings of the ICJ should be explored, including the creation of a U.N. task force that, for example, would collaborate with regional organizations to monitor and seek compliance with the Court's rulings. Another U.N. body could be created to survey overall compliance with the Charter and international law by Member States and deliver periodic reports to the General Assembly, Security Council, and ICJ.

If amendments to the Charter gain traction as a plausible opportunity, particularly if upgrading membership in the Security Council gathers steam, the Charter could be amended to freshly empower the General Assembly as a limited lawmaking body to adopt binding resolutions (perhaps with supermajority votes) on certain issues of global reach, such as international environmental law, pandemics, and transnational crimes. Far short of amending the Charter, governments could support expanding U.N. programs to promote education in international law and thus foster respect for legal norms and their enforcement.

Pillar III: Maintain International Peace and Security

The Charter's future will be defined by how the document proves its purpose and utility in taming the worst instincts of rulers who act with force to achieve illegal aims. There likely will be no shortage of such challenges to regional and global security in the years ahead, so the Charter will be tested many times over. Will the language of the Charter, both in its aspirational character and in its implementation on the world stage, demonstrate its relevance as the stress tests of the 21st Century continue to unfold?

The key provisions on international peace and security in the Charter still deliver the mandate that the United Nations can enforce to tame the beast of hostilities. Article 2(4) of the Charter requires a modern understanding of "force" in international affairs. Whereas this guiding "Principle" of the Charter originally was viewed through the World War II prism of the clash of vast armies, the meaning of "force" is so multidimensional now that a multitude of playing fields have opened to the provision's relevance. Beyond conventional use of military forces, munitions, and advanced weaponry, the "threat or use of force" can encompass cyber warfare, disinformation, human-induced ecological catastrophes, viral outbreaks, energy blackouts, financial manipulations, space-based disrupters, and waves of migrants forcibly shoved onto the sovereign territories of other countries. Far from becoming an antiquated throwback to another era, Article 2(4) is more relevant and meaningful than ever before.

National leaders need to broaden their understanding of the prohibition on "the threat or use of force" in Article 2(4) to include the full range of actions that violate the peace and "sovereign equality" of nations which Article 2(1) enshrines as another guiding Principle of the Charter.

The Charter's Article 2(5) holds potential for improving the effectiveness of the United Nations if nations were to interpret it as the means by which to significantly support U.N. actions and programs across the spectrum of security, humanitarian, economic, social, cultural, and international law responsibilities. The reference to "any action" taken by the United Nations need not be limited to actions relating to international peace and security but to the broader body of activities undertaken by the United Nations. Governments also need to boldly call out those nations that are seeking to thwart U.N. "preventive or enforcement action" against a state and thus honor Article 2(5)'s aim to unify states behind the United Nations. In sum, this Principle of the Charter should be resurrected to stir collective action among states to advance the work of the United Nations.

Perhaps the most significant interpretative puzzle of the Charter is Article 2(7), which prohibits the United Nations from intervening in "matters which are essentially within the domestic jurisdiction of any state..." A modern interpretation of those words would take into account the shrinking parameters of what truly constitutes internal affairs, namely the "domestic jurisdiction," of any state. The trans-border realities of international trade, environmental phenomena, social media, many types of human rights violations, expanding telecommunications, cyberattacks, irregular warfare, migrations, epidemics and pandemics, and educational and cultural exchanges and events do not occupy the exclusive domain of internal affairs and they point to a turbulent and risky future. A government's reliance on Article 2(7) to keep the United Nations, and hence its agencies and Member States, at arms length is losing its relevance as global phenomena swamp people's lives and the economies, cultures, and ecology of nations.

The General Assembly can become a true engine of preventing armed hostilities by interpreting more aggressively Articles 11(2), 11(3) and 14 as together a mandate for action among Member States. The body could quickly evolve as a far more prickly thorn in the backside of the Security Council on issues of peace and security by convening for discussions and by making recommendations (when not sidelined by Article 12).

Another provision that awaits a modernizing push is Article 26 which authorizes the Security Council to regulate armaments, a term that in a modern context can reach a vast array of advanced technological weaponry, including drones and laser weapons. If the political will can be discovered once again for meaningful Security Council action in this respect, then Article 26 awaits to be tapped for an enormous range of initiatives in the Council.

Article 29, empowering the Security Council to establish subsidiary organs, invites collaborative efforts that would have to be launched by the P-5 and the nonpermanent members of the Council, but on rising issues of deep concern to the fate of all nations.

All of Chapter VII (Articles 39–51) retains powerful meaning and potential long after these provisions were drafted in 1944 and 1945 to utilize non-military and military responses to threats to international peace and security. Article 39 elevates three events that also frame the title of Chapter VII: "threat to the peace, breach of the peace, or act of aggression." How each one of these events is interpreted requires a pragmatic understanding of such actions as they unfold under complex modern circumstances, where innovative technological advancements in weaponry and cyber capabilities can instantly imperil a nation's security and where one leader's view of national destiny can still unleash massive cross-border aggression thought, until recently, to be relegated to the history books. Article 39 is open to unlimited challenges of interpretation that require keen appreciation of how science, technology, disinformation, and unchecked authoritarianism can disrupt the peace and launch highly destructive acts of aggression.

Still lacking is the full-scale implementation of all articles of Chapter VII which would occur if and when sufficient political will be achieved by the permanent Council members. That prospect awaits the shift, perhaps over generations, from authoritarianism to constitutional democracies among all of the P-5 or whatever new composition of powers an enlarged Security Council may someday require. For example, the 80-year impotency of Article 43 and concluding military assistance agreements thereunder need not point to its permanent irrelevance, as the logic of its rapid force capability for the Security Council only builds with each successive year of wars and mass atrocities. The challenge is how to turn such logic into practical necessity and action in a highly fractured and multipolar world that still strives, despite the aggressive and illegal aims of autocrats, for the maintenance of international peace and security.

Article 51 of Chapter VII requires modern interpretations of the "inherent right of individual or collective self-defence" and the meaning of "an armed attack against a Member of the United Nations." The "inherent right" has evolved along with customary international law and the practice of the Security Council over the years either to rise to the challenge of meeting the threat to a nation and its people, as contemplated by Article 51, or of falling short of that imperative. The very nature of warfare, particularly in the technology of weaponry and the use of cyberspace, keeps moving the goalposts of an "inherent right" beyond the more conventional acts of warfare that were envisioned in 1945 to trigger Security Council attention and, if politically achievable, action that would catapult the Council's determination alongside that of the nation under attack.

Pillar IV: Promote Economic and Social Progress

The United Nations is *not* a vast commercial enterprise or governing body responsible for the world's economic prosperity or social well-being among the countless cultures and peoples spanning the globe. Those primarily are the responsibilities of the private and government sectors of 193 sovereign nations. But the U.N. Charter maps out the goals that should be pursued in the pursuit of normalcy in global society, in contrast to the disruptive character of hostilities and peace endeavors and how they are to be managed, that characterize many other provisions in the Charter.

The guiding principles of economic and social co-operation are deeply embedded in the Charter's language and there is no need to ponder crafting amendments to revise the wording of, for example, Chapters IX and X of the Charter. The specialized agencies authorized by Article 57 and guided under Article 63 are pursuing economic development and investment, agricultural, humanitarian, environmental, educational, health, maritime, and telecommunications priorities among nations. They act under the umbrella of the Charter and their own constitutional mandates.

However, there is one particular term—self-determination—found in the Charter (Articles 1 and 55) that requires a modern interpretation when applied to today's world. For much of its history, international law has provided legitimacy to achieving the self-determination of peoples through the use of force. Even in the 1974 U.N. General Assembly resolution that defines prohibited acts of aggression, there is a carve-out exempting self-determination goals. Nonetheless, the decolonization movement following World War II and greatly enabled by the Charter (particularly Chapters XI, XII, and XIII) accommodated much of what needed to be done to achieve self-determination for peoples in scores of newly liberated lands in the world, and did so in a largely peaceful manner. Modern quests for self-determination—whether, for example, they be of the character sought by parties in Scotland or Catalonia through constitutional means of detachment from larger nations (the United Kingdom and Spain, respectively) or the often violent and conflicting aspirations of the Israeli and Palestinian populations of the Middle East or those who will determine the fate of Western Sahara—should be pursued by peaceful and not violent means.

The principle of self-determination, which remains a *jus cogens* principle under international law (and thus inviolable), should be interpreted as expressive of the will of "peoples" who are often a minority population dominating a regional part of a country, to achieve the full protection of their rights within or by territorial detachment from such nation, but in either case ideally through peaceful means. Wars of self-determination have had their time and place in world history, but now the principle of self-determination should be honored upon the foundation of peaceful change. The United Nations remains a forum in which to advocate the right of self-determination whether or not it results in a new sovereign nation admitted to the United Nations. The Republic of Kosovo in the Balkans has long exemplified this challenge, which has proven difficult because of Russia's refusal to approve its membership in the United Nations.

Pillar V: Enable the Peacemakers

In a hypothetical world, the peaceful settlement of disputes would be the singular methodology described in the U.N. Charter for the achievement of world peace. But of course that is not the real world. Nonetheless, the Charter encourages a robust effort at waging peace and avoiding armed conflicts under various Charter authorities vested upon the General Assembly, the Security Council, the International Court of Justice, and the Secretary-General.

We reiterate here our earlier emphasis in Chapter 6 on several of these Charter authorities in the quest for peace. First, Article 14 empowers the General Assembly to "recommend measures for the peaceful adjustment of any situation, regardless of origin" for a wide range of situations in the world. The language of Article 14 is essentially open-ended and ought to become a far more explicit and dynamic means for the General Assembly to influence parties to choose peaceful remedies for their difficulties. Second, Article 33, which prioritizes seeking peaceful solutions to disputes endangering the maintenance of international peace and security, places initial responsibility on the parties to the disputes. The General Assembly, the Security Council, and the Secretary-General should press disputing parties to honor this responsibility as a legal obligation under the Charter.

Third, the Security Council should more frequently activate its clear authority under Article 34 to investigate emerging situations that might slide into "international friction or give rise to a dispute…". The power of an official investigation, which can untap channels of truth-telling and diplomatic pressures, can be used to deeply influence parties that are on the verge of armed conflict. The parties must realize that a Security Council investigation could lead to required cooperation by Member States and to Chapter VII enforcement action none of the disputing parties would wish to see happen or endure. Fourth, the Security Council has ample authority and flexibility under Article 36 to steer parties towards a peaceful settlement of a dispute with recommendations for action, including deference to "procedures" (namely, deals) already adopted by the parties themselves. The Council also could make far better use of its power under Article 36 to persuade parties to refer legal disputes (and almost all inter-state disputes are legal disputes) to the International Court of Justice. Additionally, Article 96 empowers the Security Council, when political realities permit, to request advisory opinions from the ICJ, whose judges could clarify how disputing parties should understand the legal issues at stake.

Fifth, the Security Council holds considerable authority under Article 38 to press parties to a dispute with recommendations for a peaceful settlement. This provides the Council with another opportunity to steer the parties away from conflict, including war, but it must be used with the determined emphasis only the Council can muster and, in a sense, shame the parties towards negotiating a settlement.

Sixth, the Charter clearly favors regional means and solutions relating to international peace and security and to forging peaceful settlement of local disputes. Articles 52 and 53 provide the platform for those priorities but also recognize the Security Council's primacy of enforcement action under the Charter. While this authority has been occasionally invoked by the Council during its 80-year history, there are ample opportunities in modern times to activate Articles 52 and 53 more robustly.

Finally, the Secretary-General's power under Article 99 of the Charter to bring to the attention of the Security Council "any matter which in his opinion may threaten the maintenance of international peace and security" could prove to be an unpopular initiative to take as viewed by at least some Council members, but there may be no credible choice otherwise. Exercising Article 99 authority is like thrusting a cattle prod at the Security Council, and it should be exercised more often to energize the Council, and hence the Member States of the United Nations, to react far more effectively to an international crisis.

The U.N. Charter remains a vibrant document, under siege by legions of skeptics and understandably so (Fig. 7.1). Many of the expectations and procedures that undergirded the Charter in 1945 have not been met, but the principles in the document remain undefeated and, we argue, hold more importance today than they did 80 years ago. The tripwires for calamities unimagined even in the aftermath of a catastrophic world war now endanger nations and peoples across the globe. Binding us all together

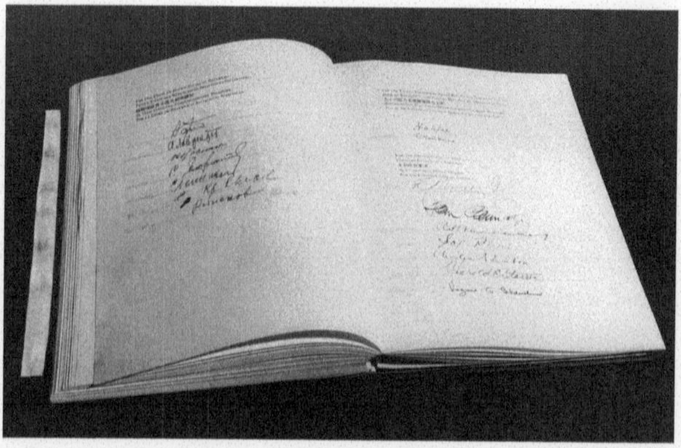

Fig. 7.1 The U.N. Charter opened to the signatory page on June 26, 1945 (*Source* UN Photo/ Rosenberg)

is one document—the Charter—that, despite some outdated provisions and fragility in a multipolar world of stubborn ideologies and nationalist power grabs, retains the essential principles of global cooperation and engagement we cannot afford to abandon. "The future" is still etched across the global constitution we call the "Charter."

Reference

U.S. Department of State (2024) Reforming the UN Security Council with Ambassador Linda Thomas-Greenfield. https://www.state.gov/briefings-foreign-press-centers/unga79/reforming-the-un-security-council. Accessed 7 Dec 2024

Appendix

United Nations Charter (Full Text)

Source: UN

Preamble

WE THE PEOPLES OF THE UNITED NATIONS DETERMINED

to save succeeding generations from the scourge of war, which twice in our lifetime has brought untold sorrow to mankind, and
to reaffirm faith in fundamental human rights, in the dignity and worth of the human person, in the equal rights of men and women and of nations large and small, and
to establish conditions under which justice and respect for the obligations arising from treaties and other sources of international law can be maintained, and
to promote social progress and better standards of life in larger freedom.

AND FOR THESE ENDS

to practice tolerance and live together in peace with one another as good neighbours, and
to unite our strength to maintain international peace and security, and
to ensure, by the acceptance of principles and the institution of methods, that armed force shall not be used, save in the common interest, and
to employ international machinery for the promotion of the economic and social advancement of all peoples.

D. J. Scheffer and M. S. Ellis, *The UN Charter*,
https://doi.org/10.1007/978-3-031-94866-4

HAVE RESOLVED TO COMBINE OUR EFFORTS TO ACCOMPLISH THESE AIMS.

Accordingly, our respective Governments, through representatives assembled in the city of San Francisco, who have exhibited their full powers found to be in good and due form, have agreed to the present Charter of the United Nations and do hereby establish an international organization to be known as the United Nations.

Chapter I: Purposes and Principles

Article 1

The Purposes of the United Nations are:

1. To maintain international peace and security, and to that end: to take effective collective measures for the prevention and removal of threats to the peace, and for the suppression of acts of aggression or other breaches of the peace, and to bring about by peaceful means, and in conformity with the principles of justice and international law, adjustment or settlement of international disputes or situations which might lead to a breach of the peace;
2. To develop friendly relations among nations based on respect for the principle of equal rights and self-determination of peoples, and to take other appropriate measures to strengthen universal peace;
3. To achieve international co-operation in solving international problems of an economic, social, cultural, or humanitarian character, and in promoting and encouraging respect for human rights and for fundamental freedoms for all without distinction as to race, sex, language, or religion; and
4. To be a centre for harmonizing the actions of nations in the attainment of these common ends.

Article 2

The Organization and its Members, in pursuit of the Purposes stated in Article 1, shall act in accordance with the following Principles.

1. The Organization is based on the principle of the sovereign equality of all its Members.
2. All Members, in order to ensure to all of them the rights and benefits resulting from membership, shall fulfill in good faith the obligations assumed by them in accordance with the present Charter.
3. All Members shall settle their international disputes by peaceful means in such a manner that international peace and security, and justice, are not endangered.
4. All Members shall refrain in their international relations from the threat or use of force against the territorial integrity or political independence of any state, or in any other manner inconsistent with the Purposes of the United Nations.

5. All Members shall give the United Nations every assistance in any action it takes in accordance with the present Charter, and shall refrain from giving assistance to any state against which the United Nations is taking preventive or enforcement action.
6. The Organization shall ensure that states which are not Members of the United Nations act in accordance with these Principles so far as may be necessary for the maintenance of international peace and security.
7. Nothing contained in the present Charter shall authorize the United Nations to intervene in matters which are essentially within the domestic jurisdiction of any state or shall require the Members to submit such matters to settlement under the present Charter; but this principle shall not prejudice the application of enforcement measures under Chapter VII.

Chapter II: Membership

Article 3

The original Members of the United Nations shall be the states which, having participated in the United Nations Conference on International Organization at San Francisco, or having previously signed the Declaration by United Nations of 1 January 1942, sign the present Charter and ratify it in accordance with Article 110.

Article 4

1. Membership in the United Nations is open to all other peace-loving states which accept the obligations contained in the present Charter and, in the judgment of the Organization, are able and willing to carry out these obligations.
2. The admission of any such state to membership in the United Nations will be effected by a decision of the General Assembly upon the recommendation of the Security Council.

Article 5

A Member of the United Nations against which preventive or enforcement action has been taken by the Security Council may be suspended from the exercise of the rights and privileges of membership by the General Assembly upon the recommendation of the Security Council. The exercise of these rights and privileges may be restored by the Security Council.

Article 6

A Member of the United Nations which has persistently violated the Principles contained in the present Charter may be expelled from the Organization by the General Assembly upon the recommendation of the Security Council.

Chapter III: Organs

Article 7

1. There are established as principal organs of the United Nations: a General Assembly, a Security Council, an Economic and Social Council, a Trusteeship Council, an International Court of Justice and a Secretariat.
2. Such subsidiary organs as may be found necessary may be established in accordance with the present Charter.

Article 8

The United Nations shall place no restrictions on the eligibility of men and women to participate in any capacity and under conditions of equality in its principal and subsidiary organs.

Chapter IV: The General Assembly

COMPOSITION

Article 9

1. The General Assembly shall consist of all the Members of the United Nations.
2. Each Member shall have not more than five representatives in the General Assembly.

FUNCTIONS AND POWERS

Article 10

The General Assembly may discuss any questions or any matters within the scope of the present Charter or relating to the powers and functions of any organs provided for in the present Charter, and, except as provided in Article 12, may make recommendations to the Members of the United Nations or to the Security Council or to both on any such questions or matters.

Article 11

1. The General Assembly may consider the general principles of co-operation in the maintenance of international peace and security, including the principles governing disarmament and the regulation of armaments, and may make recommendations with regard to such principles to the Members or to the Security Council or to both.

2. The General Assembly may discuss any questions relating to the maintenance of international peace and security brought before it by any Member of the United Nations, or by the Security Council, or by a state which is not a Member of the United Nations in accordance with Article 35, paragraph 2, and, except as provided in Article 12, may make recommendations with regard to any such questions to the state or states concerned or to the Security Council or to both. Any such question on which action is necessary shall be referred to the Security Council by the General Assembly either before or after discussion.
3. The General Assembly may call the attention of the Security Council to situations which are likely to endanger international peace and security.
4. The powers of the General Assembly set forth in this Article shall not limit the general scope of Article 10.

Article 12

1. While the Security Council is exercising in respect of any dispute or situation the functions assigned to it in the present Charter, the General Assembly shall not make any recommendation with regard to that dispute or situation unless the Security Council so requests.
2. The Secretary-General, with the consent of the Security Council, shall notify the General Assembly at each session of any matters relative to the maintenance of international peace and security which are being dealt with by the Security Council and shall similarly notify the General Assembly, or the Members of the United Nations if the General Assembly is not in session, immediately the Security Council ceases to deal with such matters.

Article 13

1. The General Assembly shall initiate studies and make recommendations for the purpose of:

   a. promoting international co-operation in the political field and encouraging the progressive development of international law and its codification;
   b. promoting international co-operation in the economic, social, cultural, educational, and health fields, and assisting in the realization of human rights and fundamental freedoms for all without distinction as to race, sex, language, or religion.

2. The further responsibilities, functions and powers of the General Assembly with respect to matters mentioned in paragraph 1 (b) above are set forth in Chapters IX and X.

Article 14

Subject to the provisions of Article 12, the General Assembly may recommend measures for the peaceful adjustment of any situation, regardless of origin, which it deems likely to impair the general welfare or friendly relations among nations, including situations resulting from a violation of the provisions of the present Charter setting forth the Purposes and Principles of the United Nations.

Article 15

1. The General Assembly shall receive and consider annual and special reports from the Security Council; these reports shall include an account of the measures that the Security Council has decided upon or taken to maintain international peace and security.
2. The General Assembly shall receive and consider reports from the other organs of the United Nations.

Article 16

The General Assembly shall perform such functions with respect to the international trusteeship system as are assigned to it under Chapters XII and XIII, including the approval of the trusteeship agreements for areas not designated as strategic.

Article 17

1. The General Assembly shall consider and approve the budget of the Organization.
2. The expenses of the Organization shall be borne by the Members as apportioned by the General Assembly.
3. The General Assembly shall consider and approve any financial and budgetary arrangements with specialized agencies referred to in Article 57 and shall examine the administrative budgets of such specialized agencies with a view to making recommendations to the agencies concerned.

VOTING

Article 18

1. Each member of the General Assembly shall have one vote.
2. Decisions of the General Assembly on important questions shall be made by a two-thirds majority of the members present and voting. These questions shall include: recommendations with respect to the maintenance of international peace and security, the election of the non-permanent members of the Security Council, the election of the members of the Economic and Social Council, the election of members of the Trusteeship Council in accordance with paragraph 1 (c) of Article 86, the admission of new Members to the United Nations, the suspension of the rights and privileges of membership, the expulsion of Members, questions relating to the operation of the trusteeship system, and budgetary questions.
3. Decisions on other questions, including the determination of additional categories of questions to be decided by a two-thirds majority, shall be made by a majority of the members present and voting.

Article 19

A Member of the United Nations which is in arrears in the payment of its financial contributions to the Organization shall have no vote in the General Assembly if the amount of its arrears equals or exceeds the amount of the contributions due from it for the preceding two full years. The General Assembly may, nevertheless, permit such a Member to vote if it is satisfied that the failure to pay is due to conditions beyond the control of the Member.

PROCEDURE

Article 20

The General Assembly shall meet in regular annual sessions and in such special sessions as occasion may require. Special sessions shall be convoked by the Secretary-General at the request of the Security Council or of a majority of the Members of the United Nations.

Article 21

The General Assembly shall adopt its own rules of procedure. It shall elect its President for each session.

Article 22

The General Assembly may establish such subsidiary organs as it deems necessary for the performance of its functions.

Chapter V: The Security Council

COMPOSITION

Article 23

1. The Security Council shall consist of fifteen Members of the United Nations. The Republic of China, France, the Union of Soviet Socialist Republics, the United Kingdom of Great Britain and Northern Ireland, and the United States of America shall be permanent members of the Security Council. The General Assembly shall elect ten other Members of the United Nations to be non-permanent members of the Security Council, due regard being specially paid, in the first instance to the contribution of Members of the United Nations to the maintenance of international peace and security and to the other purposes of the Organization, and also to equitable geographical distribution.

2. The non-permanent members of the Security Council shall be elected for a term of two years. In the first election of the non-permanent members after the increase of the membership of the Security Council from eleven to fifteen, two of the four additional members shall be chosen for a term of one year. A retiring member shall not be eligible for immediate re-election.
3. Each member of the Security Council shall have one representative.

FUNCTIONS AND POWERS

Article 24

1. In order to ensure prompt and effective action by the United Nations, its Members confer on the Security Council primary responsibility for the maintenance of international peace and security, and agree that in carrying out its duties under this responsibility the Security Council acts on their behalf.
2. In discharging these duties the Security Council shall act in accordance with the Purposes and Principles of the United Nations. The specific powers granted to the Security Council for the discharge of these duties are laid down in Chapters VI, VII, VIII, and XII.
3. The Security Council shall submit annual and, when necessary, special reports to the General Assembly for its consideration.

Article 25

The Members of the United Nations agree to accept and carry out the decisions of the Security Council in accordance with the present Charter.

Article 26

In order to promote the establishment and maintenance of international peace and security with the least diversion for armaments of the world's human and economic resources, the Security Council shall be responsible for formulating, with the assistance of the Military Staff Committee referred to in Article 47, plans to be submitted to the Members of the United Nations for the establishment of a system for the regulation of armaments.

VOTING

Article 27

1. Each member of the Security Council shall have one vote.
2. Decisions of the Security Council on procedural matters shall be made by an affirmative vote of nine members.
3. Decisions of the Security Council on all other matters shall be made by an affirmative vote of nine members including the concurring votes of the permanent members; provided that, in decisions under Chapter VI, and under paragraph 3 of Article 52, a party to a dispute shall abstain from voting.

PROCEDURE

Article 28

1. The Security Council shall be so organized as to be able to function continuously. Each member of the Security Council shall for this purpose be represented at all times at the seat of the Organization.
2. The Security Council shall hold periodic meetings at which each of its members may, if it so desires, be represented by a member of the government or by some other specially designated representative.
3. The Security Council may hold meetings at such places other than the seat of the Organization as in its judgment will best facilitate its work.

Article 29

The Security Council may establish such subsidiary organs as it deems necessary for the performance of its functions.

Article 30

The Security Council shall adopt its own rules of procedure, including the method of selecting its President.

Article 31

Any Member of the United Nations which is not a member of the Security Council may participate, without vote, in the discussion of any question brought before the Security Council whenever the latter considers that the interests of that Member are specially affected.

Article 32

Any Member of the United Nations which is not a member of the Security Council or any state which is not a Member of the United Nations, if it is a party to a dispute under consideration by the Security Council, shall be invited to participate, without vote, in the discussion relating to the dispute. The Security Council shall lay down such conditions as it deems just for the participation of a state which is not a Member of the United Nations.

Chapter VI: Pacific Settlement of Disputes

Article 33

1. The parties to any dispute, the continuance of which is likely to endanger the maintenance of international peace and security, shall, first of all, seek a solution by negotiation, enquiry, mediation, conciliation, arbitration, judicial settlement,

resort to regional agencies or arrangements, or other peaceful means of their own choice.

2. The Security Council shall, when it deems necessary, call upon the parties to settle their dispute by such means.

Article 34

The Security Council may investigate any dispute, or any situation which might lead to international friction or give rise to a dispute, in order to determine whether the continuance of the dispute or situation is likely to endanger the maintenance of international peace and security.

Article 35

1. Any Member of the United Nations may bring any dispute, or any situation of the nature referred to in Article 34, to the attention of the Security Council or of the General Assembly.
2. A state which is not a Member of the United Nations may bring to the attention of the Security Council or of the General Assembly any dispute to which it is a party if it accepts in advance, for the purposes of the dispute, the obligations of pacific settlement provided in the present Charter.
3. The proceedings of the General Assembly in respect of matters brought to its attention under this Article will be subject to the provisions of Articles 11 and 12.

Article 36

1. The Security Council may, at any stage of a dispute of the nature referred to in Article 33 or of a situation of like nature, recommend appropriate procedures or methods of adjustment.
2. The Security Council should take into consideration any procedures for the settlement of the dispute which have already been adopted by the parties.
3. In making recommendations under this Article the Security Council should also take into consideration that legal disputes should as a general rule be referred by the parties to the International Court of Justice in accordance with the provisions of the Statute of the Court.

Article 37

1. Should the parties to a dispute of the nature referred to in Article 33 fail to settle it by the means indicated in that Article, they shall refer it to the Security Council.
2. If the Security Council deems that the continuance of the dispute is in fact likely to endanger the maintenance of international peace and security, it shall decide whether to take action under Article 36 or to recommend such terms of settlement as it may consider appropriate.

Article 38

Without prejudice to the provisions of Articles 33 to 37, the Security Council may, if all the parties to any dispute so request, make recommendations to the parties with a view to a pacific settlement of the dispute.

Chapter VII: Action with Respect to Threats to the Peace, Breaches of the Peace, and Acts of Aggression

Article 39

The Security Council shall determine the existence of any threat to the peace, breach of the peace, or act of aggression and shall make recommendations, or decide what measures shall be taken in accordance with Articles 41 and 42, to maintain or restore international peace and security.

Article 40

In order to prevent an aggravation of the situation, the Security Council may, before making the recommendations or deciding upon the measures provided for in Article 39, call upon the parties concerned to comply with such provisional measures as it deems necessary or desirable. Such provisional measures shall be without prejudice to the rights, claims, or position of the parties concerned. The Security Council shall duly take account of failure to comply with such provisional measures.

Article 41

The Security Council may decide what measures not involving the use of armed force are to be employed to give effect to its decisions, and it may call upon the Members of the United Nations to apply such measures. These may include complete or partial interruption of economic relations and of rail, sea, air, postal, telegraphic, radio, and other means of communication, and the severance of diplomatic relations.

Article 42

Should the Security Council consider that measures provided for in Article 41 would be inadequate or have proved to be inadequate, it may take such action by air, sea, or land forces as may be necessary to maintain or restore international peace and security. Such action may include demonstrations, blockade, and other operations by air, sea, or land forces of Members of the United Nations.

Article 43

1. All Members of the United Nations, in order to contribute to the maintenance of international peace and security, undertake to make available to the Security Council, on its call and in accordance with a special agreement or agreements,

armed forces, assistance, and facilities, including rights of passage, necessary for the purpose of maintaining international peace and security.
2. Such agreement or agreements shall govern the numbers and types of forces, their degree of readiness and general location, and the nature of the facilities and assistance to be provided.
3. The agreement or agreements shall be negotiated as soon as possible on the initiative of the Security Council. They shall be concluded between the Security Council and Members or between the Security Council and groups of Members and shall be subject to ratification by the signatory states in accordance with their respective constitutional processes.

Article 44

When the Security Council has decided to use force it shall, before calling upon a Member not represented on it to provide armed forces in fulfilment of the obligations assumed under Article 43, invite that Member, if the Member so desires, to participate in the decisions of the Security Council concerning the employment of contingents of that Member's armed forces.

Article 45

In order to enable the United Nations to take urgent military measures, Members shall hold immediately available national air-force contingents for combined international enforcement action. The strength and degree of readiness of these contingents and plans for their combined action shall be determined within the limits laid down in the special agreement or agreements referred to in Article 43, by the Security Council with the assistance of the Military Staff Committee.

Article 46

Plans for the application of armed force shall be made by the Security Council with the assistance of the Military Staff Committee.

Article 47

1. There shall be established a Military Staff Committee to advise and assist the Security Council on all questions relating to the Security Council's military requirements for the maintenance of international peace and security, the employment and command of forces placed at its disposal, the regulation of armaments, and possible disarmament.
2. The Military Staff Committee shall consist of the Chiefs of Staff of the permanent members of the Security Council or their representatives. Any Member of the United Nations not permanently represented on the Committee shall be invited by the Committee to be associated with it when the efficient discharge of the Committee's responsibilities requires the participation of that Member in its work.

3. The Military Staff Committee shall be responsible under the Security Council for the strategic direction of any armed forces placed at the disposal of the Security Council. Questions relating to the command of such forces shall be worked out subsequently.
4. The Military Staff Committee, with the authorization of the Security Council and after consultation with appropriate regional agencies, may establish regional sub-committees.

Article 48

1. The action required to carry out the decisions of the Security Council for the maintenance of international peace and security shall be taken by all the Members of the United Nations or by some of them, as the Security Council may determine.
2. Such decisions shall be carried out by the Members of the United Nations directly and through their action in the appropriate international agencies of which they are members.

Article 49

The Members of the United Nations shall join in affording mutual assistance in carrying out the measures decided upon by the Security Council.

Article 50

If preventive or enforcement measures against any state are taken by the Security Council, any other state, whether a Member of the United Nations or not, which finds itself confronted with special economic problems arising from the carrying out of those measures shall have the right to consult the Security Council with regard to a solution of those problems.

Article 51

Nothing in the present Charter shall impair the inherent right of individual or collective self-defence if an armed attack occurs against a Member of the United Nations, until the Security Council has taken measures necessary to maintain international peace and security. Measures taken by Members in the exercise of this right of self-defence shall be immediately reported to the Security Council and shall not in any way affect the authority and responsibility of the Security Council under the present Charter to take at any time such action as it deems necessary in order to maintain or restore international peace and security.

Chapter VIII: Regional Arrangements

Article 52

1. Nothing in the present Charter precludes the existence of regional arrangements or agencies for dealing with such matters relating to the maintenance of international peace and security as are appropriate for regional action provided that such arrangements or agencies and their activities are consistent with the Purposes and Principles of the United Nations.
2. The Members of the United Nations entering into such arrangements or constituting such agencies shall make every effort to achieve pacific settlement of local disputes through such regional arrangements or by such regional agencies before referring them to the Security Council.
3. The Security Council shall encourage the development of pacific settlement of local disputes through such regional arrangements or by such regional agencies either on the initiative of the states concerned or by reference from the Security Council.
4. This Article in no way impairs the application of Articles 34 and 35.

Article 53

1. The Security Council shall, where appropriate, utilize such regional arrangements or agencies for enforcement action under its authority. But no enforcement action shall be taken under regional arrangements or by regional agencies without the authorization of the Security Council, with the exception of measures against any enemy state, as defined in paragraph 2 of this Article, provided for pursuant to Article 107 or in regional arrangements directed against renewal of aggressive policy on the part of any such state, until such time as the Organization may, on request of the Governments concerned, be charged with the responsibility for preventing further aggression by such a state.
2. The term enemy state as used in paragraph 1 of this Article applies to any state which during the Second World War has been an enemy of any signatory of the present Charter.

Article 54

The Security Council shall at all times be kept fully informed of activities undertaken or in contemplation under regional arrangements or by regional agencies for the maintenance of international peace and security.

Chapter IX: International Economic and Social Cooperation

Article 55

With a view to the creation of conditions of stability and well-being which are necessary for peaceful and friendly relations among nations based on respect for the principle of equal rights and self-determination of peoples, the United Nations shall promote:

1. higher standards of living, full employment, and conditions of economic and social progress and development;
2. solutions of international economic, social, health, and related problems; and international cultural and educational cooperation; and
3. universal respect for, and observance of, human rights and fundamental freedoms for all without distinction as to race, sex, language, or religion.

Article 56

All Members pledge themselves to take joint and separate action in co-operation with the Organization for the achievement of the purposes set forth in Article 55.

Article 57

1. The various specialized agencies, established by intergovernmental agreement and having wide international responsibilities, as defined in their basic instruments, in economic, social, cultural, educational, health, and related fields, shall be brought into relationship with the United Nations in accordance with the provisions of Article 63.
2. Such agencies thus brought into relationship with the United Nations are hereinafter referred to as specialized agencies.

Article 58

The Organization shall make recommendations for the co-ordination of the policies and activities of the specialized agencies.

Article 59

The Organization shall, where appropriate, initiate negotiations among the states concerned for the creation of any new specialized agencies required for the accomplishment of the purposes set forth in Article 55.

Article 60

Responsibility for the discharge of the functions of the Organization set forth in this Chapter shall be vested in the General Assembly and, under the authority of the General Assembly, in the Economic and Social Council, which shall have for this purpose the powers set forth in Chapter X.

Chapter X: The Economic and Social Council

COMPOSITION

Article 61

1. The Economic and Social Council shall consist of fifty-four Members of the United Nations elected by the General Assembly.
2. Subject to the provisions of paragraph 3, eighteen members of the Economic and Social Council shall be elected each year for a term of three years. A retiring member shall be eligible for immediate re-election.
3. At the first election after the increase in the membership of the Economic and Social Council from twenty-seven to fifty-four members, in addition to the members elected in place of the nine members whose term of office expires at the end of that year, twenty-seven additional members shall be elected. Of these twenty-seven additional members, the term of office of nine members so elected shall expire at the end of one year, and of nine other members at the end of two years, in accordance with arrangements made by the General Assembly.
4. Each member of the Economic and Social Council shall have one representative.

FUNCTIONS AND POWERS

Article 62

1. The Economic and Social Council may make or initiate studies and reports with respect to international economic, social, cultural, educational, health, and related matters and may make recommendations with respect to any such matters to the General Assembly to the Members of the United Nations, and to the specialized agencies concerned.
2. It may make recommendations for the purpose of promoting respect for, and observance of, human rights and fundamental freedoms for all.
3. It may prepare draft conventions for submission to the General Assembly, with respect to matters falling within its competence.
4. It may call, in accordance with the rules prescribed by the United Nations, international conferences on matters falling within its competence.

Article 63

1. The Economic and Social Council may enter into agreements with any of the agencies referred to in Article 57, defining the terms on which the agency concerned shall be brought into relationship with the United Nations. Such agreements shall be subject to approval by the General Assembly.
2. It may co-ordinate the activities of the specialized agencies through consultation with and recommendations to such agencies and through recommendations to the General Assembly and to the Members of the United Nations.

Article 64

1. The Economic and Social Council may take appropriate steps to obtain regular reports from the specialized agencies. It may make arrangements with the Members of the United Nations and with the specialized agencies to obtain reports on the steps taken to give effect to its own recommendations and to recommendations on matters falling within its competence made by the General Assembly.
2. It may communicate its observations on these reports to the General Assembly.

Article 65

The Economic and Social Council may furnish information to the Security Council and shall assist the Security Council upon its request.

Article 66

1. The Economic and Social Council shall perform such functions as fall within its competence in connection with the carrying out of the recommendations of the General Assembly.
2. It may, with the approval of the General Assembly, perform services at the request of Members of the United Nations and at the request of specialized agencies.
3. It shall perform such other functions as are specified elsewhere in the present Charter or as may be assigned to it by the General Assembly.

VOTING

Article 67

1. Each member of the Economic and Social Council shall have one vote.
2. Decisions of the Economic and Social Council shall be made by a majority of the members present and voting.

PROCEDURE

Article 68

The Economic and Social Council shall set up commissions in economic and social fields and for the promotion of human rights, and such other commissions as may be required for the performance of its functions.

Article 69

The Economic and Social Council shall invite any Member of the United Nations to participate, without vote, in its deliberations on any matter of particular concern to that Member.

Article 70

The Economic and Social Council may make arrangements for representatives of the specialized agencies to participate, without vote, in its deliberations and in those of the commissions established by it, and for its representatives to participate in the deliberations of the specialized agencies.

Article 71

The Economic and Social Council may make suitable arrangements for consultation with non-governmental organizations which are concerned with matters within its competence. Such arrangements may be made with international organizations and, where appropriate, with national organizations after consultation with the Member of the United Nations concerned.

Article 72

1. The Economic and Social Council shall adopt its own rules of procedure, including the method of selecting its President.
2. The Economic and Social Council shall meet as required in accordance with its rules, which shall include provision for the convening of meetings on the request of a majority of its members.

Chapter XI: Declaration Regarding Non-Self-Governing Territories

Article 73

Members of the United Nations which have or assume responsibilities for the administration of territories whose peoples have not yet attained a full measure of self-government recognize the principle that the interests of the inhabitants of these territories are paramount, and accept as a sacred trust the obligation to promote to the utmost, within the system of international peace and security established by the present Charter, the well-being of the inhabitants of these territories, and, to this end:

1. to ensure, with due respect for the culture of the peoples concerned, their political, economic, social, and educational advancement, their just treatment, and their protection against abuses;
2. to develop self-government, to take due account of the political aspirations of the peoples, and to assist them in the progressive development of their free political institutions, according to the particular circumstances of each territory and its peoples and their varying stages of advancement;
3. to further international peace and security;

4. to promote constructive measures of development, to encourage research, and to co-operate with one another and, when and where appropriate, with specialized international bodies with a view to the practical achievement of the social, economic, and scientific purposes set forth in this Article; and
5. to transmit regularly to the Secretary-General for information purposes, subject to such limitation as security and constitutional considerations may require, statistical and other information of a technical nature relating to economic, social, and educational conditions in the territories for which they are respectively responsible other than those territories to which Chapters XII and XIII apply.

Article 74

Members of the United Nations also agree that their policy in respect of the territories to which this Chapter applies, no less than in respect of their metropolitan areas, must be based on the general principle of good-neighbourliness, due account being taken of the interests and well-being of the rest of the world, in social, economic, and commercial matters.

Chapter XII: International Trusteeship System

Article 75

The United Nations shall establish under its authority an international trusteeship system for the administration and supervision of such territories as may be placed thereunder by subsequent individual agreements. These territories are hereinafter referred to as trust territories.

Article 76

The basic objectives of the trusteeship system, in accordance with the Purposes of the United Nations laid down in Article 1 of the present Charter, shall be:

1. to further international peace and security;
2. to promote the political, economic, social, and educational advancement of the inhabitants of the trust territories, and their progressive development towards self-government or independence as may be appropriate to the particular circumstances of each territory and its peoples and the freely expressed wishes of the peoples concerned, and as may be provided by the terms of each trusteeship agreement;
3. to encourage respect for human rights and for fundamental freedoms for all without distinction as to race, sex, language, or religion, and to encourage recognition of the interdependence of the peoples of the world; and

4. to ensure equal treatment in social, economic, and commercial matters for all Members of the United Nations and their nationals, and also equal treatment for the latter in the administration of justice, without prejudice to the attainment of the foregoing objectives and subject to the provisions of Article 80.

Article 77

1. The trusteeship system shall apply to such territories in the following categories as may be placed thereunder by means of trusteeship agreements:
   a. territories now held under mandate;
   b. territories which may be detached from enemy states as a result of the Second World War; and
   c. territories voluntarily placed under the system by states responsible for their administration.
2. It will be a matter for subsequent agreement as to which territories in the foregoing categories will be brought under the trusteeship system and upon what terms.

Article 78

The trusteeship system shall not apply to territories which have become Members of the United Nations, relationship among which shall be based on respect for the principle of sovereign equality.

Article 79

The terms of trusteeship for each territory to be placed under the trusteeship system, including any alteration or amendment, shall be agreed upon by the states directly concerned, including the mandatory power in the case of territories held under mandate by a Member of the United Nations, and shall be approved as provided for in Articles 83 and 85.

Article 80

1. Except as may be agreed upon in individual trusteeship agreements, made under Articles 77, 79, and 81, placing each territory under the trusteeship system, and until such agreements have been concluded, nothing in this Chapter shall be construed in or of itself to alter in any manner the rights whatsoever of any states or any peoples or the terms of existing international instruments to which Members of the United Nations may respectively be parties.
2. Paragraph 1 of this Article shall not be interpreted as giving grounds for delay or postponement of the negotiation and conclusion of agreements for placing mandated and other territories under the trusteeship system as provided for in Article 77.

Article 81

The trusteeship agreement shall in each case include the terms under which the trust territory will be administered and designate the authority which will exercise the administration of the trust territory. Such authority, hereinafter called the administering authority, may be one or more states or the Organization itself.

Article 82

There may be designated, in any trusteeship agreement, a strategic area or areas which may include part or all of the trust territory to which the agreement applies, without prejudice to any special agreement or agreements made under Article 43.

Article 83

1. All functions of the United Nations relating to strategic areas, including the approval of the terms of the trusteeship agreements and of their alteration or amendment shall be exercised by the Security Council.
2. The basic objectives set forth in Article 76 shall be applicable to the people of each strategic area.
2. The Security Council shall, subject to the provisions of the trusteeship agreements and without prejudice to security considerations, avail itself of the assistance of the Trusteeship Council to perform those functions of the United Nations under the trusteeship system relating to political, economic, social, and educational matters in the strategic areas.

Article 84

It shall be the duty of the administering authority to ensure that the trust territory shall play its part in the maintenance of international peace and security. To this end the administering authority may make use of volunteer forces, facilities, and assistance from the trust territory in carrying out the obligations towards the Security Council undertaken in this regard by the administering authority, as well as for local defence and the maintenance of law and order within the trust territory.

Article 85

1. The functions of the United Nations with regard to trusteeship agreements for all areas not designated as strategic, including the approval of the terms of the trusteeship agreements and of their alteration or amendment, shall be exercised by the General Assembly.
2. The Trusteeship Council, operating under the authority of the General Assembly shall assist the General Assembly in carrying out these functions.

Chapter XIII: The Trusteeship Council

COMPOSITION

Article 86

1. The Trusteeship Council shall consist of the following Members of the United Nations:
   a. those Members administering trust territories;
   b. such of those Members mentioned by name in Article 23 as are not administering trust territories; and
   c. as many other Members elected for three-year terms by the General Assembly as may be necessary to ensure that the total number of members of the Trusteeship Council is equally divided between those Members of the United Nations which administer trust territories and those which do not.
2. Each member of the Trusteeship Council shall designate one specially qualified person to represent it therein.

FUNCTIONS AND POWERS

Article 87

The General Assembly and, under its authority, the Trusteeship Council, in carrying out their functions, may:

1. consider reports submitted by the administering authority;
2. accept petitions and examine them in consultation with the administering authority;
3. provide for periodic visits to the respective trust territories at times agreed upon with the administering authority; and
4. take these and other actions in conformity with the terms of the trusteeship agreements.

Article 88

The Trusteeship Council shall formulate a questionnaire on the political, economic, social, and educational advancement of the inhabitants of each trust territory, and the administering authority for each trust territory within the competence of the General Assembly shall make an annual report to the General Assembly upon the basis of such questionnaire.

VOTING

Article 89

1. Each member of the Trusteeship Council shall have one vote.

2. Decisions of the Trusteeship Council shall be made by a majority of the members present and voting.

PROCEDURE

Article 90

1. The Trusteeship Council shall adopt its own rules of procedure, including the method of selecting its President.
2. The Trusteeship Council shall meet as required in accordance with its rules, which shall include provision for the convening of meetings on the request of a majority of its members.

Article 91

The Trusteeship Council shall, when appropriate, avail itself of the assistance of the Economic and Social Council and of the specialized agencies in regard to matters with which they are respectively concerned.

Chapter XIV: The International Court of Justice

Article 92

The International Court of Justice shall be the principal judicial organ of the United Nations. It shall function in accordance with the annexed Statute, which is based upon the Statute of the Permanent Court of International Justice and forms an integral part of the present Charter.

Article 93

1. All Members of the United Nations are ipso facto parties to the Statute of the International Court of Justice.
2. A state which is not a Member of the United Nations may become a party to the Statute of the International Court of Justice on conditions to be determined in each case by the General Assembly upon the recommendation of the Security Council.

Article 94

1. Each Member of the United Nations undertakes to comply with the decision of the International Court of Justice in any case to which it is a party.
2. If any party to a case fails to perform the obligations incumbent upon it under a judgment rendered by the Court, the other party may have recourse to the Security Council, which may, if it deems necessary, make recommendations or decide upon measures to be taken to give effect to the judgment.

Article 95

Nothing in the present Charter shall prevent Members of the United Nations from entrusting the solution of their differences to other tribunals by virtue of agreements already in existence or which may be concluded in the future.

Article 96

1. The General Assembly or the Security Council may request the International Court of Justice to give an advisory opinion on any legal question.
2. Other organs of the United Nations and specialized agencies, which may at any time be so authorized by the General Assembly, may also request advisory opinions of the Court on legal questions arising within the scope of their activities.

Chapter XV: The Secretariat

Article 97

The Secretariat shall comprise a Secretary-General and such staff as the Organization may require. The Secretary-General shall be appointed by the General Assembly upon the recommendation of the Security Council. He shall be the chief administrative officer of the Organization.

Article 98

The Secretary-General shall act in that capacity in all meetings of the General Assembly, of the Security Council, of the Economic and Social Council, and of the Trusteeship Council, and shall perform such other functions as are entrusted to him by these organs. The Secretary-General shall make an annual report to the General Assembly on the work of the Organization.

Article 99

The Secretary-General may bring to the attention of the Security Council any matter which in his opinion may threaten the maintenance of international peace and security.

Article 100

1. In the performance of their duties the Secretary-General and the staff shall not seek or receive instructions from any government or from any other authority external to the Organization. They shall refrain from any action which might reflect on their position as international officials responsible only to the Organization.
2. Each Member of the United Nations undertakes to respect the exclusively international character of the responsibilities of the Secretary-General and the staff and not to seek to influence them in the discharge of their responsibilities.

Article 101

1. The staff shall be appointed by the Secretary-General under regulations established by the General Assembly.
2. Appropriate staffs shall be permanently assigned to the Economic and Social Council, the Trusteeship Council, and, as required, to other organs of the United Nations. These staffs shall form a part of the Secretariat.
3. The paramount consideration in the employment of the staff and in the determination of the conditions of service shall be the necessity of securing the highest standards of efficiency, competence, and integrity. Due regard shall be paid to the importance of recruiting the staff on as wide a geographical basis as possible.

Chapter XVI: Miscellaneous Provisions

Article 102

1. Every treaty and every international agreement entered into by any Member of the United Nations after the present Charter comes into force shall as soon as possible be registered with the Secretariat and published by it.
2. No party to any such treaty or international agreement which has not been registered in accordance with the provisions of paragraph 1 of this Article may invoke that treaty or agreement before any organ of the United Nations.

Article 103

In the event of a conflict between the obligations of the Members of the United Nations under the present Charter and their obligations under any other international agreement, their obligations under the present Charter shall prevail.

Article 104

The Organization shall enjoy in the territory of each of its Members such legal capacity as may be necessary for the exercise of its functions and the fulfilment of its purposes.

Article 105

1. The Organization shall enjoy in the territory of each of its Members such privileges and immunities as are necessary for the fulfilment of its purposes.
2. Representatives of the Members of the United Nations and officials of the Organization shall similarly enjoy such privileges and immunities as are necessary for the independent exercise of their functions in connection with the Organization.
3. The General Assembly may make recommendations with a view to determining the details of the application of paragraphs 1 and 2 of this Article or may propose conventions to the Members of the United Nations for this purpose.

Chapter XVII: Transitional Security Arrangements

Article 106

Pending the coming into force of such special agreements referred to in Article 43 as in the opinion of the Security Council enable it to begin the exercise of its responsibilities under Article 42, the parties to the Four-Nation Declaration, signed at Moscow, 30 October 1943, and France, shall, in accordance with the provisions of paragraph 5 of that Declaration, consult with one another and as occasion requires with other Members of the United Nations with a view to such joint action on behalf of the Organization as may be necessary for the purpose of maintaining international peace and security.

Article 107

Nothing in the present Charter shall invalidate or preclude action, in relation to any state which during the Second World War has been an enemy of any signatory to the present Charter, taken or authorized as a result of that war by the Governments having responsibility for such action.

Chapter XVIII: Amendments

Article 108

Amendments to the present Charter shall come into force for all Members of the United Nations when they have been adopted by a vote of two thirds of the members of the General Assembly and ratified in accordance with their respective constitutional processes by two thirds of the Members of the United Nations, including all the permanent members of the Security Council.

Article 109

1. A General Conference of the Members of the United Nations for the purpose of reviewing the present Charter may be held at a date and place to be fixed by a two-thirds vote of the members of the General Assembly and by a vote of any nine members of the Security Council. Each Member of the United Nations shall have one vote in the conference.
2. Any alteration of the present Charter recommended by a two-thirds vote of the conference shall take effect when ratified in accordance with their respective constitutional processes by two thirds of the Members of the United Nations including all the permanent members of the Security Council.
3. If such a conference has not been held before the tenth annual session of the General Assembly following the coming into force of the present Charter, the proposal to call such a conference shall be placed on the agenda of that session

of the General Assembly, and the conference shall be held if so decided by a majority vote of the members of the General Assembly and by a vote of any seven members of the Security Council.

Chapter XIX: Ratification and Signature

Article 110

1. The present Charter shall be ratified by the signatory states in accordance with their respective constitutional processes.
2. The ratifications shall be deposited with the Government of the United States of America, which shall notify all the signatory states of each deposit as well as the Secretary-General of the Organization when he has been appointed.
3. The present Charter shall come into force upon the deposit of ratifications by the Republic of China, France, the Union of Soviet Socialist Republics, the United Kingdom of Great Britain and Northern Ireland, and the United States of America, and by a majority of the other signatory states. A protocol of the ratifications deposited shall thereupon be drawn up by the Government of the United States of America which shall communicate copies thereof to all the signatory states.
4. The states signatory to the present Charter which ratify it after it has come into force will become original Members of the United Nations on the date of the deposit of their respective ratifications.

Article 111

The present Charter, of which the Chinese, French, Russian, English, and Spanish texts are equally authentic, shall remain deposited in the archives of the Government of the United States of America. Duly certified copies thereof shall be transmitted by that Government to the Governments of the other signatory states.

In Faith Whereof the representatives of the Governments of the United Nations have signed the present Charter. DONE at the city of San Francisco the twenty-sixth day of June, one thousand nine hundred and forty-five.

Note on Amendments to Articles 23, 27, 61, 109

Amendments to Articles 23, 27 and 61 of the Charter were adopted by the General Assembly on 17 December 1963 and came into force on 31 August 1965. A further amendment to Article 61 was adopted by the General Assembly on 20 December 1971, and came into force on 24 September 1973. An amendment to Article 109, adopted by the General Assembly on 20 December 1965, came into force on 12 June 1968.

The amendment to Article 23 enlarges the membership of the Security Council from eleven to fifteen. The amended Article 27 provides that decisions of the Security Council on procedural matters shall be made by an affirmative vote of nine members (formerly seven) and on all other matters by an affirmative vote of nine members (formerly seven), including the concurring votes of the five permanent members of the Security Council.

The amendment to Article 61, which entered into force on 31 August 1965, enlarged the membership of the Economic and Social Council from eighteen to twenty-seven. The subsequent amendment to that Article, which entered into force on 24 September 1973, further increased the membership of the Council from twenty-seven to fifty-four.

The amendment to Article 109, which relates to the first paragraph of that Article, provides that a General Conference of Member States for the purpose of reviewing the Charter may be held at a date and place to be fixed by a two-thirds vote of the members of the General Assembly and by a vote of any nine members (formerly seven) of the Security Council. Paragraph 3 of Article 109, which deals with the consideration of a possible review conference during the tenth regular session of the General Assembly, has been retained in its original form in its reference to a "vote, of any seven members of the Security Council", the paragraph having been acted upon in 1955 by the General Assembly, at its tenth regular session, and by the Security Council.

The manufacturer's authorised representative in the EU is Springer Nature Customer Service Centre GmbH, Europaplatz 3, 69115 Heidelberg, Germany. If you have any concerns regarding our products, please contact ProductSafety@springernature.com

Printed and bound by CPI Group (UK) Ltd, Croydon, CR0 4YY

05/10/2026

02228157-0004